P9-ELF-774

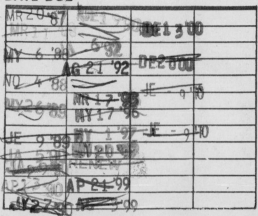

A ROBERT LOUIS STEVENSON
COMPANION

In the same series

A COLERIDGE COMPANION *J. S. Hill*

A KIPLING COMPANION *Norman Page*

A WORDSWORTH COMPANION *F. B. Pinion*

A ROBERT LOUIS STEVENSON COMPANION

A guide to the novels, essays
and short stories

J. R. HAMMOND

MACMILLAN PUBLISHING COMPANY
NEW YORK

First published in the United States 1984 by
MACMILLAN PUBLISHING CO., INC.
866 Third Avenue
New York, NY 10022

Library of Congress Catalog Card Number 83–82620
ISBN 0–02–913790–X

Printed in Hong Kong

Most vain, most generous, sternly critical,
Buffoon and poet, lover and sensualist:
A deal of Ariel, just a streak of Puck,
Much Antony, of Hamlet most of all,
And something of the Shorter Catechist.

W. E. HENLEY, 'RLS'

With all my romance, I am a realist and
a prosaist, and a most fanatical lover of
plain physical sensations plainly and
expressly rendered.

R. L. STEVENSON
(1 May 1892)

Contents

List of Plates

For the provision of illustrations, and permission to reproduce them, grateful acknowledgements are made to: the Mansell Collection (frontispiece); Lady Stair's House Museum, Edinburgh (plates 1–8).

Preface

Stevenson, in common with H. G. Wells and Arnold Bennett, is today paying the price for having been so immensely popular during and immediately following his lifetime. For many years he has been regarded as the author of a number of stirring adventure stories for boys, of a handful of pleasing essays and one or two travel books written in a vein of antique charm. So well known have been these aspects of his work, and so constantly in demand, that his more solid achievement as a novelist and short story writer has tended to be overlooked.

There are signs, however, that a dispassionate critical reassessment of his work is under way and it is hoped that this *Companion* will contribute towards that process. In recent years a number of new biographies have appeared – notably James Pope Hennessy's *Robert Louis Stevenson* and Jenni Calder's *RLS: A Life Study* – which have demonstrated for the first time the full extent of his creative achievement and the odds against which he fought throughout his life. The American scholar Roger G. Swearingen has in preparation a full-scale critical biography, the first attempt to write a definitive *Life* since that of Graham Balfour in 1901. A complete edition of Stevenson's letters is also in preparation, edited by Bradford Booth.

The present *Companion* aims to be a guide to the whole range of his prose – novels, romances, essays and short stories – and to enable the reader to follow his writings with a keener appreciation. It is my hope that it will be a 'companion' in the fullest sense, a book to have at one's elbow and on the reference shelf, a source of information, ideas and stimulus. Though Stevenson was only forty-four when he died he wrote an immense amount, far more than is generally realised; a guide to his work has been long overdue.

I am indebted in particular to two reference works. First, *The Prose Writings of Robert Louis Stevenson: A Guide*, by Roger G. Swearingen – an excellent bibliography of Stevenson's writings. Second, *Robert Louis Stevenson: The Critical Heritage*, edited by Paul Maixner – a compendium of critical responses to the novels and essays, fully and helpfully annotated. Full details of these and other scholarly works will be found in the Select Bibliography.

For the texts of Stevenson's works I have consulted the best extant critical editions, though in some cases a variorum edition is not available. For the letters I have relied on the edition prepared by Sidney Colvin, particularly the revised and enlarged arrangement published in four volumes. I have also consulted a wide selection of critical, biographical and bibliographical works and reread the whole of Stevenson's fiction in the order in which it was written: I commend the latter experience to all who would seek a closer understanding of his art.

I wish to express my thanks to the National Library of Scotland, the City of Edinburgh District Council and Lady Stair's House Museum, Edinburgh, for their helpfulness and courtesy at all times. My appreciation is due to Mrs Carol Staves for typing the manuscript with such care, to Mrs Julia Steward for her encouragement and guidance on behalf of the publishers, and to my wife for her constant interest.

J. R. HAMMOND

Part I

The Life of Robert Louis Stevenson

The forces which mould the life and character of an imaginative writer are many and complex. It is a fascinating process to disentangle the combination of factors — hereditary, temperamental and psychological — which contribute towards the making of a novelist and shape the attitude of mind that permeates his writings. In the case of Stevenson the process is unusually interesting for in his life, his philosophy and his work he represents a fusion of emotions and attitudes which are at once peculiarly Scottish and highly relevant to the literature of our age. At the same time he marks a significant departure from the nineteenth century literary tradition whose work anticipates the didactic fiction of Conrad and Wells.

Robert Louis Balfour Stevenson was born on 13 November 1850 at 8 Howard Place, Edinburgh, the only son of respectable middle-class parents. His father, Thomas Stevenson, was a lighthouse engineer, the heir of a long family tradition of civil and marine engineering. Thomas was a strict Presbyterian but a kindly man, not without imagination or a sense of humour, who intended to bring up his son in accordance with the orthodox principles of mid-Victorian Edinburgh. His mother, Margaret, was the daughter of a minister, Lewis Balfour, whose manse at Colinton became one of Louis's favourite childhood haunts. Margaret shared her husband's strict religious views but tempered this with a more optimistic attitude to life and a refusal to dwell on unpleasant realities. During much of Louis's childhood she suffered from persistent ill-health and he inherited from her a susceptibility to tuberculosis.

As Louis had no brothers or sisters his boyhood was a lonely one, but it must not be assumed that it was necessarily unhappy. It is true that he was dogged by illnesses – for years he suffered from coughs and fevers and a variety of chest complaints which continually interrupted his schooling – but he was lovingly cared for by his mother and by his devoted nurse, Alison Cunningham, to whom he later dedicated *A Child's Garden of Verses.* 'Cummy', as she was called, joined the family when he was eighteen months old and throughout his childhood was his constant companion, nurse and teacher. From her, even more than from his father, he derived an atmosphere of intense Calvinism with its emphasis on evil, sin and the works of the devil. The formative literary influences on his childhood were the Old Testament and Bunyan's *Pilgrim's Progress* – both of which were read aloud to him by his nurse – and the pious verses, recited by 'Cummy', which told the story of Scotland's religious and historical feuds.

Louis attended a number of schools but was never able to remain long at one establishment because of his chronic ill-health. He enjoyed playing at imaginary countries with his cousin Bob, at the normal games of boyhood (especially hide and seek) and with a toy theatre given to him when he was six. At seven he learned to read for himself and was soon browsing in his father's library. The latter consisted mainly of learned theological and scientific works, of little interest to an imaginative boy – he wrote later that 'My father's library was a spot of some austerity . . . it was only in holes and corners that anything really legible existed as by accident'[1] – but he did discover some novels and travel books which whetted his appetite for tales of adventure. Among these were *Rob Roy*, *Waverley*, *Guy Mannering*, *The Voyages of Captain Woodes Rogers*, George Sand's *La Mare au Diable* and Ainsworth's *Tower of London*. There were also four old volumes of *Punch* in which he read abundantly. Other cherished discoveries during these years were the *Arabian Nights Entertainments* and the stories of Mayne Reid.

When he entered Edinburgh University as a science student in 1867 it was tacitly assumed that he would follow in his father's footsteps and become a civil engineer. Though he spent most of his vacations accompanying his father on visits to harbours and lighthouses it soon became apparent that he was not cut out for a career in engineering; temperamentally he was imaginative and romantic rather than practical, and his interests were already revealing a decidedly literary turn of mind. Moreover, he could not bring himself to take his studies seriously. Whilst ostensibly he was working for a science degree, in practice he was reading widely outside his course of study: French literature (particularly Dumas), Scottish history, and the works of Darwin and Spencer. When at the age of twenty-one he confided to his father that he did not wish to become an engineer and wanted to become a writer instead, Thomas was naturally disappointed. As a compromise it was settled that Louis would read for the Bar; if his literary ambitions came to nothing then he would still have a respectable profession to fall back upon.

To understand Stevenson fully it is essential to understand that there were two Edinburghs, both of which played their part in moulding his personality and outlook. On the one hand was the New Town, as exemplified by the prim, solid, elegant exterior of Heriot Row, to which the family moved in 1857. This was the respectable, conventional, formal Edinburgh: deeply religious, polite, and socially correct. Alongside this was a much more bohemian Edinburgh, symbolised by the shebeens and brothels of Leith Walk and the Lothian Road. The juxtaposition of the two aspects in the sharpest contrast to one another made a deep impression on his mind and strengthened his fascination with the duality of human nature.[2] This realisation that outward probity could exist side by side with inward laxity was a powerful revelation to one who had been brought up in a sheltered religious environment. Later it provided the theme for one of his most celebrated tales, *The Strange Case of Dr. Jekyll and Mr. Hyde.*

During his student years as a young man in his late teens and early twenties he frequently sampled the louche, bohemian drinking-houses of the Old Town (a glimpse of these is given in his short story 'The Misadventures of John Nicholson') and seems to have embarked on a number of illicit affairs. There is some speculation that he experienced at least one powerful sexual relationship at this time, but critical opinion is deeply divided on this point.[3] What is not in doubt is that for some years he frequented the low haunts of the Old Town and that he found interest and happiness in these sojourns. For him the Old Town represented a freer, more honest, less hypocritical way of life than the conventional Edinburgh of his home surroundings. To the end of his life he remained unconventional in his dress, his mannerisms, and his indifference towards material possessions.

Early in 1873 the differences between Louis and his father on

matters of belief came to a head. For some time he had been
increasingly sceptical of the framework of religion and dogma
accepted so firmly by his parents. Thomas, unaware of his son's
perfervid reading, seems not to have realised the extent of his
scepticism until one day when he questioned him on religion and
theology. Horrified by Louis's agnosticism (which from Thomas's
point of view was tantamount to blatant atheism) he spent many
weeks in prayer and argument; it seemed to him that Louis had
rejected the principles and beliefs on which his own life had been
based. The atmosphere at home became extremely unpleasant. 'O
Lord,' wrote Louis to a friend, 'what a pleasant thing it is to have
just *damned* the happiness of (probably) the only two people who
care a damn about you in the world.'[4]

During these years Louis made a number of friendships which
were destined to influence his life and stimulate his literary
ambitions. Charles Baxter, his closest friend at the University, was
a young lawyer who became a lifelong confidant and ally and in
later years handled many of his dealings with publishers.
Fleeming Jenkin, by far the most understanding of the older
generation in Louis's circle, was Professor of Engineering at the
University and a regular contributor to the *Saturday Review*. He
and his wife entertained Louis in their home, encouraged him to
talk of his literary aspirations and drew him out by involving him
in critical and philosophical discussions. Frances Sitwell, whom he
met while staying with relatives in England in 1873, was a
beautiful and intelligent woman, ten years older than Louis and
separated from her husband. Louis quickly became deeply infatuated with her and embarked on a correspondence which
lasted some years, a correspondence in which he poured out his
views on life and his determination to make a name for himself in
the world of letters. She introduced Louis to her friend Sidney
Colvin (later her husband), Professor of Fine Art at Cambridge.
Colvin was then twenty-eight but already firmly established in
literary circles. He was soon charmed by Louis and give him
introductions to a number of influential editors, including Leslie
Stephen of the *Cornhill* and George Grove of Macmillan. From this
point onwards Colvin became a firm friend and adviser, offering
encouragement and counsel at each stage of his career and helping to pave his way in the world of literature. It was Colvin who,
when Stevenson was at the height of his fame, conceived the idea
of a uniform edition of his works and it was he who edited Steven-

son's letters after his death. These four – Baxter, Jenkin, Mrs Sitwell and Colvin – remained his closest circle for many years. Together with W. E. Henley, whom he met for the first time in 1874, they were of immeasurable importance in giving him encouragement and advice at a crucial phase of his career. Together they assisted him in making the transition from a gauche, unformed young man to a self-confident writer with a style and mission of his own.

In the autumn of 1873 he was taken ill with nervous exhaustion and a severe chest condition, and his doctor ordered him to take a prolonged rest abroad. For the next six months he convalesced at Mentone in the South of France, working at the essays 'Ordered South' and 'Victor Hugo's Romances' and making notes for a projected volume on *Four Great Scotsmen* (Knox, Hume, Burns and Scott). The latter was abandoned, though in later years he did publish essays on Knox and Burns. On his return to Edinburgh he spent most of his time for the next year at Heriot Row – the relationship with his parents had by this time eased somewhat – writing book reviews and articles and trying his hand at short stories. To this period belong his perceptive essay on the works of Edgar Allan Poe (*The Academy*, 2 January 1875), a number of the *Fables* including the striking 'The House of Eld', and the short story 'When the Devil was Well'. Slowly but surely he was earning a name for himself in journalism and his pieces were beginning to appear in distinguished journals such as the *Cornhill Magazine* and the *Fortnightly Review*. Many of the stories and articles written at this period were abandoned or destroyed. He did not grudge the time spent on them since he felt he was gradually evolving a style and technique that would stand him in good stead; he recognised that any worthwhile literary apprenticeship was bound to be a long and arduous process.

During 1875 and 1876 he spent much of his time at Fontainebleau, where his cousin Bob was a member of an informal colony of artists and writers. In this congenial fellowship he was completely at home, writing, talking, bathing and canoeing. Something of the atmosphere of his life at this time can be derived from his essay 'Fontainebleau' in which he describes with affection and nostalgia the pleasant landscape and friendly company in which he found so much happiness. In the summer of 1876 occurred an encounter which altered the whole tenor of his life. Returning to the inn at Grez one day (Grez-sur-Loing is a village in the Fontainebleau forest) he met an American lady, a Mrs Osbourne, together with her son and daughter. Fanny Vandegrift Osbourne was a remarkable woman who soon captivated Stevenson. Small, dark-eyed and possessing striking hair and features, she was ten years older than the struggling young writer. At the age of seventeen she had married a beguiling young man from whom she was now estranged (he had been unfaithful to her for many years); she had determined to visit Europe to detach herself from his influence and to pursue her art studies. Now thirty-six, she was a sturdy, determined woman with unconventional attitudes to life and conduct. Though her background and temperament were very different from Stevenson's – she was fiercely independent and strong-willed, and there had been nothing in her upbringing to correspond with the genteel respectability of his own – the two were powerfully drawn to one another. The story of his life for the next three years is one of an increasingly intense emotional attraction, pursued partly through correspondence and partly through renewed encounters at Paris and Grez. Stevenson recognised that he had met a very unusual woman and that he was deeply in love with her; he was also aware that the difficulties in the way of marriage were formidable. Her marriage to Sam Osbourne was still legally binding. Moreover, his own health was precarious and he was still financially dependent on his parents. But he would not abandon his pursuit of her and she became his primary inspiration during the ensuing years.

Meanwhile his literary career was beginning in earnest. In April 1878 his first book was published, *An Inland Voyage*, an engaging account of a canoeing holiday along the rivers and canals of Belgium. His first short stories, 'A Lodging for the Night', 'Will o' the Mill' and 'The Sire de Maletroit's Door' were written in the summer of 1877, as were a number of promising essays including 'Crabbed Age and Youth' and 'The English Admirals'. He was working hard at essays and stories and much of the material collected in *Virginibus Puerisque* (1881) and *New Arabian Nights* (1882) was written at this time. A second travel book, *Travels with a Donkey*, appeared in 1879: a slight but charming description of a journey through the Cevennes mountains undertaken in the previous year. He was steadily consolidating his reputation as a writer of note – not, as yet, with a distinctive approach or genre but with an unusual eye for visual detail and a gift for vivid narration. His work was beginning to catch the attention of Henry

James, Andrew Lang and Edmund Gosse and by the end of 1878 he felt he could regard himself as a professional man of letters.

In gaining a foothold in the world of journalism he had received much help and encouragement from William Ernest Henley, a poet, critic and dramatist who in later years became an extremely influential figure in the London literary scene. Henley was in turn editor of *London,* the *Magazine of Art,* the *National Observer* and the *New Review.* He collaborated with Stevenson in the writing of a number of plays and for some years acted as his unpaid literary agent. The two men had much in common and, though their friendship cooled after Stevenson's marriage, Henley's role as a stimulus and source of guidance during these years should not be underestimated. When Stevenson came to write *Treasure Island* he acknowledged his influence in creating the powerful, dogged figure of Long John Silver.

Fanny Osbourne returned to California in the autumn of 1878 and soon determined to seek a divorce from her husband. Worried by news of her ill health and unhappiness Stevenson resolved to join her and hastily set off from Scotland en route for Monterey, a journey of six thousand miles involving an eleven-day cruise across the Atlantic by ocean-steamer and an epic journey across the United States aboard an emigrant train. To Henley and Colvin it appeared that he was turning his back on a promising literary career in pursuit of a chimerical future in an unknown land. Stevenson, however, was adamant. Despite wretched health and an acute shortage of money he was determined to see Fanny and persuade her to marry him. He arrived in Monterey utterly exhausted by his travels and privations and for some weeks was close to death. After Fanny had nursed him back to health he moved into cheap lodgings in San Francisco and devoted himself to his writing and a full recovery from his illnesses. His marriage took place there in May 1880.

Despite poor health and poverty his sojourn in America was an interlude of steady literary activity. On the voyage out he had managed to write a short story, 'The Story of a Lie', and while convalescing he had written an account of his travels which later became *The Amateur Emigrant.* He also completed 'The Pavilion on the Links', one of the most remarkable short stories of this period, and worked on a number of the essays later gathered together in *Familiar Studies of Men and Books.* He eked out a precarious existence by contributing articles to a local newspaper but there was no disguising the fact that the financial outlook was extremely uncertain. The outlook was transformed by a cable from his father, 'Count on £250 annually', which at once relieved him of his financial anxieties and enabled him to settle down to his work with equanimity. In August 1880 the Stevensons, accompanied by Fanny's son Lloyd Osbourne, arrived back in England and were reconciled to his parents. Thomas and Margaret Stevenson took an immediate liking to Fanny and welcomed her as one of the family.

The story of Stevenson's life from this point onwards is a cease-less search for a climate in which he could live and work without a continual risk of haemorrhage and breakdown. The Scottish winters proved to be too much for his delicate lungs and for three years he, Fanny and Lloyd wintered in the South of France. From September 1884 to August 1887 they lived in Bournemouth, settling at 'Skerryvore', 61 Alum Chine Road (now demolished), the only part of his life in which Stevenson lived in England. His health remained extremely fragile and for some years he was a semi-invalid, spending most of the day writing in bed. Never-theless the years 1880–7 were characterised by steady literary work and many of his finest achievements were produced during this period. To these years belong such stories as 'Thrawn Janet', 'The Merry Men', 'Markheim' and Olalla': tales which have earned for him a lasting reputation as a storyteller and a worthy descen-dant in the tradition of Poe and Hawthorne. Some of his most memorable essays including 'Talk and Talkers', 'A Gossip on Romance', 'Old Mortality' and 'A Humble Remonstrance' were also written at this time. But it is in the field of the novel that he made his most notable contributions. *Treasure Island*, his first full-length work of fiction, was published in 1883. This was followed by *Dr. Jekyll and Mr. Hyde* (1886) and *Kidnapped* (1886), works which are known wherever the English language is read. For the first time in his life he was now a popular writer. *Jekyll and Hyde* sold 40,000 copies in England alone in six months and was extensively pirated in America. *Kidnapped* also enjoyed a considerable success. Increasingly he was gaining recognition as a writer of stature and began to receive commissions from editors in Britain and the United States.

His most important literary friendship during these years was with Henry James. He and James had first met in 1885 after an exchange of correspondence following the publication of 'A

Humble Remonstrance' (*Longman's Magazine*, December 1884). James was then a rising novelist who had already written *Portrait of a Lady*, *The American* and *Daisy Miller*. He became a frequent visitor to the Stevenson home at Bournemouth and for some years the two never lost an opportunity of meeting and corresponding. Janet Adam Smith has observed that 'probably both of them were more interested in the art of fiction than any other novelists in England'.[5] Though their respective approaches to literature were clearly very different they greatly admired each other's work and their correspondence represents a fascinating commentary on attitudes to the novel. The two continued to exchange letters until Stevenson's death, commenting not only on one another's work but on that of contemporaries such as Barrie and Kipling.

In May 1887 Thomas Stevenson died. At last Louis felt that the ties which had bound him to Britain could now be severed – the climate of both Scotland and England had proved far too cold and damp for his chest condition – and he sailed for America, remaining at Saranac in the Adirondack mountains (a bleak spot in the far north of New York State) until April 1888. Here he settled down to the writing of *The Master of Ballantrae* and worked away at his essays, including 'A College Magazine', 'Memoirs of an Islet', 'A Chapter on Dreams' and 'The Lantern-Bearers'. He had received an attractive offer from Samuel McClure, the newspaper magnate, for a series of articles which could be syndicated on a wide scale; McClure had suggested that a cruise in the Pacific would provide admirable material for a series of letters. Stevenson eagerly accepted the idea. The sea and islands had always held a fascination for him and he felt convinced that the open-air life would be beneficial for his health. Accordingly he set sail from San Francisco in the yacht *Casco* in May 1888, accompanied by his wife, mother and step-son, bound for the South Sea islands. This was to be the beginning of a nomadic life which continued until December 1889.

The voyage in the *Casco* had originally been intended to last seven months. With the passage of time, however, Stevenson became more and more enchanted with the life of the islands and, as his health was now greatly improved, he was in no hurry to return to civilisation. He therefore continued his journeyings in the Pacific, first in the *Casco* then in the schooner *Equator*, visiting the Marquesas, Tahiti, Honolulu, the Gilberts and Samoa. For as long as he could remember the sea and the sea-going life had exercised for him a powerful emotional appeal. His father and grandfather had both loved the sea and as early as 1875 he had confided to Mrs. Sitwell that he was 'sick with desire' to visit the South Sea islands:

> beautiful places, green for ever; perfect climate; perfect shapes of men and women, with red flowers in their hair; and nothing to do but to study oratory and etiquette, sit in the sun, and pick up the fruits as they fall. Navigator's Island (Samoa) is the place; absolute balm for the weary.[6]

It was a curious life: several weeks at sea, then a stay of a week or a month on a Pacific island, perhaps as the guest of a native chief, then off again for another destination. Stevenson revelled in it, though it cannot have been a very comfortable existence for Fanny or his mother. Somehow during these months he found time for his writing. *The Master of Ballantrae* was completed at Tahiti and Honolulu, *The Wrong Box* and *The Ebb-Tide* were put in hand, and work was commenced on *The Wrecker*. He was also planning an ambitious survey of life and customs in the Pacific islands; this was never completed on the scale he had originally envisaged but after his death was published in fragmentary form under the title *In the South Seas*. (The phrase 'Pacific islands' suggests a group of habitations with a uniform culture and tradition. In fact the islands vary widely in customs, language and way of life: the contrast fascinated Stevenson and he spent many hours delving into the history and traditions of the island peoples – time which Fanny felt should have been devoted to the writing of fiction.)

In December 1889 the *Equator* arrived at Apia, the main harbour of Samoa. Stevenson intended to remain here for some weeks as he wished to include the island in his projected study of the South Seas. The climate and setting proved more congenial than he had anticipated and he soon realised that he need travel no further in his quest for a permanent home. For some time he had been reconciled to the fact that he could never return to England or to his native Scotland and that henceforth his home must be in the Pacific. Samoa proved to be ideally suited to his needs: the climate was tropical but rarely excessively wild, even in the rainy season; the people were happy, loyal and hard working; and it possessed a good postal service (there was a regular mail route by steamer between Apia and San Francisco). In January

1890 he took the decisive step and purchased an estate of 300 acres on the hills above Apia. He named it Vailima, 'the five streams'. Here he lived and worked until his death five years later.

There now began for him a period of intensive mental and physical activity, years in which he probably experienced greater happiness than he had ever known. They were years in which he experienced frustrations and worries — the costs of upkeeping the Vailima estate were considerable and he had to work extremely hard to secure the income needed to support it — and, above all, years of unremitting literary activity. The greatest blessing from his own point of view was the dramatic improvement in his health. Whereas at Bournemouth he had been forced to lead a retired, sedentary life, now he was like a man reborn; he could indulge in hard physical work on the estate, swim, go horse riding, and lead the normal life of a healthy human being. His happiness was tempered by his wife's ill-health — for much of the time in Samoa her own health was far from normal — but he never regretted his decision to leave Europe. 'I was never fond of towns, houses, society, or (it seems) civilisation', he wrote to James. 'Nor yet it seems was I ever very fond of (what is technically called) God's green earth. The sea, islands, the islanders, the island life and climate, make and keep me truly happier.'[7]

He was now a man with considerable responsibilities. Not only was he the owner of a substantial estate (the capital expenditure on Vailima was £4000, and its annual running costs were £1500: considerable sums for those days) but he was presiding over a diverse extended family whose population tended to increase. The household consisted not only of Louis and Fanny but of Mrs. Margaret Stevenson; Fanny's son and daughter by her first marriage, Lloyd and Isobel (Belle); Belle's husband, Joe Strong; and a servant population which fluctuated between five and nineteen. Moreover, the natives regarded him as a patriarch who could be consulted on all matters where judicious arbitration was required. They came to him with their problems and soon found that he could be relied upon to listen sympathetically and give wise counsel based on his legal training and on an acute understanding of human nature. They called him 'Tusitala', the storyteller, and were proud to have him among their company. Apart from the sheer physical drudgery of clearing the estate — a task involving many hours of weeding, planting and fencing — he interested himself in the island's complicated political situation and found his sympathies powerfully engaged in the feuds and rivalries which simmered in and around Samoa. Yet despite these distractions his literary work continued apace.

The list of his writings for 1890–4 reveals an impressive range of activity. During this time he completed two of his finest novellas, 'The Beach of Falesa' and *The Ebb-Tide*, two novels, *The Wrecker* and *Catriona*, the short stories 'The Bottle Imp', 'The Isle of Voices' and 'The Waif Woman', and the short pieces collected under the title *Fables*. He also worked hard at a number of novels he did not live to complete, including *St. Ives*, *The Young Chevalier* and *Heathercat*. In addition to fiction he spent much time on a history of the Stevenson family, *Records of a Family of Engineers*, a summary of Samoan politics, *A Footnote to History*, and numerous essays and fragments. He also maintained a copious correspondence with his friends, particularly Colvin, much of which was collected after his death in the volume *Vailima Letters*.

His daily routine is well described in a letter to his cousin:

> I have a room now, a part of the twelve-foot verandah sparred in, at the most inaccessible end of the house. Daily I see the sunrise out of my bed, which I still value as a tonic, a perpetual tuning fork, a look of God's face once in the day. At six my breakfast comes up to me here, and I work till eleven. If I am quite well, I sometimes go out and bathe in the river before lunch at twelve. In the afternoon I generally work again, now alone drafting, now with Belle dictating. Dinner is at six, and I am often in bed by eight.[8]

The large number of abandoned novels written during these years suggests an inability to concentrate for sustained lengths of time and a recognition that his greatest strength lay in the single memorable effect rather than in panoramic novels in the vein of Scott or Dickens. Throughout this time he was aiming at a greater realism and clarity, 'to get out the facts of life as clean and naked and sharp as I could manage it',[9] and devoting much effort to refining his style to one of the utmost simplicity. He was also infected with an increasing nostalgia for the scenery of his beloved Scotland and a longing for the sights and sounds of Edinburgh which at times filled him with waves of emotion.

It was not until the autumn of 1892 that these two elements – affection for his native land and a desire for a sharper cutting edge in his work – fused together in an idea for a new novel, originally entitled *The Justice-Clerk* but finally published as *Weir of Hermiston*. To this project he brought all his insight into the manners and morals of Edinburgh society, his deep feeling for Scottish history and traditions and his desire to write one novel by which he would be remembered. 'Mind you,' he wrote to Charles Baxter, 'I expect the *Justice-Clerk* to be my masterpiece. My Braxfield [Adam Weir] is already a thing of beauty and a joy for ever, and so far as he has gone *far* my best character.'[10] During much of its composition he was suffering from writers' cramp and dictated each day's work to Belle Strong, who would then write out the rough drafts for his correction.

He worked on the novel with mounting enthusiasm until the day of his death, 3 December 1894. On that day he dictated a further instalment of the novel and seemed in excellent spirits, pleased with the book's progress and confident in his ability to create an enduring work of art. He was talking to his wife in the evening when he suddenly felt a violent pain in his head and almost immediately lost consciousness. He died of a cerebral haemorrhage a few hours later at the age of forty-four. He had expressed a wish to be buried at the summit of Mount Vaea, 1300 feet above the sea. On the simple tombstone were engraved the lines of his poem 'Requiem':

> Under the wide and starry sky,
> Dig the grave and let me lie.
> Glad did I live and gladly die,
> And I laid me down with a will.
>
> This be the verse you grave for me:
> Here he lies where he longed to be;
> Home is the sailor, home from sea,
> And the hunter home from the hill.

The strongest single impression one derives from a study of his life is one of courage. 'No man is any use until he has dared everything', he wrote while travelling in the emigrant train, and to another correspondent he confided that he was 'a person who prefers life to art, and who knows it is a far finer thing to be in love, or to risk a danger, than to paint the finest picture or write the noblest book'.[11] The phrase *prefers life to art* is interesting and suggests that had he enjoyed normal health he would have preferred to be a man of action rather than a writer. His wife was convinced that he hankered after the life of a soldier. As it was, almost his whole life was dogged by ill-health; he was compelled to sublimate his craving for adventure and express his love of romance through his writing. He achieved this consummately in *Treasure Island*, a tale which has earned for him a niche in literary history as the creator of one of the enduring myths of our literature, one which belongs with *Robinson Crusoe* and *Don Quixote* as a continually fertile source of symbols and archetypes. But there was a darker side to his mind, a profound pessimism which found its expression in *Dr. Jekyll and Mr. Hyde*, *The Master of Ballantrae* and *Weir of Hermiston*. 'We are disbelievers in the morrow', he wrote to his cousin Bob, 'The future is *always* black to us.'[12] It is this coexistence in the same personality of wholly opposing attitudes – on the one hand, a courage which refused to be thwarted by adversity, however harsh; and on the other, a deep pessimism concerning human fallibilities, a stark acknowledgement of man's animal nature – which makes Stevenson one of the most rewarding writers of his generation. It is one of the tragedies of his short life that he did not complete *Weir of Hermiston*, the one novel which might have demonstrated his full stature as an imaginative writer. But in his life and work, incomplete as they are, there is abundant testimony to the vigour of his personality and his promise as one of the most original and forceful writers of his time.

Stevenson's Literary Achievement

Critical reactions to the life and work of Robert Louis Stevenson fall into three phases. His death in 1894 was followed by two decades of excessive adulation, fostered unwittingly by his family and friends. During this period appeared a number of hagiographical studies and appreciations which sedulously fostered the legend of the upright, manly Stevenson – a saint-like figure who could do no wrong and whose writings, including the most ephemeral, were held to be worthy of literary immortality. This phase came to an end in 1914 with the publication of Frank Swinnerton's *R. L. Stevenson: A Critical Study*, a work which sought to redress the balance by presenting a dispassionate critique of the works and concentrating discussion on the writings as distinct from the personality. Swinnerton's was the first of a series of depreciatory studies which, partly as a reaction against the exaggerated praise following Stevenson's death, sought to demolish the wholly uncritical image fostered by his supporters and to draw attention to the more fallible aspects of his life and achievement. The effect of these works, however, was to swing the critical pendulum too far in the opposite direction. For a long period he was regarded as a writer who represented values and attitudes which were now outmoded; a writer who had been over-rated in his own lifetime and now was completely out of favour. It was not until the publication of J. C. Furnas's perceptive biography *Voyage to Windward* (1952) that a third phase began: a phase in which, for the first time for many years, Stevenson became the subject of serious critical discussion. Furnas, by demonstrating that many previous biographies had been based upon misconceptions or inadequate research, was able to present a balanced picture which paved the way for a number of fine and intelligent studies of his life and work. Such works as Robert Kiely's *Robert Louis Stevenson and the Fiction of Adventure* (1964), Edwin Eigner's *Robert Louis Stevenson and the Romantic Tradition* (1966) and James Pope Hennessy's *Robert Louis Stevenson* (1974) reawakened scholarly interest in his life and achievement and insisted on a more dispassionate assessment of his writings. More recently Jenni Calder's *RLS: A Life Study* (1980) has explored in depth the factors which helped to shape his distinctive personality and give him such an acute insight into the ambiguities of the late Victorian age. Today it is possible, arguably for the first time since his death, to attempt a balanced appraisal of his achievement – freed from both uncritical adulation and insensitive disparagement – which seeks to place his works in their literary context and assess his significance for the twentieth century.

A question which continues to exercise literary critics is to what extent he was an original writer. His use of the phrase 'sedulous ape' in a youthful essay[13] has led to the assumption that he was in part a pasticheur, that the element of originality in his work is less than in other novelists of his generation, and that he was content to follow in the tradition of Scott and Defoe rather than explore fresh approaches to the novel. In fact these assumptions do less than justice to Stevenson. Through an examination of his work in its totality it is possible to identify four main strands in his writings, to each of which he brought to bear an invigorating freshness of approach. First, his unceasing concern with moral ambiguity and the duality of man's nature; second, his unusual approach to the presentation of character, a far more original approach than is usually acknowledged; third, his powerful emotional response to Scotland, a response which coloured all his work and gave it breadth and continuity; fourth, his willingness to experiment in a continual search for a satisfying means of expression. In each of these directions his contribution was significant.

In his novels and romances Stevenson continually explores his lifelong concern with problems of duality and moral ambiguity. Again and again he returns to the theme of the ambiguities of human behaviour, of the coexistence in one person of selfish and attractive motives, of the thin dividing line separating rational from irrational conduct. This is achieved through the sympathetic presentation of individual behaviour over long periods, and the highlighting of moments of crisis. Through the study of particular individuals – the Durie brothers, Adam Weir, Loudon Dodd, Alan Breck – he is able to demonstrate the inconsistencies inherent in human actions and the ambivalence which lies at the heart of superficially clear-cut situations. Continually the reader is compelled to examine his own responses and to evaluate alternative courses of behaviour. Is this character good or bad? Was that action right or wrong? Is this man wholly evil? Is this issue really as simple as it appears?

But his especial skill is in the presentation of incidents and scenes which crystallise moral ambiguities in moments of drama. In 'A Gossip on Romance' he wrote:

> The threads of a story come from time to time together and make a picture in the web; the characters fall from time to time into some attitude to each other or to nature, which stamps the story home like an illustration. . . . This is the plastic part of literature: to embody character, thought, or emotion in some act or attitude that shall be remarkably striking to the mind's eye.

The phrase 'stamps the story home like an illustration' is interesting and illustrates the visual and dramatic quality of his imagination. The novels and stories contain numerous examples of this penchant for placing his characters in moments of crisis. One thinks, for example, of David Balfour on board the brig *Covenant* and his realisation that the crew are plotting to murder Alan Breck; of the dialogue between the Durie brothers immediately preceding their momentous duel; of Herrick's meditation as he contemplates suicide; of the nocturnal conversation between Kirstie and Archie Weir. Instances of this kind occur throughout his fiction. The effect of these moments of crisis, these scenes depicting 'some act or attitude that shall be remarkably striking to the mind's eye', is to compel his characters to reach a decision on courses of action: a decision frequently involving a choice between competing moral considerations.

A continuing theme in his fiction is the equivocal nature of human character, the shifting allegiances which affect behaviour and determine our responses to unforeseen situations. John Silver in *Treasure Island* and Northmour in 'A Pavilion on the Links' are both presented as ruthless men motivated by cunning and greed;

yet both possess other qualities – courage, resourcefulness and loyalty – which counterbalance their selfishness. Henry Durie in *The Master of Ballantrae* is fundamentally a kindly, sensitive man but becomes so consumed with hatred and jealousy for his brother that he destroys his own good nature and in the process forfeits much of the reader's sympathy. Attwater in *The Ebb-Tide* is a tyrant who rules his island with utter ruthlessness yet is guided in his actions by principles of justice based ultimately on a religious ethic. Adam Weir in *Weir of Hermiston* is outwardly a dour and undemonstrative man oblivious of human considerations, yet inwardly longs to express his affection for his son.

The theme is also explored through the dichotomies implicit in his fiction. Superficially each of the novels presents a choice between clearly defined alternatives; pirates versus honest men (*Treasure Island*), English versus Scots, and Highland versus Lowland (*Kidnapped*), York versus Lancaster (*The Black Arrow*), good versus evil (*Dr. Jekyll and Mr. Hyde*), English versus French (*St. Ives*), convention versus rebellion (*Weir of Hermiston*). In each instance Stevenson demonstrates that the conflict is by no means clear-cut; that the dividing line separating 'good' from 'evil' conduct is frequently blurred, and that it is possible to shift one's allegiance in the light of changing circumstances. Silver, for example, veers between honesty and dishonesty so that to the end his ultimate allegiance is in doubt; Dick Shelton transfers his loyalty from Lancaster to York; Archie Weir deplores his father's intransigence yet becomes more and more inflexible in his dealings with others. Continually the point is being made that human nature is not a constant, that it is *changing* in response to events, that such apparently simple concepts as 'vice', 'virtue', 'disloyalty' and 'evil' are capable of differing interpretations in the light of circumstances. Though he rebelled against the restrictive morality of his parents, generation he well knew that no morality at all could be an equally dangerous alternative. Implicit in his fiction is a continual process of questioning which obliges the reader to examine such concepts as good and evil and to re-evaluate the principles by which one's life is guided. This preoccupation with the mainsprings of human conduct and motivation may prove to be his most enduring contribution to our literature.

Stevenson spent the first half of his life in Scotland and for the remainder of his days Scottish scenes, people and history were never far from his thoughts. It is an apparent paradox that much

of his finest work with a Scottish setting was composed in locations utterly remote from the land of his birth. *Kidnapped* and 'The
Misadventures of John Nicholson' were written at Bournemouth;
The Master of Ballantrae was written in the United States and Tahiti;
Catriona, *St. Ives* and *Weir of Hermiston* were written at Samoa. It was
as if the emotional and psychological experience of Scotland was
so intense, so difficult to assimilate, that it was only when he was
in exile, detached from the sights and sounds he loved so much,
that he was able to express his true feelings for the country which
had always been his deepest inspiration. 'O for ten Edinburgh
minutes,' he wrote to Charles Baxter from Davos, 'sixpence
between us, and the ever-glorious Lothian Road, or dear mysterious Leith Walk!'[14] From his childhood days at Howard Place and
Heriot Row, Edinburgh, to the last years of his life in the South
Seas he was fascinated by the history, atmosphere and character
of Scotland and sought to express this fascination through his
personality and writings.

It is important to understand that his attachment to Scotland
was not only a deep affection for its scenery and people – though
his love of Edinburgh and the Pentland Hills remained with him
throughout his life – but a profound sense of its past, an emotional
awareness of its history and spirit which coloured all his work. In
this sense he was a world removed from the Kailyard school of
Scottish writers, deeply though he admired their works. (Kailyard
means 'kitchen garden' or 'cabbage patch', and is a term applied to
a group of authors of stories about Scottish cottagers, including
J. M. Barrie and S. R. Crockett.) Though Stevenson enthused over
Barrie's *The Little Minister* and *A Window in Thrums* he must have
been aware that his own response to Scotland was much more
emotional than physical, much more rooted in a sense of the past
and of the powerful forces which had moulded Scotland's history.
There is a key passage in *Weir of Hermiston* in which he expresses
this awareness of his inheritance:

> For that is the mark of the Scot of all classes: that he stands in
> an attitude towards the past unthinkable to Englishmen, and
> remembers and cherishes the memory of his forebears, good or
> bad; and there burns alive in him a sense of identity with the
> dead even to the twentieth generation.... The power of
> ancestry on the character is not limited to the inheritance of
> cells ... some Barbarossa, some old Adam of our ancestors,

sleeps in all of us till the fit circumstance shall call it into action.   (Chapter v, 3)

This powerful sense of the ancestral past, of the brooding forces which sleep in all of us 'till the fit circumstance shall call it into action' colours all his fiction and gives his writing a psychological depth that makes it strangely apposite to the twentieth century. Few novelists of his generation were so conscious of the 'old Adam of our ancestors', of the deep strands of violence and irrationality in the human make-up: it is not until the work of Wells and, later, of William Golding that one finds a similar awareness of man's animality.[15]

As a child Stevenson had spent many hours imbibing tales of violence and hatred from Scotland's turbulent past. These had been coloured by the profound Calvinistic pessimism of his nurse and his parents and strengthened by a religious background rooted in the Old Testament and *Pilgrim's Progress*. This immersion in stories of evil and bloodshed, in tales of revenge and intolerance, was for him an integral part of the Scottish experience. For him it was not possible to admire the Scottish landscape, to sympathise with its people or be charmed by its atmosphere without at the same time being aware of its long and bloody history, of the immense weight of violence, carnage, passion and hatred which had moulded its distinctive character. For Stevenson Scotland's present and past were inseparable.

The dark, almost satanic quality which underlies much of his fiction has its roots in this consciousness of the past, this preoccupation with the 'power of ancestry' which could well up and dominate at any time. This can be seen in the sombre parable of Jekyll and Hyde, in the devilry of the Master of Ballantrae, in the atavism of Olalla and her mother, and in the Mephistophelian quality of Frank Innes. It can be seen in the aura of evil which hangs over many of his characters, from Huish in *The Ebb-Tide* to Case in 'The Beach of Falesá', from Blind Pew in *Treasure Island* to Uncle Ebenezer in *Kidnapped*. This brooding sense of evil was firmly embedded in his temperament and, allied to his love of romance and adventure and his feeling for Scotland's history, made him one of the finest interpreters of the Scottish spirit.

His attitudes towards Scotland were never straightforward and cannot be summarised in a single sentence. All his life he was bewitched by the beauty of its scenery, fascinated by its people and their canniness and intrigued by the romance of its history. His feelings towards his homeland were complicated by the know-ledge that, though it remained the country of his birth and the inspiration for much of his best work, its climate spelt ruin for his health and he must be a permanent exile from its shores. This detachment meant that for him Scotland remained a 'lost domain', a secret country he could regard with nostalgia and affec-tion but must be forever cut off from his deepest longings.

Stevenson has been consistently underrated as a novelist of character. One of the strongest factors militating against his accep-tance as a serious novelist has been his posthumous reputation as a writer of boys' adventure stories. The success of *Treasure Island* and *Kidnapped* has had a twofold effect on his reputation: it has strengthened the widely held view that he was basically an adolescent writer, and diverted attention from his very substantial achievement as a novelist *per se* – most notably as the author of *The Master of Ballantrae* and *Weir of Hermiston*. It is undeniable that the yearning for adventure and romance exercised for him a very strong appeal. This can be seen in such essays as 'A Gossip on Romance', in his lifelong enthusiasm for Scott and Dumas, in his continual desire for novels of adventure and in the fact that he frequently began (and later abandoned) stories of romance and adventure set in the historical past.[16] Henry James wrote in this connection: 'It all comes back to his sympathy with the juvenile.'[17] The view that Stevenson was emotionally immature, that it was only at the end of his life that he outgrew the comparative safety of his adolescence, has been fuelled by these facts and by the continuing popularity of his early romances.

Yet it can be demonstrated that both *Treasure Island* and *Kid-napped* are rather more than boys' adventure stories, that both contain elements of characterisation which are extremely signifi-cant in the light of his subsequent development as a creative writer. Each is examined in detail in later chapters of the present study. Suffice it here to draw attention to the two principal characters, Jim Hawkins and David Balfour. Neither is a *static* character: each commences his narrative in a state of innocence and slowly gains in maturity through a process of experience and interaction. Each comes into contact with a spectrum of adult values and measures his own view of the world against that experience. Through one relationship in particular – Hawkins with Long John Silver, and Balfour with Alan Breck – each gains immeasurably in understanding and emerges from the encounter with a tried and tested appreciation of human worth. Both *Treasure Island* and *Kidnapped* are narrated in the first person. The effect of this is that the author cannot describe the thoughts and emotions of his characters, with the exception of the narrator; the impact of one character upon another and the manner in which attitudes are changed as a result of experience has to be revealed in the story itself. The manner in which this is achieved in both novels is interesting and illustrates the technique of explicating an inner drama through an outward action: a technique Stevenson employed to great effect in his later novels and short stories. In *Treasure Island*, for example, one thinks of the stockade sequence (Chs 16–21), the encounter with Israel Hands (26) and the unmasking of John Silver (33, appropriately entitled 'The Fall of a Chieftain'). In *Kidnapped* one recalls the meeting with Uncle Ebenezer (Ch. 3), the encounter with Alan Breck (9), the quarrel with Alan (24) and the interview with Mr Rankeillor (27). Each of these incidents represents a focal point in the novel, a climax which brings to a head the attitudes and perceptions of the narrator and clarifies these in relation to the values of others. Whilst superficially then both are stories of adventure, both are fundamentally novels of character. That is to say, whilst both contain action and incident in abundance, their characters are not mere ciphers but are believable human beings who *change* in response to experience and reflection.

It can be seen then that *Treasure Island* and *Kidnapped* are both less straightforward than appears on first reading, that each contains a greater depth of subtlety in characterisation than one would normally associate with an adventure story. In his later novels and stories he continued to experiment in approaches to the presentation of character. Each of his fictions, whether related in the first person, as in *Catriona* and *St. Ives*, or in the third person, as in *Weir of Hermiston*, represents a fresh approach to the delineation of character.

Ephraim Mackellar, the narrator of *The Master of Ballantrae*, is one of the most interesting examples of his technique in presenting character. Though the narrator of the story Mackellar is not a major participant in the action; he is simply a family servant whose principal qualities are pedantry, dourness and a shrewd appreciation of human worth. Yet long before the novel reaches its conclusion he succeeds in gaining the reader's sympathy:

beneath the dour, matter-of-fact exterior the reader detects a sense of humour and qualities of humanity which are at once engaging and true. It would have been entirely possible for the story to have been narrated by one of the Durie brothers or by Alison Durie; some instinct told Stevenson to reject any of these courses and to opt instead for unfolding the drama through the prosaic eyes of Mackellar. As a result the novel gains immeasurably in conviction, not least because the reader is aware of the narrator's inward struggle between his dry, legal training and the romantic capacity for devotion which leads him into unquestioning loyalty to his master. In choosing Mackellar as the narrator rather than one of the main protagonists Stevenson added significantly to his own technical problems in welding the novel together but added an important dimension of credibility. Mackellar is a living character, solidly based on close observation of Edinburgh and its people.

Examples of this kind recur throughout the novels and romances. Rankeillor in *Kidnapped*, Prestongrange in *Catriona*, Pinkerton in *The Wrecker* and, above all, the Lord Justice-Clerk in *Weir of Hermiston*, are each solid and rounded creations, firmly rooted in observation of human traits. The same care is devoted to the creation of many of the minor characters. Even those characters who play insignificant roles – Lord Glenalmond in *Weir of Hermiston*, for example, or Thomas Dudgeon in *St. Ives* – are drawn with an attention to detail stemming from a deep fascination with human behaviour.

His critics are on firmer ground in drawing attention to the lack of credibility in his female characters. There is a curious unreality about most of his women characters which underlines an interesting aspect of Stevenson's personality. Five of his novels – *Treasure Island*, *Kidnapped*, *Dr. Jekyll and Mr. Hyde*, *The Wrecker* and *The Ebb-Tide* possess no major female characters. Of the remainder, the Countess Rosen in *Prince Otto*, Catriona Drummond and Barbara Grant in *Catriona* and Flora Gilchrist in *St. Ives* are all believable creations but one has the impression that each has been drawn from the outside rather than with inner conviction. The love scenes between Catriona and David Balfour, and between Flora and St. Ives are characterised by a lack of conviction, as if he is reluctant or unable to describe the passionate feelings of one adult for another. It is not until the creation of Uma in 'The Beach of Falesa' and, supremely, the two Kirsties in *Weir of Hermiston* that he succeeds in depicting credible female characters capable of expressing adult emotions with total conviction. Writing to a correspondent in 1890 he remarked: 'I have never pleased myself with any women of mine save two character parts, one of only a few lines', and to Colvin he expressed his satisfaction with 'The Beach of Falesa' because 'It is really good, well fed with facts, true to the manners, and (for once in my works) rendered pleasing by the presence of a heroine who is pretty. Miss Uma is pretty; a fact. All my other women have been as ugly as sin.'[18]

The culmination of his achievement in the delineation of female character is Christina in *Weir of Hermiston*: a wholly rounded portrait of thwarted love, of a young woman determined to express her personality in an age of convention. Consider the scene in the ninth chapter, 'At the Weaver's Stone', in which Christina and Archie meet for their assignation:

The revulsion of feeling in Christina's heart was violent. To have longed and waited these weary hours for him, rehearsing her endearments – to have seen him at last come – to have been ready there, breathless, wholly passive, his to do what he would with – and suddenly to have found herself confronted with a grey-faced, harsh schoolmaster – it was too rude a shock. She could have wept, but pride withheld her. She sat down on the stone, from which she had arisen, part with the instinct of obedience, part as though she had been thrust there. What was this? Why was she rejected? Had she ceased to please? She stood there offering her wares, and he would none of them! And yet they were all his! His to take and keep; not his to refuse, though! In her quick petulant nature, a moment ago on fire with hope, thwarted love and wounded vanity wrought. The schoolmaster that there is in all men, to the despair of all girls and most women, was now completely in possession of Archie. He had passed a night of sermons; a day of reflection; he had come wound up to do his duty; and the set mouth, which in him only betrayed the effort of his will, to her seemed the expression of an averted heart. It was the same with his constrained voice and embarrassed utterance; and if so – if it was all over – the pang of the thought took away from her the power of thinking.

Rarely if ever has he succeeded in presenting the torments of adolescent passion with such feeling, rarely does one sense such an undercurrent of suppressed desire, of the fragile structure of longing and self-abandon on which such relationships are based. It is with an effort that one reminds oneself that the scene stems from the same pen as *Prince Otto* and *St. Ives*: that the author of this and other superb scenes wrote the embarrassingly wooden encounters between Flora and her lover. The reasons for this deep-rooted shyness about adult relationships are complex. In part it may have had its origins in his puritanical upbringing, in part in a natural reticence, and in part because he genuinely feared to offend against the tacit avoidance of sexual matters which prevailed in the English novels of the period.[19] In his constant urge for manliness, for action and adventure he may, too, have suppressed unconsciously the more gentle, 'female' aspects of his own temperament. It was not until the end of his life, in *Weir of Hermiston*, that he was able to write with absolute conviction of tenderness and passion.

The whole of Stevenson's work, from *Treasure Island* to *Weir of Hermiston*, was a continual process of experiment — in the presentation of character, in style, in structure, balance and tone. Henry James wrote of him: 'Each of his books is an independent effort — a window opened to a different view.'[20] Stevenson himself, in 'A Humble Remonstrance', asserted that 'the true artist will vary his method and change the point of attack. That which was in one case an excellence, will become a defect in another; what was the making of one book will in the next be impertinent or dull.' This insistence that each work of fiction is a unique work of art underlay all his writings. To the end of his life he held to the view that each novel 'exists by and for itself', that each could only be judged by its own criteria and raised its own distinctive problems of presentation and approach. It is this constant desire for experiment which accounts for the extraordinary diversity of his work (and incidentally for the large number of fragmentary novels left uncompleted on his death).[21] Thus, *Treasure Island*, *Kidnapped* and *The Black Arrow* are cast in the form of historical romances; *Dr. Jekyll and Mr. Hyde* is at once a mystery story in the vein of Wilkie Collins or Sheridan Le Fanu and a profound study of human psychology; *The Master of Ballantrae* is an epic tragedy, conceived on a vast scale, spanning several generations and continents; *The Wrong Box* is a lighthearted humorous novel with no pretensions to seriousness; *The Ebb-Tide* is a complex study of human fallibility which anticipates the work of Conrad and Wells. A comparable diversity of style and theme is found in the short stories. 'The Pavilion on the Links' is a fast-moving narrative of mystery and adventure which might almost have been written by John Buchan or Conan Doyle; 'Markheim' and 'Olalla' are sustained studies in horror after the manner of Poe; 'The Misadventures of John Nicholson' is a novel in miniature, rich in observation of the manners and morals of Victorian Edinburgh; 'The Beach of Falesa' is a profound allegory on the themes of intolerance and loyalty. This wide range of styles and themes permitted a variety of approaches to characterisation, treatment and tone. It enabled Stevenson to examine human behaviour from a multiplicity of angles, to experiment with points of view and methods of narration, and to present situations depicting a range of attitudes and problems.

Whilst superficially much of his work follows in the tradition of the historical romance as exemplified by Scott, he was not content simply to emulate his predecessors but sought continually to open fresh approaches to the novel as a literary form. James's analogy of a Stevenson novel being 'a window opened to a different view' is extremely apt in this connection. *Treasure Island*, whilst on the surface a conventional romance, employs the interesting device of two narrators: a device which enables the reader to view the events being narrated from widely differing perspectives. *Kidnapped* begins in the form of an autobiographical novel in the manner of *Great Expectations* but widens to embrace elements of the *Bildungsroman* and the historical romance in a skilfully blended whole. *The Wrecker*, conceived as a mystery novel after the pattern of *The Woman in White*, embodies a number of extremely interesting experiments in narration and structure, including a 'story within a story' – the investigation of the deserted wreck on Midway Island. *The Ebb-Tide*, one of his finest yet least-known works, explores human fallibility in a narrative which fuses the compact form of 'The Beach of Falesa' with the sustained approach to character of a full-length novel. *Weir of Hermiston*, though left uncompleted at his death, embodies sufficient departures from convention – including the fascinating interlude 'A Border Family', which might almost be regarded as a short story in its own right – to indicate that it would have been a major contribution to the novel as an experiment in statement. Each of his novels, then, opens a different vantage point on life and character and each raises problems of presentation and structure that are unique to itself. (It should be noted in this connection that with the single exception of *Catriona*, a not wholly successful experiment, he did not write sequels to any of his novels – however tempting it may have been to do so.)

Stevenson and Henry James both had a background of European rather than English literature. His grounding in European, particularly French, novels gave him a facility of language, a love of precise statement, which found its fullest expression in his novels and stories. 'The main characteristic of Stevenson', wrote Conan Doyle, 'is his curious instinct for saying in the briefest space just those few words which stamp the impression upon the reader's mind.'[22] His precision as a stylist and his willingness to experiment with a variety of styles has paradoxically weakened rather than strengthened his reputation, for it has led to the assertion that he was a technician, a manipulator of language rather than a novelist with an instinctive feel for words. Stevenson was a craftsman above all else, an artist who cared deeply about words and was never satisfied until he felt he had achieved precisely the right expression. G. B. Stern wrote of him: 'he alone could blend a passionate *caring* with ardent industry, till at last, more for rejection than for use, he had all words at his command'.[23] As an instance of his painstaking precision as a literary artist one need look no further than *The Ebb-Tide*, a novella on which he toiled for long periods towards the end of his life and which is in itself a fascinating case-study in the techniques of narration and characterisation. It is in an altogether different world from *Treasure Island*, yet both stem from the same concern with human fallibilities.

It was this constant search for a satisfying medium of expression which led him to experiment with the writing of poetry. Though he was never a serious poet in the sense of Poe or Whitman – he wrote simply for his own enjoyment and with no literary pretensions – he produced several volumes of verse, much of which remains readable and interesting. The poetry is chiefly of interest for the insight it affords into his personality and attitude to life and because in his verse he returned to themes and ideas he had aired in his fiction. Thus, 'A Song of the Road' and 'The Vagabond' give eloquent expression to that love of the open air, that yearning for life and adventure which is epitomised in *Travels with a Donkey*; 'To My Old Familiars' is a moving statement of his affection for the people and scenes of his native Edinburgh; 'The Sick

Child' is a reminder of his frequent boyhood illnesses and the devotion of his mother; 'To a Youth' is a powerful declaration (probably addressed to his cousin R. A. M. Stevenson) of his attitudes to adolescence. Whilst much of the poetry is *vers d'occasion* there is evident in his verse an attitude of mind which is refreshing and which complements the view of the writer implicit in the fiction. It is that of a fundamentally lonely man longing for companionship and solace, a man imbued with a yearning for the roving life and a love of the passing seasons, a man possessing an instinctive understanding for the mind and outlook of a child. In his poetry as in his prose he experimented with language as a means of expression and illuminated many dark corners of the mind.

Yet a reading of the poems, engaging though they are, confirms the impression that prose was his true medium. He possessed the authentic poetic vision in the sense that he could write feelingly and with precision of scenes of natural beauty and of the emotions but he put this vision to far more effective use in the novels, short stories and essays where he was free to express himself on a broad canvas, unrestricted by conventions of rhyme and metre.

There remains the question: is there an attitude, a view of life, underlying his fiction which gives coherence and relevance to his work? What, in essence, is Stevenson's relevance to the twentieth century?

The single overriding impression one derives from a reading of the novels and stories is a sense of life as a journey: an exilarating sense of casting off and embarking on a voyage to an unknown land. All his most memorable essays of travel – *An Inland Voyage*, *Travels with a Donkey*, *The Amateur Emigrant*, *In the South Seas* – are descriptions of journeys to unusual or romantic locations. His finest novels – *Treasure Island*, *Kidnapped*, *The Master of Ballantrae*, *Weir of Hermiston* – all involve the concept of a journey and the contrast of the familiar with the unfamiliar, the known with the untried. Similarly with the short stories: 'The Pavilion on the Links', 'The Beach of Falesá', 'The Merry Men', 'Olalla' and others are set in unusual and interesting locations which involve descriptions of landscapes different from those encountered in the world of everyday.

There is also a sense in which, on entering a Stevenson novel, one is moving outside the world of reality and entering a domain with its own laws and conventions. Thus, much of the action of *Treasure Island* is set on an island remote from the pressures and problems of urban civilisation. *Kidnapped, The Master of Ballantrae* and *Weir of Hermiston* are all set in previous centuries far removed from contemporary society. *Prince Otto* is set in an imaginary European state akin to Ruritania; *The Black Arrow* is set at the time of the Wars of the Roses; and so on. This deliberate distancing from the climate of the late nineteenth century permitted Stevenson to examine the problems of morality, evil and the duality of man without any of the extraneous considerations a novel set in contemporary England would have involved. It permitted an *isolation* of the problem of moral ambiguity, a stripping to its essentials of the dilemma implicit in all his fiction: that of the accountability of man's behaviour in an age of doubt and questioning. (It is significant in this connection that when, at the end of his life, he began to write stories placed in a contemporary framework – 'The Beach of Falesa' and *The Ebb-Tide* – he chose to give them an island setting: this again permitted the isolation of his characters and threw into starker contrast the ethical dilemmas involved.)

Insofar as any single attitude can be deduced from the novels it is fundamentally one of courage: that one should endeavour to live one's life to the utmost in spite of adversity and do one's utmost to overcome obstacles of health and circumstance. The whole of his life, from childhood onwards, was an unending struggle against ill-health: this is clearly reflected in the courage and determination emanating from his fiction. There is also present throughout the novels, essays and short stories an attitude of mind which can best be expressed as *realism*. Implicit in his work is a recognition of human fallibility, of the deep layers of irrationality, fear and greed in the human make-up and the veneer of civilisation disguising man's fundamental animality. I use the word 'realism' rather than 'pessimism' since it is fundamentally neither an optimistic nor a pessimistic attitude: it is a recognition that man is neither wholly good nor wholly evil, that in an age when religious belief has been eroded the area of moral ambivalence will inevitably increase, that there can be no simplistic solutions to the problems of conduct.

It is this pragmatic element in Stevenson's thought, this refusal to be circumscribed by dogma or convention, which makes him so untypical of his age. His work looks ahead to Conrad and Greene rather than behind to Scott and Dumas. For too long he has been regarded as the author of stirring adventure stories for boys, a kind of Scottish Rider Haggard. The time is long overdue for a reassessment of his life and achievement, for an appraisal which acknowledges the peculiar difficulties against which he fought and his important contribution to our literary heritage. It is only now, ninety years after his passing, that we are beginning to understand the significance and stature of this most unusual man.

A Robert Louis Stevenson Dictionary

This dictionary is an alphabetically arranged guide to the short stories and essays. With its aid it is possible to identify the volume containing any particular story or essay. The number of the appropriate volume in the Tusitala Edition is also given after each entry.

The following abbreviations are used throughout the dictionary:

Arabian	*New Arabian Nights*
Island Nights	*Island Nights Entertainments*
Memories	*Memories and Portraits*
Merry Men	*The Merry Men and Other Tales and Fables*
Plains	*Across the Plains with Other Memories and Essays*
Studies	*Familiar Studies of Men and Books*
T	Tusitala Edition
Tales	*Tales and Fantasies*
Vailima	*Vailima Papers*
Virginibus	*Virginibus Puerisque and Other Papers*
Writing	*Essays in the Art of Writing*

ACROSS THE PLAINS An account of Stevenson's journey by emigrant train from New York to San Francisco in August 1879. (*Plains*, *T*18)

ADVENTURES OF HENRY SHOVEL An unfinished novel, of which three chapters only were written. It was originally conceived as an ambitious panorama spanning several generations. (*T*16)

AES TRIPLEX   Reflections on death and on attitudes towards it. It is characteristic of Stevenson that the essay becomes a plea for living life to the full: 'To be deeply interested in the accidents of our existence, to enjoy keenly the mixed texture of human experience, rather leads a man to disregard precautions and risk his neck against a straw.' (*Virginibus*, *T*25)

AN APOLOGY FOR IDLERS   A critique of the notion that one's primary object in life should be the pursuit of industry and material success, and an assertion of the opposite view: that the quest for happiness should be man's overriding objective. (*Virginibus*, *T*25)

AT AUTUMN EFFECT   A description of a walking tour in the Chiltern Hills, Buckinghamshire, in October 1874: originally entitled 'In the Beechwoods'. (*T*30)

BAGSTER'S 'PILGRIM'S PROGRESS'   Review of an edition of *Pilgrim's Progress* with illustrations by Eunice Bagster. In his essay 'The Ideal House' Stevenson lists *Pilgrim's Progress* as one of the 'eternal books that never weary'. (*T*28)

THE BALLADS AND SONGS OF SCOTLAND   Review of *The Ballads and Songs of Scotland* by J. Clarke Murray. Stevenson castigates the author for his ignorance of Scottish literature. (*T*28)

THE BEACH OF FALESA   Short story set in the Pacific islands, relating the experiences of a white trader and his marriage to a native girl. The tale marked a new departure in Stevenson's work and a move towards greater realism in a contemporary setting. (*Island Nights*, *T*13)

BEGGARS   Character sketches of youthful encounters with seamen and vagabonds in and around Edinburgh. (*Plains*, *T*25)

BERANGER   An appraisal of the life and achievement of Pierre Jean de Beranger, 'the national song-writer of France', an article written for the *Encyclopaedia Britannica*. (*T*28)

THE BODY-SNATCHER   Short story inspired by the murderers Burke and Hare and the Edinburgh anatomist Robert Knox. The story was considered to be in poor taste and was not republished until 1905. (*Tales*, *T*11)

THE BOOK OF JOSEPH   A summary of the Biblical narrative of Joseph, dictated by Stevenson to his mother at the age of six. (*T*28)

BOOKS WHICH HAVE INFLUENCED ME   A discussion of the writers who had most influenced Stevenson's life and outlook, including Shakespeare, Dumas, Bunyan, Whitman and Herbert Spencer. (*Writing, T*28)

THE BOTTLE IMP Short story set in Hawaii and relating the adventures of a genie imprisoned in a bottle. (*Island Nights, T*13)

BYWAYS OF BOOK ILLUSTRATION A commentary on the illustra· tions in two Japanese romances: *Chiushingura, or the Loyal League* and *Les Fideles Ronins*. 'Pictorial art in the West is still following false gods, literary gods . . . and, in common with all our arts, it labours under the desire of the artist to represent, before all things, his own ability and knowledge.' (*T*28)

CANNONMILLS A fragment of a novel set in Edinburgh, apparently intended as a love story. Both this and 'The Story of a Recluse' are interesting for their insight into Stevenson's youthful outlook. (*T*16)

A CHAPTER ON DREAMS An account of the role of dreams and nightmares in stimulating the imagination. The essay includes interesting background on the origin of *Dr. Jekyll and Mr. Hyde* and 'Olalla'. (*Plains, T*30)

A CHARACTER A slight sketch of a stranger encountered on the streets of Edinburgh, one of a series of early fragments. (*T*30)

THE CHARACTER OF DOGS A description of the various dogs which were Stevenson's companions during his early married life. (*Memories, T*29)

THE CHARITY BAZAAR An allegorical sketch privately printed in Edinburgh in 1875. (*T*5)

CHARLES OF ORLEANS An appreciation of the life and work of a French fifteenth·century poet. The essay reveals Stevenson's fascination with French medieval literature. (*Studies, T*27)

CHILD'S PLAY A description of childhood games and of the atti· tude of the child towards the world of the imagination (cf. 'The Lantern-Bearers'). (*Virginibus, T*25)

A CHRISTMAS SERMON A plea for happiness and an assertion of the idea that happiness is a virtue in itself, to be continually striven for, not expected as a reward for virtue. 'If your morals make you dreary, depend upon it they are wrong.' (*Plains, T*26)

COCKERMOUTH AND KESWICK A description of a walking tour of Cumberland undertaken in 1871. (*T*30)

COLLEGE FOR MEN AND WOMEN A description of the College for Working Women, Bloomsbury, of which Stevenson's friend Mrs. Sitwell served as secretary. (*T*28)

A COLLEGE MAGAZINE An account of Stevenson's literary apprenticeship and of his early contributions to the *Edinburgh University Magazine*. 'All through my boyhood and youth, I was known and pointed out for the pattern of an idler; and yet I was always busy on my own private end, which was to learn to write.' The paper includes an account of his membership of the Speculative Society. (*Memories, T*29)

COLLEGE PAPERS   A series of essays contributed to the *Edinburgh University Magazine* in 1871. The titles are: 'Edinburgh Students in 1824', 'The Modern Student Considered Generally', 'Debating Societies', 'The Philosophy of Umbrellas' and 'The Philosophy of Nomenclature' (cf. 'A College Magazine'). (*T*25)

CRABBED AGE AND YOUTH   A contrast between the attitudes and behaviour of the young and the old, arguing the case that the outlook of youth is entitled to as much respect as experience and caution. (*Virginibus, T*25)

THE DAY AFTER TOMORROW   One of Stevenson's rare excursions into political prophecy, in which he reviews the forces tending to disintegrate a socialist state. (*T*26)

DIOGENES   Two sketches, 'Diogenes in London' and 'Diogenes at the Savile Club', satirising the work of Matthew Arnold, W. S. Gilbert and Oscar Wilde. (*T*5)

EL DORADO   A meditation on desire and curiosity as spurs to endeavour. The essay includes the much quoted passage 'to travel hopefully is a better thing than to arrive'. (*Virginibus, T*25)

THE ENGLISH ADMIRALS   A stirring account of admirals and their heroic deeds in which Stevenson expresses his love of adventure and the sea. (*Virginibus, T*25)

EPILOGUE TO AN INLAND VOYAGE   A description of Stevenson's arrest on suspicion of being a spy. The incident occurred during a walking tour in the valley of the Loing in 1875. (*Plains, T*17)

FABLES   A series of short sketches, each containing a moral, commenced as early as 1874. The titles are:

> 'The Persons of the Tale'
> 'The Sinking Ship'
> 'The Two Matches'
> 'The Sick Man and the Fireman'
> 'The Devil and the Innkeeper'
> 'The Penitent'
> 'The Yellow Paint'
> 'The House of Eld'

'The Four Reformers'
'The Man and his Friend'
'The Reader'
'The Citizen and the Traveller'
'The Distinguished Stranger'
'The Cart Horses and the Saddle Horse'
'The Tadpole and the Frog'
'Something In It'
'Faith, Half-Faith and No Faith At All'
'The Touchstone'
'The Poor Thing'
'The Song of the Morrow'

FATHER DAMIEN   An open letter taking issue with a Dr. Hyde of Honolulu who had criticised the leper settlement of Molokai which Stevenson knew well. (*Vailima, T*21)

FONTAINEBLEAU   An idyllic description of the colony of painters at Barbizon in the forest of Fontainebleau and the scenery surrounding the village. (*Plains, T*30)

A FOOTNOTE TO HISTORY   Subtitled 'Eight Years of Trouble in Samoa', this is a series of essays on aspects of Samoan political and social history. (*Vailima, T*21)

THE FOREIGNER AT HOME   Reflections on the divisions of races and nations. The essay reviews the differences between the English and Scottish character and contrasts the attitudes of the Highland and Lowland Scot. (*Memories, T*29)

FOREST NOTES   A description of the topography and natural history of the Fontainebleau forest (cf. 'Fontainebleau'). (*T*30)

FRANÇOIS VILLON: STUDENT, POET AND HOUSEBREAKER   A review of the life and career of Villon, a poet and rascal in fifteenth-century Paris. Stevenson's fascination with Villon is also revealed in his short story 'A Lodging for the Night' (q.v.). (*Studies, T*27)

A FRENCH LEGEND   A fragment, unpublished during Stevenson's lifetime, intended as part of the essay 'Forest Notes'. (*T*25)

THE GENESIS OF 'THE MASTER OF BALLANTRAE'   An account of the literary and autobiographical sources of *The Master of Ballantrae*. (*Writing, T*10)

A GOSSIP ON A NOVEL OF DUMAS'S   A discussion of the novels of Dumas with particular reference to *The Vicomte de Bragelonne*. The essay contains a discussion of Stevenson's favourite books and the reasons for his choice. (*Memories, T*29)

A GOSSIP ON ROMANCE   One of his most important literary essays, this discusses the difference between the romance and the novel and comments *inter alia* on *Robinson Crusoe, Clarissa Harlowe* and *The Count of Monte Cristo.* 'In anything fit to be called by the name of reading, the process itself should be absorbing and voluptuous.' (*Memories, T*29)

THE GREAT NORTH ROAD   An uncompleted novel, of which eight chapters were written, begun at Bournemouth in 1884. The fragment, written between *Treasure Island* and *Kidnapped*, reveals a growing mastery in the art of narrative. (*T*16)

HEATHERCAT   An unfinished novel, of which only three chapters were written, set in Scotland in the late seventeenth century. (*T*16)

HENRY DAVID THOREAU   An appraisal of Thoreau's philosophy and writings with particular reference to *Walden.* The essay reveals Stevenson's complete lack of sympathy for the life of quiet contemplation. (*Studies, T*27)

THE HISTORY OF MOSES   An account of Moses and the Israelites, dictated by Stevenson to his mother at the age of six. (*T*28)

A HUMBLE REMONSTRANCE   This reply to an article by Henry James on 'The Art of Fiction' led to a lasting friendship between the two writers. The essay contrasts the novel of adventure, the novel of character, and the dramatic novel and discusses the relative value novelists attach to incident (cf. 'A Gossip on Romance'). (*Memories, T*29)

THE IDEAL HOUSE   An unfinished essay describing Stevenson's conception of an ideal home. It is of particular interest for its list of his favourite books. (*T*25)

THE ISLE OF VOICES   Short story set in Hawaii and intended as a companion piece for 'The Bottle Imp'. The story is based on Stevenson's recollections of the Marquesas islands. (*Island Nights, T*13)

JOHN KNOX AND HIS RELATIONS TO WOMEN   A lengthy study of John Knox, the Scottish churchman and reformer. Stevenson had originally planned to write a biography of Knox as part of a work to be called 'Four Great Scotsmen'. (*Studies, T*27)

JULES VERNE'S STORIES   Review of eight stories by Jules Verne in which Stevenson welcomes the emergence of the scientific romance as a literary genre. (*T*28)

THE LANTERN-BEARERS   A nostalgic account of boyhood games

with bull's-eye lanterns. The essay is one of Stevenson's most deeply felt sermons on the theme of the romantic imagination: 'no man lives in the external truth, among salts and acids, but in the warm phantasmagoric chamber of his brain'. (*Plains, T*30)

THE LATE SAM BOUGH, R.S.A.   A study of the Cumberland painter Samuel Bough, whose work and personality Stevenson greatly admired. (*T*28)

LAY MORALS   An essay on morals and philosophy on which Stevenson worked intermittently between 1879–83. Throughout his life he was fascinated by ethical questions and referred to the study of ethics as being his 'veiled mistress'. (*T*26)

LETTER TO A YOUNG GENTLEMAN WHO PROPOSES TO EMBRACE THE CAREER OF ART   This paper, described by Henry James as 'a little mine of felicities', contains advice for aspiring writers and cautions them against undue expectations. (*Plains, T*28)

A LODGING FOR THE NIGHT   Short story, set in Paris in 1456, an episode in the life of François Villon. Stevenson's first short story, written at the age of twenty-seven, this demonstrates his gift for communicating physical sensations – cold, panic and fear – through the medium of prose. (*Arabian, T*1)

THE MANSE   A loving description of his grandfather, the Revd Lewis Balfour, and of the manse at Colinton which was the scene of many of his boyhood adventures. (*Memories, T*29)

MARKHEIM   One of Stevenson's most memorable short stories, a brilliant exercise in the Poe manner which was also influenced by Dostoevsky's *Crime and Punishment*. An antique dealer is murdered by a visitor posing as a customer. (*Merry Men, T*8)

MEMOIRS OF AN ISLET   An affectionate description of Earraid, a small island off the coast of Mull, which Thomas Stevenson chose as his headquarters during the building of the Dhu Heartach lighthouse. The essay vividly expresses Stevenson's fascination with the island, the setting for one of the key episodes in *Kidnapped*. (*Memories, T*29)

MEMOIRS OF HIMSELF   An autobiographical fragment begun in 1880 and augmented at Vailima. Some of the material is quoted in Balfour's *Life*. (*T*29)

THE MERRY MEN   Short story set in and around Earraid, an islet off the coast of Mull. Stevenson described the tale as 'a fantastic sonata of the sea and wrecks'. It owes something of its atmosphere to Poe's short story 'A Descent into the Maelstrom'.

(*Merry Men*, *T*8)

THE MISADVENTURES OF JOHN NICHOLSON   Short story remarkable for the verisimilitude of its Edinburgh setting and for its por-trayal of a difficult relationship between a strict father and a wayward son – a theme drawn on a fuller scale in *Weir of Hermiston*. (*Tales, T*13)

MR. BASKERVILLE AND HIS WARD   Fragment of a novel, originally entitled 'Robin Run the Hedge', concerning a magistrate and his ward Robin Rutledge. (*T*16)

A MODERN COSMOPOLIS   A description of San Francisco, a city Stevenson knew well from his residence there (December 1879–May1880). He was fascinated by the contrast between the city and Monterey (cf. 'The Old Pacific Capital'). (*T*18)

THE MORALITY OF THE PROFESSION OF LETTERS   A discussion of the ideals and qualities of the professional writer. (*Writing, T*28)

MY FIRST BOOK: 'TREASURE ISLAND'   An account of the genesis of *Treasure Island*, the first of Stevenson's works to bring him fame. 'Men are born with various manias: from my earliest childhood, it was mine to make a plaything of imaginary series of events.' (*Writing, T*2)

A NIGHT IN FRANCE   An early draft of the essay 'Forest Notes', unpublished during Stevenson's lifetime. (*T*30)

NOCTES AMBROSIANAE   Review of *The Comedy of the Noctes Ambrosianae* by John Wilson (Christopher North), edited by John Skelton. (*T*28)

A NOTE AT SEA   A fragment, unpublished during Stevenson's life-time, intended as part of the essay 'Forest Notes'. (*T*30)

A NOTE ON REALISM   A discussion of the difference between realism and idealism in literature. (*Writing, T*28)

NOTES ON THE MOVEMENTS OF YOUNG CHILDREN   Reflections on the gracefulness of childhood games such as dancing and skip-ping. (*T*25)

NUITS BLANCHES   A description of the sleepless nights of child-hood, one of a series of sketches written *circa* 1870. (*T*30)

NURSES   Reflections on the nurses of one's childhood, one of a series of sketches written *circa* 1870. (*T*30)

OLALLA   Short story in the Poe manner set in a remote Spanish valley. A wounded officer takes lodgings in a villa to convalesce but becomes emotionally involved with the strange daughter of the household. (*Merry Men, T*8)

OLD MORTALITY   A meditation on death prompted by his reflections on Greyfriars Cemetery, Edinburgh, and by the passing of his college friend Walter Ferrier in 1883 (cf. 'The Wreath of Immortelles'). (*Memories*, *T*29)

THE OLD PACIFIC CAPITAL   An account of the Californian town of Monterey, where Stevenson lived in poverty (September–October 1879) prior to his marriage. The essay illustrates his fascination with history and tradition. (*Plains*, *T*18)

AN OLD SCOTCH GARDENER   An affectionate description of the gardener at Swanston, written at the age of 20 (March 1871). This is the only example of his early work which Stevenson considered worthy of reprinting. (*Memories*, *T*29)

AN OLD SONG   A novella published in four weekly instalments in *London*, 24 February–17 March 1877. See Appendix: Posthumously Published Works.

ON A NEW FORM OF INTERMITTENT LIGHT FOR LIGHTHOUSES   A scientific paper read before the Royal Scottish Society of Arts on 27 March 1871. (*T*28)

ON LORD LYTTON'S 'FABLES IN SONG'   Review of *Fables in Song* by Edward Robert Bulwer-Lytton. (*T*28)

ON SOME TECHNICAL ELEMENTS OF STYLE IN LITERATURE   A critical discussion of the elements of prose literature with particular reference to pattern, rhythm and phrasing. 'There is nothing more disenchanting to man than to be shown the springs and mechanism of any art.' (*Writing*, *T*28)

ON THE ENJOYMENT OF UNPLEASANT PLACES   An essay inspired by a visit to Wick in the autumn of 1868. 'Wherever a man is, he will find something to please and pacify him'. (*T*25)

ON THE THERMAL INFLUENCE OF FORESTS   A scientific paper on the climatic influence of forests, read before the Royal Society, Edinburgh, on 19 May 1873. (*T*28)

ORDERED SOUTH   Reflections on the life of an invalid. The essay was written at Mentone on the Riviera where Stevenson convalesced for six months in the winter of 1873–4. (*Virginibus*, *T*25)

THE OWL   One chapter only of this novel was written, set in Brittany in 1793. Stevenson abandoned it to work on *The Ebb-Tide*. (*T*16)

PAN'S PIPES   A short paper speculating on the mythical figure of Pan as the god of nature and stressing man's need for nonscientific explanations: 'there will always be hours when we refuse to be put off by the feint of explanation, nicknamed science, and demand instead some palpitating image of our estate'. (*Virginibus*, T25)

PASTORAL   An affectionate description of an old Pentland shepherd, John Todd, whose tales of the old droving days provided the inspiration for the account of Sim and Candlish in *St. Ives*. (*Memories*, T29)

THE PAVILION ON THE LINKS   Short story written at Monterey (1878–9), one of Stevenson's earliest narratives of any length. The story is set in a pavilion on a lonely stretch of the East Lothian coast and reveals his gift for creating an atmosphere of suspense. (*Arabian*, T1)

A PENNY PLAIN AND TWOPENCE COLOURED   A nostalgic account of the toy theatre which had provided Stevenson with much happiness as a child. (*Memories*, T29)

THE PENTLAND RISING   An account of the Pentland revolt of 1666, published as a pamphlet at the expense of Thomas Stevenson in November 1866. (*T*28)

A PLEA FOR GAS LAMPS   A nostalgic plea for the cosy glow of gas lamps instead of electric lighting. (*Virginibus*, T25)

THE POETS AND POETRY OF SCOTLAND   Review of *The Poets and Poetry of Scotland* edited by James Grant Wilson. Stevenson does not praise Scottish poetry, as might have been expected, but instead deprecates the editor's uncritical adulation of Burns and others. (*T*28)

POPULAR AUTHORS   In this paper Stevenson reveals his lifelong addiction to popular fiction and admits to having been brought up on *Cassell's Family Paper*. The reader of popular romances 'escapes the narrow prison of the individual career, and sates his avidity for other lives'. (*T*28)

PROTEST ON BEHALF OF BOER INDEPENDENCE   A letter to the press supporting the Transvaal rebellion of Paul Kruger and arguing against British Jingoism. 'We are in the wrong, or all that we profess is false; blood has been shed, glory lost, and, I fear, honour also.' (*T*28)

PROVIDENCE AND THE GUITAR   Short story describing the adventures of a pair of strolling actors, apparently based on an incident related to Stevenson by a penniless actor while staying at Barbizon. (*Arabian*, T1)

PULVIS ET UMBRA   One of Stevenson's rare excursions into philosophy, this essay affirms the existence of a moral motive running through all forms of life. (*Plains*, T26)

A QUIET CORNER OF ENGLAND   Review of *A Quiet Corner of England* by Basil Champneys, a study of landscape and architecture in the Romney Marsh district of Kent. (*T*28)

THE RAJAH'S DIAMOND   Short story consisting of four sections —'Story of the Bandbox', 'Story of the Young Man in Holy Orders', 'Story of the House with the Green Blinds' and 'The Adventure of Prince Florizel and a Detective'. (*Arabian*, *T*1)

RANDOM MEMORIES   Two autobiographical pieces, 'The Coast of Fife' and 'The Education of an Engineer', describing boyhood journeys with his father. (*Plains*, *T*30)

A RETROSPECT   An account of a visit to Dunoon in 1870. The essay contains interesting evidence of Stevenson's fascination with childhood. 'The future is nothing; but the past is myself, my own history, the seed of my present thoughts, the mould of my present disposition.' (*T*30)

ROADS   Stevenson's first paid contribution to a periodical (December 1873), planned during walks at Cockfield, Co. Durham. (*T*25)

ROSA QUO LOCORUM   An account of his childhood discovery of the world of literature. 'To pass from hearing literature to reading it is to take a great and dangerous step ... it involves coming of age; it is even a kind of second weaning.' (*T*30)

SALVINI'S 'MACBETH'   Review of a performance of *Macbeth* given by the Italian actor Salvini. (*T*28)

SAMUEL PEPYS   A review of Pepys's life and achievement, contrasting the diarist's outward respectability with his private laxity. (*Studies*, *T*27)

THE SATIRIST   A slight description of a satirical companion, one of a series of sketches written *circa* 1870. (*T*30)

SCOTTISH RIVERS   Review of *Scottish Rivers* by Sir Thomas Lauder, a book which deeply impressed Stevenson by its sincerity and charm. (*T*28)

THE SIRE DE MALETROIT'S DOOR   Short story set in medieval France, originally entitled 'The Sire of Maletroit's Mousetrap'. A nobleman traps a chance visitor in his house and asks his prisoner to choose between marrying his niece or forfeiting his own life. (*Arabian*, *T*1)

SOME ASPECTS OF ROBERT BURNS   A critical appreciation of Burns's life and work, notable for its frankness in discussing the poet's moral lapses. (*Studies*, *T*27)

SOME COLLEGE MEMORIES   Reminiscences of student days at

Edinburgh University, commenting on student and staff attitudes past and present. (*Memories, T*29)

SOME GENTLEMEN IN FICTION   A discussion of the concept of the gentleman in fiction, with particular reference to the novels of Dickens. (*T*26)

SOME PORTRAITS BY RAEBURN   An appreciation of the works of the Scottish artist whose portraits were exhibited at Edinburgh. The paper includes a notable description of Braxfield, the Lord Justice-Clerk, who later served as the inspiration for Adam Weir. (*Virginibus, T*25)

STEVENSON'S COMPANION TO THE COOK BOOK   Brief sketches including anecdotes on the lives of Fielding, Richardson, Sterne, Burns, Judge Jeffries, St Athanasius and John Knox. (*T*5)

THE STORY OF A LIE   Short story written on the steerage passage to New York in August 1879. The tale is apparently based on Stevenson's experiences in Paris as a young man. (*Tales, T*14)

THE STORY OF A RECLUSE   An unfinished story concerning the adventures of a medical student of Edinburgh University (cf. 'Cannonmills'). (*T*16)

THE SUICIDE CLUB   Short story consisting of three sections – 'Story of the Young Man with the Cream Tarts', 'Story of the Physician and the Saratoga Trunk' and 'The Adventure of the Hansom Cabs' – set in Victorian London. (*Arabian, T*1)

SWISS NOTES   A series of articles on aspects of Switzerland, inspired by his prolonged convalescence at Davos. The titles are: 'Health and Mountains', 'Davos in Winter', 'Alpine Diversions' and 'The Stimulation of the Alps'. (*T*30)

TALK AND TALKERS   A description of six friends and their conversational gifts. The friends are: R. A. M. Stevenson (Spring-heel'd Jack), W. E. Henley (Burly), Fleeming Jenkin (Cockshot), Walter Simpson (Athelred), J. A. Symonds (Opalstein), and Edmund Gosse (Purcel). (*Memories, T*29)

THOMAS STEVENSON: CIVIL ENGINEER   A moving account of Stevenson's father written shortly after the latter's death in May 1887. The account should be compared with the description of Thomas Stevenson as a boy in *A Family of Engineers*. (*Memories, T*29)

THRAWN JANET   A supernatural short story, planned as one of a series of tales of psychological terror, and the only one of Stevenson's stories written entirely in Scottish dialect. He confided to Colvin that the writing of it 'frightened me to death'. (*Merry Men*, *T*8)

TIME Reflections on the differing attitudes to time on the part of adults and children. 'Time doesn't exist for us while we are children; we are unconscious of any progression, and live in a large place not measured out by hours.'.(*T*25)

THE TREASURE OF FRANCHARD Short story set in rural France. The central character, Anastasie Desprez, is a portrait of Madame La Chevre, the wife of a painter at whose house in Barbizon Stevenson was a frequent guest. The story displays his understanding of the French life and spirit. (*Merry Men*, *T*8)

TUTUILA A description of the Samoan island of Tutuilu, originally intended for inclusion in *In the South Seas*. (*Vailima*, *T*21)

TWO JAPANESE ROMANCES: *See* BYWAYS OF BOOK ILLUSTRATION

VICTOR HUGO'S ROMANCES A study of Hugo's novels, tracing the development of the romantic tradition through the work of Fielding and Scott. (*Studies*, *T*27)

VIRGINIBUS PUERISQUE Four essays dealing respectively with courtship, marriage, falling in love and conversation. The first two are untitled, but three and four are headed 'On Falling in Love' and 'Truth and Intercourse'. (*Virginibus*, *T*25)

THE WAIF WOMAN Short story set in Iceland, originally intended for inclusion in *Island Nights*. (*T*5)

WALKING TOURS As a young man Stevenson was an enthusiastic walker in England, Scotland and France and in this essay he expresses his delight in the roving life. The paper reveals his love of open-air adventure and his admiration for Hazlitt. (*Virginibus*, *T*25)

WALT WHITMAN An appreciation of the poetry and outlook of Whitman, whose work made a deep impression on Stevenson as a young man. (*Studies*, *T*27)

WELLINGTON A fragment of a life of the Duke of Wellington, originally conceived as part of a full-length study commissioned in 1885 but never completed. (*T*28)

WHEN THE DEVIL WAS WELL A short story set in Italy in the fifteenth century, one of Stevenson's earliest surviving pieces of fiction. (*T*5)

WILL O' THE MILL Short story, cast in the form of an allegory, and set in a valley in Germany or Austria. The setting was apparently inspired by memories of the Brenner Pass. (*Merry Men*, *T*8)

A WINTER WALK IN CARRICK AND GALLOWAY A description of a walking tour in January 1876, unpublished during his lifetime. (*T*30)

THE WORKS OF EDGAR ALLAN POE   Review of the edition of Poe's works edited by John H. Ingram. The review is of considerable literary interest in the light of Stevenson's indebtedness to Poe as a storyteller. (*T*28)

THE WREATH OF IMMORTELLES   One of a series of sketches written *circa* 1870, this is an account of reflections in Old Greyfriars Cemetery, Edinburgh: a favourite childhood haunt of Stevenson. (*T*30)

YOSHIDA-TORAJIRO   An appraisal of the life and work of Yoshida, a Japanese reformer whose struggle for emancipation held a deep appeal for Stevenson. (*Studies, T*27)

THE YOUNG CHEVALIER   An unfinished novel, of which only a fragment survives, set in France and Scotland in 1749. The Master of Ballantrae was to have been one of the central characters. (*T*16)

Part II
THE ESSAYS

The Essays

Though Stevenson's reputation rests principally on his novels, romances and short stories it should be remembered that he began his literary career as an essayist, and that throughout his life he continued to write essays and *belles-lettres* on numerous aspects of life, literature and ideas. In recent years this aspect of his work has received comparatively little critical attention. This is due to a combination of factors: changing tastes in literary fashion, the mannered style of the essays, their occasional posturing and artificiality, perhaps above all to a feeling that his essays are clever rather than profound and that they do not contribute materially to an understanding of Stevenson as a creative writer.

With the passage of time since his death and the growing appreciation of his stature as a serious imaginative artist it is possible to attempt a balanced appraisal of his achievement as an essayist which acknowledges their limitations and at the same time recognises their thematic and artistic significance. An examination of his essays reveals continuing attention to themes and ideas he explored in the novels and stories: the contrast between the man of action and the philosophy of resignation, life as a pilgrimage towards disillusionment, the dichotomy between the veneer of civilisation and man's animal impulses, the impact of circumstances on behaviour and attitudes. These ideas are approached in differing forms and from diverse angles. The effect is to illuminate the novels and tales by a continuous process of discussion and commentary. Thus, themes which are approached indirectly or by implication in the novels are examined at fuller length in the essays, and vice versa. It is possible to discern behind

49

the essays an attitude of mind, a personality, with a distinctive approach to matters of conduct and belief. It is a voice which insists on living life to the full, on extracting the utmost from every facet of experience, on the necessity for aspiration and effort as an antidote to stagnation, on a vigorous intellectual curiosity towards endeavour and diversity. The underlying attitude fluctuates between a fatalistic stoicism and insistence on individual effort as the key to human happiness. Common to them all is the assertion that life is worth living, or rather can be and ought to be made worth living: a value judgement implicit in all his work.

The principal essays are contained in seven volumes: *An Inland Voyage* (1878), *Travels with a Donkey* (1879), *Virginibus Puerisque* (1881), *Familiar Studies of Men and Books* (1882), *Memories and Portraits* (1887), *Across the Plains* (1892) and *In the South Seas* (1896). To read these in the order in which they were written is to appreciate afresh Stevenson's growth as a literary craftsman, the extraordinary range of style and topic at his command, and the importance of the essays as an expression of his personal philosophy.

An Inland Voyage, his first published book, is an account of a canoe journey in Belgium and France during September 1876. In company with his friend Sir Walter Simpson (the 'Cigarette' of the book) he journeyed by canal from Antwerp to Brussels, then on the rivers Sambre and Oise to Pointoise, eighteen miles from the Seine. Here, abruptly, the voyage terminated. 'I was weary of dipping the paddle', he wrote, 'I was weary of living on the skirts of life; I wished to be in the thick of it once more; I wished to get to work.'[1] Much of the book is a transcription from his log-book written daily on the journey. The log-book was carefully rewritten on his return to Scotland – the substance of the work being carried out in Edinburgh during the autumn of 1877 – and the task was completed in January 1878. On its publication the book attracted slight though on the whole favourable attention from reviewers. Perhaps of more importance than the reviews was the fact that it attracted the attention of a number of distinguished literary figures including George Meredith and Henry James and was widely praised by his friends. Stevenson himself summed up his reaction to its critical reception in a letter to his mother: 'I read *Inland Voyage* the other day: what rubbish these reviewers did talk! It is not badly written, thin, mildly cheery, and strained.'[2]

The book is a readable and light-hearted account of his travels, interspersed with vivid character sketches, descriptions of landscapes and philosophical reflections. The account of the canoe voyage which forms the linking thread is written in a genial tone which anticipates such works as *Three Men in a Boat* (1889) and is remarkable for its humour and individuality. (Stevenson's reference to the book being 'mildly cheery, and strained' is an acknowledgement that at times the humour *is* a little forced: it is known from the letters he wrote during his travels that the weather was mainly wet and miserable.) The reader's attention is held by the flowing style of the language and the striking descriptions of people, places and incidents encountered on the journey. Thus, in 'The Royal Sport Nautique' there is an engaging account of a meeting with a group of boating enthusiasts; in 'The Oise in Flood' there is a powerful description of being struck by a fallen tree whilst racing along a swollen river; in 'The Company at Table' there is a fascinating glimpse of the guests at a wayside inn, written with a novelist's insight into nuance and character. Whether he is describing the interior of a cathedral, rural scenery, an itinerant pedlar ('The Travelling Merchant') or the changing climate, one is aware of a highly idiosyncratic voice, a writer possessing unusual powers of observation and with the gift of approaching the familiar through fresh eyes. The account of the way of life of a canal bargee ('On the Willebroek Canal') is a characteristic example of his ability to describe familiar sights and to invest them with a romantic charm. Continually one senses the voice of the romantic:

To know what you prefer, instead of humbly saying Amen to what the world tells you you ought to prefer, is to have kept your soul alive.

I am sure I would rather be a bargee than occupy any position under heaven that required attendance at an office.

There is some life in humanity yet; and youth will now and again find a brave word to say in dispraise of riches, and throw up a situation to go strolling with a knapsack.

This emphasis on the virtues of the nomadic life, this 'protest against offices and the mercantile spirit', runs through the book as a leitmotiv. There can be no question that the idea of living as a vagabond, freed from all considerations of routine and predictability, held for Stevenson a very powerful appeal. 'There is nobody under thirty so dead', he wrote, 'but his heart will stir a little at sight of a gypsies' camp.' The idea of embarking on a canoe voyage on the rivers and canals of Europe, of journeying with a donkey in the Cevennes mountains, of setting out on a cruise among the islands of the South Seas – all these were expressions of this romantic yearning for the life of the nomad, this unceasing quest for the roving life in preference to all that was safe, secure and certain.

From the point of view of his subsequent development as a novelist and essayist, the most interesting aspects of *An Inland Voyage* are its indications of an imaginative writer in embryo. At numerous points in the book there are passages capable of much fuller treatment, paragraphs which, though undeveloped, offer convincing evidence of his search for a satisfying means of expression. In the chapter entitled 'Changed Times' there is a paragraph (beginning 'I suppose none of us recognise the great part that is played in life by eating and drinking') in which he is clearly tempted to digress into a separate essay on food and drink. In 'Canal Boats 'there is a fascinating speculation on the way of life aboard a canal barge; in 'Precy and the Marionnettes' he embarks on a description of the inn which quickly shades into a detailed account of a marionnette performance; the highlight of 'At Maubeuge' is a discussion of the contrast between living in a town where one is known and a place where one is a stranger. This continual tendency to digress and philosophise is characteristic of Stevenson's early writings and is a reminder that each of his works – whether cast in the form of a novel, short story or essay – is an experiment in statement, a crucible in which he tested out alternative approaches to life and literature.

An Inland Voyage is capable of both a literal and a metaphorical interpretation. Literally the journey is an attempt to escape from the routines of everyday life, to withdraw from the claustrophobia of respectability and seek happiness in the life of a traveller. Metaphorically it is a journey into the self, a voyage of exploration into the human psyche. The idea of life as a journey in quest of self-freedom is implicit throughout and is raised explicitly towards the end:

There is no coming back ... on the impetuous stream of life. And we must all set our pocket-watches by the clock of fate. There is a headlong, forthright tide, that bears away man with his fancies like a straw, and runs fast in time and space.

Stevenson senses that the search for freedom, for a total release from commitments and conventionalities, is a chimera which is bound to prove illusory in the end. Hence his use of mist imagery: 'There is a sense in which those mists [the mists of illusion] never rose from off our journey; and from that time forth they lie very densely in my note-book.' The desire for a total withdrawal from conventional life is, then, an illusion which can be entertained for short periods but sooner or later there has to be a return to the demands of society. 'To the civilised man', he writes on the final page, 'there must come, sooner or later, a desire for civilisation.' This recognition that complete self-freedom is an impossibility, that there can be no escape from obligations, tempers the humorous tone of the book with a sombre note of realism and anticipates the theme of *Travels with a Donkey* and the later essays.

An Inland Voyage occupies an important place in the Stevenson canon, not simply because it was the first of his books to be published. It has weaknesses common to many first books by young writers still in the process of learning their craft – unevenness, occasional immaturities, a tendency on the part of the author to play the part of a poseur. But in its originality, its refusal to be bound by convention (for example, in its criticism of established religion), its engaging descriptions of natural beauty and its penetrating insight into human character it marked the arrival of a new and significant literary talent. Stevenson's cousin reported to him that a society at Oxford had chosen the book as 'the best specimen of the writing of English of this century'.[3]

Travels with a Donkey in the Cevennes, an account of a twelve-day walking tour (22 September–2 October 1878) in the mountains of central France, is one of Stevenson's most characteristic excursions in the field of the travel essay. During his journey he kept a detailed journal of his daily experiences and wrote these up on his return to England. The book was published in June 1879 and was on the whole favourably reviewed. Critics were impressed with its charm and freshness and the evidence of a narrator intensely

curious concerning the world about him and eager to communicate his reflections on life and behaviour.

The book is cast in the form of a journal recording his journey
of 120 miles from Monastier to St. Jean du Gard, accompanied by
an intractable but engaging donkey, Modestine. One of the most
attractive features of the book is the description of the gradually
deepening relationship between Stevenson and the donkey. At the
outset the animal is barely tolerated; she is stubborn, wayward
and has to be beaten to extract obedience. During the course of
the twelve days the relationship between them deepens to one of
mutual affection. When the moment for parting arrives Stevenson
cannot conceal his emotion :

> After the first day, although sometimes I was hurt and distant in
> manner, I still kept my patience; and as for her, poor soul! She
> had come to regard me as a god. She loved to eat out of my
> hand. She was patient, elegant in form, the colour of an ideal
> mouse, and inimitably small. Her faults were those of her race
> and sex; her virtues were her own. Farewell, and if for ever –

The charm of the book lies in its lyrical descriptions of natural
beauty, of dawns and sunsets and the stark grandeur of the
mountainous terrain, intertwined with fascinating glimpses of
peasants, innkeepers and travellers by the way. He confided to his
cousin that much of the book 'is mere protestations to F[Fanny
Osbourne, later to become his wife] most of which I think you will
understand. That is to me the main thread of interest.'4 Implicit in
the narrative is a continual awareness of a missing communion, of
a longing for the company of the woman he loved. 'I wished a
companion to lie near me in the starlight', he wrote, 'silent and
not moving, but ever within touch.' Continually one has a sense
that the narrator is thinking aloud, that he is addressing an unseen
yet intimately known friend and recording his innermost
thoughts. In his comments on Cistercian monks, on Roman
Catholicism and on the way of life of the Cevennes peasants can
be discerned a characteristically Stevensonian voice and an insistence on courage, activity (as opposed to the life of contemplation)
and freedom of thought.

It seems clear that he intended both a literal and a symbolic
interpretation of the book. In the dedication he wrote: 'But we are
all travellers in what John Bunyan calls the wilderness of this

world – all, too, travellers with a donkey; and the best that we find
in our travels is an honest friend. He is a fortunate voyager who
finds many.'

The explicit reference to *Pilgrim's Progress* is a reminder that life
itself is a journey in quest of companionship and enlightenment.
In the whole of his journey in the mountains Stevenson does not
find any friendship; he finds instead dishonesty, rudeness and
indifference. Even at Monastier he had been struck by the uncivil,
argumentative people who all 'hate, loathe, decry, and calumniate
each other'. The one companion he has is a dumb animal; his
affection for the donkey is in the sharpest contrast to the unap-
pealing shallowness of the human society he has encountered.

The implication is not simply that solitude is preferable to
society (in his essay 'Walking Tours' he openly asserted 'to be
properly enjoyed, a walking tour should be gone upon alone') but
that affection, companionship and loyalty are much rarer qualities
than is commonly supposed and have to be consciously sought.
This conception of life as a journey, as a series of explorations
through 'the wilderness of this world' was always with him. In a
sense each of his novels and stories is a variation on this theme
and he returned to it for the last time in the profound characterisation of *Weir of Hermiston*.

Travels with a Donkey is a young man's book. It possesses in
abundance the naive, innocent, enthusiastic tone of a young writer
eager to communicate his impressions of unfamiliar sights and
sounds. It is also an essentially romantic work: the idea of setting
off into the mountains, discarding civilisation and all its comforts,
was a romantic conception which held a strong appeal for one
who always yearned for the life of the vagabond. The actual
materials of which the book is composed are slight yet the overall
impression is one of a compact and satisfying narrative, intimate
but not egotistical. Through these early travel narratives Stevenson was gaining confidence in expression and acquiring increasing mastery over vocabulary. Already critics were coming to
recognise his graceful, lucid, flowing style and to acknowledge the
emergence of a new force in English literature.

Stevenson began in 1876 the series of essays later collected under
the title *Virginibus Puerisque and Other Papers*. His original intention,
as he expressed it in the dedication (to his friend W. E. Henley),

was 'to state temperately the beliefs of youth as opposed to the contentions of age; to go over all the field where the two differ, and produce at last a little volume of special pleadings which I might call, without misnomer, *Life at Twenty-five*'. The title, literally translated, means 'young men and maidens', and the volume was conceived as the voice of youth addressing young people on their hopes and problems, the claims of youth against age and the pit-falls on the road to maturity. The first four sections, collectively entitled 'Virginibus Puerisque', deal with love, marriage and truth-fulness. Then follow a series of essays ranging over aspects of life which specially interested him: activity versus contentment, the point of view of the invalid, attitudes towards death, definitions of happiness, the romance of the sea, the outlook of a child, and walking tours. The book concludes with two essays on characteris-tically Stevensonian themes: the spirit of romance ('Pan's Pipes') and a lament for the passing of the lamplighter ('A Plea for Gas Lamps'). The tone throughout is genial and discursive. In these gentle, elegant, cultured essays – essays which display a striking maturity for one so young – there is evidence of a man of wide reading who has observed for himself and formed his own conclu-sions on the fundamentals of life.

On its publication in 1881 *Virginibus Puerisque* was warmly praised for its fine writing, its courage and restraint, but it was recognised that, despite the charm of the graceful prose and the reflective, didactic tone, the volume as a whole suffers from a number of weaknesses. Stevenson himself in his essay 'Fontaine-bleau' (1883) wrote with evident approval of those artists and writers who 'are at that stage of education, for the most part, when a man is too much occupied with style to be aware of the necessity for any matter'. The essays are open to the criticism that they are too artificial, too carefully polished, and that their read-ability and erudition conceals an obsession with style at the expense of any serious moral or intellectual concern. The essays were written for the most part between 1876–8 when Stevenson was in his late twenties. At this time he was still feeling his way as a man of letters and unsure in which direction his real talents lay. This basic uncertainty is evident in his tendency towards affecta-tion, in the rather forced tone of some passages; one has the impression of a lack of spontaneity, of a striving for stylistic excel-lence which obscures a fundamental indecision.

Beneath the pleasant, delicate tone, however, there is also

evidence of an acute psychological insight and a shrewd practical judgement on matters concerning human behaviour. Moreover the essays contain a number of indications of the novelist Stevenson was to become. 'A Plea for Gas Lamps', for example, ostensibly a straightforward exercise in nostalgia, is also capable of an allegorical interpretation: as a symbol of man's unending struggle against the darkness of ignorance and fear. In such essays as 'The English Admirals', 'Walking Tours' and 'Pan's Pipes' there is evidence of that quest for adventure, that yearning for romance which underlies so much of his work as a novelist and storyteller. There is also present a more serious element: in 'Aes Triplex' and 'Ordered South' there is a recognition of man's fundamental lone-liness, an awareness that the human condition is an endless struggle between conflicting forces – a tension he described later as 'the war in the members'.[5] It is this philosophical element underlying the outward geniality of the volume which compels the reader to return to it and to recognise the hand of a novelist in embryo.

Virginibus Puerisque is the work of a young man still experiment-ing to find a satisfying medium of expression. It is also the work of a writer possessing an unusually perceptive eye for descriptive detail. In 'Some Portraits by Raeburn', for example, there is a strik-ing description of Braxfield, the Lord Justice-Clerk whose persona-lity was later to inspire the novel *Weir of Hermiston*:

> The tart, rosy, humorous look of the man, his nose like a cudgel, his face resting squarely on the jowl. . . . A peculiarly subtle expression haunts the lower part, sensual and incredulous, like that of a man tasting good Bordeaux with half a fancy it has been somewhat too long uncorked. From under the pendulous eyelids of old age the eyes look out with a half-youthful, half-frosty twinkle. Hands, with no pretence to distinction, are folded on the judge's stomach.

It is in passages such as this that Stevenson displayed that fascination with human character and gift for the vivid metaphor which so characterised his fiction. In these early pieces he was not simply experimenting in style but was perfecting techniques of irony, hyperbole and humour which found their full expression in the novels and romances. In doing so he was fashioning a distinc-tive manner, a voice which his readers came to recognise. Review-

ing the book in *Academy* Edmund Purcell, one of his shrewdest
critics, had to admit that it revealed 'that undefinable but surely
unmistakeable feeling of affectionate cameraderie, that strong
sense of a personality whom one would like to know in the flesh as
well as in the book'.[6]

Stevenson described *Familiar Studies of Men and Books* as 'the read-
ings of a literary vagrant'.[7] The volume consists of nine essays —
contributed for the most part to the *Cornhill Magazine* during
1876–81 — in which he discusses the life and work of a range of
literary figures. The subjects include such diverse personalities as
Victor Hugo, Robert Burns, Walt Whitman, Henry Thoreau and
Samuel Pepys. In each case his approach is to review the subject's
literary achievement and to discuss the relevance of his work
within the wider context of English and European literature.

Perhaps the most interesting aspect of the book is that it high-
lights his lifelong fascination with the contrast between the life of
activity and the life of contemplation. Several of his subjects could
be described as men of action: such figures as Walt Whitman and
François Villon; others, including Thoreau, Charles of Orleans and
John Knox withdrew from active life in order to pursue a philosophy of meditation and resignation. The implicit contrast
between the two approaches forms one of the book's most significant underlying themes and makes the book as a whole a rewarding example of his ability to be judicious even when writing of
men with whom he can have had little sympathy. (The essay on
Thoreau, for example, contains many indications of Stevenson's
instinctive dislike for the life of contemplation, yet he cannot
conceal the attraction of the idea of Thoreau's sojourn by Walden
Pond.) He wrote in the Preface: 'For these were all men whom, for
one reason or another, I loved; or when I did not love the men,
my love was the greater to their books . . . and behold, when I
came to write them, my tone was sometimes hardly courteous and
seldom wholly just.'

The technique of writing a short essay appraising a writer's life
and work is in practice an extremely difficult one, as Stevenson
was the first to acknowledge. Defining his intention at the outset
he wrote:

The writer of short studies, having to condense in a few pages

the events of a whole lifetime, and the effect on his own mind
of many various volumes, is bound, above all things, to make
that condensation logical and striking. For the only justification
of his writing at all is that he shall present a brief, reasoned, and
memorable view. . . . Short studies are, or should be, things
woven like a carpet, from which it is impossible to detach a
strand.

The assertion that the primary object of a short study was to
achieve a single 'logical and striking' effect, to present a 'brief,
reasoned, and memorable view' to which each sentence contributed was central to his view of the essay as a literary form and
was one which never left him.[8] From his earliest essay 'Roads'
(1873) to his last 'My First Book: *Treasure Island*' (1893) he
continued to refine his style and approach but did not depart in
essence from this basic conception.

Familiar Studies continued the process of recognition begun by
his earlier volumes of essays. Henley, reviewing the book in
Academy, summed up the general reaction: 'He thinks critically and
dispassionately; he writes as his thoughts have made him feel. . . .
He is a critic in method and intelligence, and an advocate in
manner and temperament.'[9] (The use of the word 'advocate' here
is of course deliberate; Stevenson's legal training had given him
valuable training in the art of dispassionate appraisal.) In these
early essays, written whilst he was still in his twenties, he was
acquiring increasing experience in the use of language and in
methods of presentation. He was gaining added confidence in
expression and in techniques of style, approach and tone which
affected all his literary work.

Writing to Henley apropos *Memories and Portraits* Stevenson commented: 'Its interest will be largely autobiographical, Mr. S. having
sketched there the lineaments of many departed friends, and
dwelt fondly, and with a mistened eye, upon bygone pleasures.'[10]
His use of the phrase 'largely autobiographical' is interesting in
that the essays brought together in this volume represent his
mature reflections on the friendships and experiences of his early
life in Edinburgh. 'Some College Memories' and 'A College
Magazine' dwell on his memories of Edinburgh University; 'An
Old Scotch Gardener' is a fond sketch of the Swanston gardener,

whom he recalled with such nostalgia from his youth; 'The Manse' is an idyllic description of the manse at Colinton, every detail of which was fixed in his memory; 'Memoirs of an Islet' conveys the enchantment he felt for the island of Earraid, off the coast of Mull (the scene of a memorable episode in *Kidnapped*); 'Talk and Talkers' is a fascinating portrait of some of his closest friends from Edinburgh days; and so on. The entire volume is written with a novelist's insight into human character and with a warm affection for the scenes and personalities of his youth.

As an illustration of his skill in depicting scenes and characters with maximum economy and fidelity the essays describing John Todd, a Pentland shepherd, and his own father, Thomas Stevenson, are of exceptional interest. In the former, 'Pastoral', there is a masterly sketch of Todd's physical appearance:

> He laughed not very often, and when he did, with a sudden, loud haw-haw, hearty but somehow joyless, like an echo from a rock. His face was permanently set and coloured; ruddy and stiff with weathering; more like a picture than a face; yet with a certain strain and a threat of latent anger in the expression, like that of a man trained too fine and harassed with perpetual vigilance.

There are numerous touches here which reveal the hand of a craftsman with an acute eye for telling detail. Thus, the shepherd's laugh was 'hearty but somehow joyless, like an echo from a rock'; his face contained a threat of anger 'like that of a man trained too fine and harassed with perpetual vigilance'; his features were 'more like a picture than a face'. Instances of this kind can be found throughout the whole range of Stevenson's essays. In such passages he demonstrates his gift for the vivid portrayal of character and his skill in deploying language to the utmost effect. Notice in passing the peculiar appositeness of the phrase 'harassed with perpetual vigilance'. John Todd had had a lifetime's experience in looking after sheep. As a young man he had driven flocks of sheep along the drovers' roads to England and had a fund of memories of his lonely, pastoral life. Through observing such characters, talking with them and listening to their tales of a wilder, more dangerous past Stevenson was both absorbing the atmosphere and *feel* of the past and storing a wealth of impressions of the varieties of human experience.

The sketch of the wise old shepherd should be compared with the loving description of his father in the essay 'Thomas Stevenson: Civil Engineer':

He was a man of a somewhat antique strain: with a blended sternness and softness that was wholly Scottish and at first somewhat bewildering; with a profound essential melancholy of disposition and (what often accompanies it) the most humorous geniality in company; shrewd and childish; passionately attached, passionately prejudiced; a man of many extremes, many faults of temper, and no very stable foothold for himself among life's troubles.

It would be difficult to better this paragraph as an encapsulation of Thomas Stevenson's personality. The passage conveys the combination of 'sternness and softness' that was such an essential part of his temperament, the unusual combination of a sense of humour and a melancholiness of outlook, the contradictory elements which together made up his complex personality: childishness and shrewdness, strong prejudices and wise counsel, anger and affection. The description also conveys the complex of emotions with which Stevenson regarded his father: the blend of love and bewilderment with which he looked back on this most tender and devout of men. The essay as a whole is a profound statement of his feelings towards his father and a masterly summary of Thomas Stevenson's character and achievements.

Much of the interest of the volume stems from this strong autobiographical element, from the intrinsic fascination of a writer reviewing the personalities, scenes and reminiscences of his childhood and youth. The collection concludes with two essays which depart from this predominant theme and which review his approach to the art of fiction. In the first of these, 'A Gossip on Romance', he argues that romance (defined as 'the poetry of circumstance') is a fundamental human need; that the field of the romance is activity rather than contemplation; that its interest lies 'not on the passionate slips and hesitations of the conscience, but on the problems of the body and of the practical intelligence, in clean, open-air adventure, the shock of arms or the diplomacy of life'. In developing his argument he draws a comparison between Defoe's *Robinson Crusoe* and Richardson's *Clarissa Harlowe*, speculating on the reasons for the continuing popularity of *Crusoe* and the comparative neglect of *Clarissa*. The difference lies, for Stevenson, in the fact that Richardson's novel, whilst possessing many literary qualities, lacks the quality of pictorial romance, while *Crusoe* 'depends for the most part and with the overwhelming majority of its readers on the charm of circumstance'. His theme is summarised in these terms:

> This, then, is the plastic part of literature: to embody character, thought, or emotion in some act or attitude that shall be remarkably striking to the mind's eye. This is the highest and hardest thing to do in words; the thing which, once accomplished, equally delights the schoolboy and the sage and makes, in its own right, the quality of epics.

In this essay Stevenson is not simply justifying his own attitude to the romance but is attempting to define a profound truth of literature: that a romance is distinguished from other literary forms precisely in its quality of immediacy: that an individual is placed in circumstances to which he must respond with the minimum of hesitation. Seen in this light a romance is a series of incidents, each one a test of human character; the interest lies 'not upon what a man shall choose to do, but on how he manages to do it'. This, for him, was the central challenge of his art: 'to embody character, thought, or emotion in some act or attitude that shall be remarkably striking to the mind's eye' and which would illuminate aspects of psychology in such a way as to compel the reader to reflect on the mainsprings of human activity. 'A Gossip on Romance' is arguably the most important essay in the collection since in it he is thinking aloud on some primary aspects of his work and in doing so is ranging widely over literature and art. The fact that it took him two weeks to write it is indicative of the care and seriousness with which he approached his theme.

The theme is continued in the final essay, 'A Humble Remonstrance', in which Stevenson takes issue with Henry James over the latter's paper 'The Art of Fiction' (*Longman's Magazine*, September 1884). Though James and Stevenson were later to become close friends and maintained a genial correspondence for years, the two had very different conceptions of the novel. For Stevenson the art of narrative resided in 'the clear conception of certain characters of man, the choice and presentation of certain incidents out of a great number that offered, and the invention . . . of a certain key in dialogue'. Literature was essentially a process of selection, a sifting process in which a chaos of incidents and scenes was ordered into a neat and structured pattern. It was a distillation of life, an artefact through which the author seeks to illuminate and comment on the endless variety of human experience. In a memorable passage from the essay he summarises his conception of the novel:

> From all its chapters, from all its pages, from all its sentences, the well written novel echoes and re-echoes its one creative and controlling thought; to this must every incident and character contribute; the style must have been pitched in unison with this; and if there is anywhere a word that looks another way, the book would be stronger, clearer, and (I had almost said) fuller without it.

This conception of the 'one creative and controlling thought' of the novel was central to his artistic vision. Throughout the remaining ten years of his life he remained steadfast to his view that each work of fiction was a unique experiment in statement, that each was designed to achieve a single dominant effect, that fiction was a device which permitted the manipulation of actuality beyond the limited permutations of everyday living. In his insistence that fiction could both comment on life and change the reader's attitudes towards it – by helping him to see aspects of human behaviour from fresh vantage points – he was postulating a truth of profound significance and contributing to that debate on the functions of literature which still continues in our own century.

During 1888 Stevenson published a series of reminiscent and philosophical articles in *Scribner's Magazine*. These ranged from memories of his childhood ('The Coast of Fife' and 'The Lantern-Bearers') to descriptions of his nightmares ('A Chapter on Dreams'), from advice to aspiring writers ('Letter to a Young Gentleman') to a discussion of the idea of happiness ('A Christmas Sermon'). In 1891 Sidney Colvin suggested the idea of bringing these together in volume form; Stevenson readily concurred, entrusting Colvin with the selection and arrangement of the book and with overseeing its production. To the *Scribner's* essays Colvin added a number of earlier pieces including a lengthy account of his journey by emigrant train from New York to San Francisco ('Across the Plains') and an account of his experiences in Monterey ('The Old Pacific Capital'). The resulting volume, *Across the Plains with Other Memories and Essays* was published in 1892 and attracted wide attention.

Writing to Colvin on 29 May 1892 Stevenson expressed his appreciation:

> I don't know if I remembered to say how much pleased I was with *Across the Plains* in every way, inside and out, and you and me. The critics seem to taste it, too, as well as could be hoped, and I believe it will continue to bring me in a few shillings a year for a while.

His comment 'the critics seem to taste it, too' refers to its largely favourable critical reception. It was reviewed by influential writers such as William Archer in the *Pall Mall Gazette* and Richard le Gallienne in the *Academy*, and was the subject of a lengthy unsigned review in the *Scottish Leader*. The critics recognised in *Across the Plains* impressive evidence of his powers of observation and descriptive gifts and were agreed that it marked further confirmation of his distinctive style and approach as an essayist.

The most striking aspect of *Across the Plains* is its diversity: the essays range from travel to reminiscence, from philosophical reflection to literary discussion. Whether he is describing the Wyoming desert or the cliffs of Caithness, whether he is reflecting on the joy of existence or on the implications of the Darwinian theory, there is a sense of passionate involvement, of a distinctive voice looking at familiar things in a fresh and individual way. In 'The Lantern-Bearers', for example, his childhood games with bull's-eye lanterns become the basis for a discussion of the intangible nature of happiness; 'A Chapter on Dreams' discusses the genesis of *Dr. Jekyll and Mr. Hyde*; 'Pulvis et Umbra' is a sombre affirmation of a moral motive in the evolution of man. Behind and through each of the essays one is aware of a highly individual intelligence, a creative writer looking at the world and commenting on experience with originality and insight.

At a number of points in the book there are indications of that sense of loss which is never far from the surface in his writings. In 'Fontainebleau', a nostalgic meditation on his sojourn among the artists' community at Barbizon, there is a direct reference to the idea of a 'lost domain' – an elusive world glimpsed in childhood or adolescence but never recaptured:

> We are not content to pass away entirely from the scenes of our delight; we would leave, if but in gratitude, a pillar and a legend. One generation after another fall like honey-bees upon this memorable forest, rifle its sweets, pack themselves with vital memories, and when the theft is consummated depart again into life richer, put poorer also. The forest, indeed, they have possessed, from that day forward it is theirs indissolubly, and they will return to walk in it at night in the fondest of their dreams, and use it for ever in their books and pictures. ... A projection of themselves shall appear to haunt unfriended these scenes of happiness, a natural child of fancy, begotten and forgotten unawares.

Again, in 'The Coast of Fife', there is a haunting sense of lost happiness, an awareness of memories which can only be recalled with regret:

> The area railings, the beloved shop-window, the smell of semi-suburban tanpits, the song of the church bells upon a Sunday, the thin, high voices of compatriot children in a playing-field – what a sudden, what an overpowering pathos breathes to him from each familiar circumstance!

This sense of loss, of happinesses which can never be regained, accounts for the surprisingly modern quality of much of Stevenson's writing and anticipates the mood of such seminal novels as Alain-Fournier's *Le Grand Meaulnes*. (It is significant that Stevenson was one of the strongest influences on Alain-Fournier.)[11]

Linked with this is a tinge of pessimism, a faint but definite air of disillusionment which pervades the book as a whole. In his preface Colvin had drawn attention to this, reminding the reader that certain of the essays 'were written under circumstances of especial gloom and sickness'. Thus, in 'A Christmas Sermon', after commenting that life is rich in pleasures and rewards Stevenson adds the illuminating conclusion:

> Friendships fall through, health fails, weariness assails him; year after year, he must thumb the hardly varying record of his

own weakness and folly. It is a friendly process of detachment. When the time comes that he should go, there need be few illusions left about himself.

Across the Plains, the last collection of his philosophical essays to be published, is a mature work in striking contrast to the engaging *naïveté* of his early essays. It is permeated with an awareness of the passing of time, of the stripping away of illusions, of the fact that never again would he set eyes on the scenes of his childhood and youth. For these reasons it is one of his most intimate and revealing works, encapsulating both the range of his interests and the diversity of styles at his command.

Writing to his friend Henry James apropos his literary work since making his home at Vailima Stevenson observed:

> Gracious, what a strain is a long book! The time it took me to design this volume, before I could dream of putting pen to paper, was excessive; and then think of writing a book of travels on the spot, when I am continually extending my information, revising my opinions, and seeing the most finely finished portions of my work come part by part in pieces.[12]

The 'long book' on which he toiled intermittently from October 1889 to the autumn of 1891 was the volume which ultimately became *In the South Seas*. As originally conceived by Stevenson it was to be a comprehensive survey of life and traditions in the Pacific islands – part personal impressions, part sociological commentary, part historical summary. He was overwhelmed by the range and fascination of the material at his command – 'Such wild stories, such beautiful scenes, such singular intimacies, such manners and traditions, so incredible a mixture of the beautiful and horrible, the savage and civilised'[13] – and struggled for many months to fashion his theme into a manageable literary project. From the outset there was a sharp divergence of views between Stevenson and his wife and friends regarding the shape of the book. Stevenson saw it as a review of the life, customs and culture of Polynesia: a book in which he personally would figure only as a shaping presence and which would illuminate the impact of civilisation on the people of the islands. His family and friends on the other hand wished it to be a book of anecdotes, a *Travels with a Donkey* on the tropics, and tried to persuade him that what his readers wanted was an account of his own emotional and personal response to the South Seas. Though convinced that his own approach was the only possible way of tackling such an ambitious scheme he eventually realised that such a vast subject could not be brought within the compass of a single volume and reluctantly abandoned it. The volume as we know it today was edited from his individual chapters by Sidney Colvin and published after his death.

Though it is an uneasy hybrid between the engaging tone of the early travel books and the serious tone of Stevenson at his most sociological, it remains one of his most revealing and idiosyncratic works and essential reading for all who seek to understand his fascination with the life and people of the Pacific. From the opening chapter 'An Island Landfall' – an idyllic description of his first landing on the Marquesas – through the chapters on Tahiti, Hawaii and the Gilbert Islands, the book reveals his sensitivity to his environment and his anxiety to convey to the reader not simply the outward substance of the life of the islands but its distinctive atmosphere and flavour. As an exiled Scot travelling for the first time out of the Western world he was able to describe the life and culture of the islands with an unusual degree of freshness. Moreover, he did not make the mistake of judging the island culture by the standards of Victorian civilisation; he recognised that the Pacific islands represented an ancient civilisation which must be approached with sympathetic understanding and not measured by the values of a more artificial commercial society. His deep understanding of Scottish history and acute grasp of the attitude of the Scots towards the English enabled him to view the islanders – many of whom were living under alien rule – with insight and compassion. The resulting chapters, though uneven in manner and disappointing to his first readers (the sections were serialised in the New York *Sun*, which broke them off when the editor became dissatisfied with their lack of personal incident), convey all his fascination with the scenes and legends of the Pacific and the impact of the West upon an older, more dignified, more simple way of life.

Throughout the book one is aware of a mind shaping the diverse material and speaking to the reader in vivid flashes of observation and portraiture:

The first experience can never be repeated. The first love, the first sunrise, the first South Sea Island, are memories apart, and touched a virginity of sense. . . . Eight degrees south, and the day two hours a-coming. The interval was passed on deck in the silence of expectation, the customary thrill of landfall height-ened by the strangeness of the shores that we were then approaching (Part 1, 1)

In this place the annular isle was mostly under water, carrying here and there on its submerged line a wooded islet. Over one of these the birds hung and flew with an incredible density like that of gnats or hiving bees; the mass flashed white and black, and heaved and quivered, and the screaming of the creatures rose over the voice of the surf in a shrill clattering whirr. (Part 2, 1)

Crime, pestilence and death are in the day's work; the imagina-tion readily accepts them. . . . And yet to be just to barbarous islanders we must not forget the slums and dens of our cities; I must not forget that I have passed dinnerward through Soho, and seen that which cured me of my dinner. (Part 4, 4)

Neither the newspaper articles nor the published book were a commercial success yet in time it came to be acknowledged as a work of stature. Janet Adam Smith described it as 'the most solid of his general writings, and far from being the least readable'.[14] The book was greatly admired by Conrad who recognised beneath its fragmentary nature the immensity of Stevenson's vision and the impact of the South Seas on his intrinsically curious and specu-lative mind.[15] There were essentially two Stevensons: one was the romantic, the swashbuckling adventurer, the author of *Treasure Island* and *Kidnapped*; the other was the realist, the observer acutely interested in patterns of life and behaviour, the author of *A Footnote to History*. At the end of his life he confessed to Colvin 'With all my romance, I am a realist and a prosaist, and a most fanatical lover of plain physical sensations plainly and expressly rendered.'[16] These two aspects of his personality fused in the making of *In the South Seas* to produce a work of originality and haunting power.

Stevenson's primary achievement as an essayist was to restore the essay as a distinctive literary form. Since Lamb, Hazlitt and Leigh Hunt there had been few practitioners writing in English able to invest the genre with fresh vitality and insight. With the publication of such volumes as *Virginibus Puerisque, Familiar Studies* and *Memories and Portraits* he brought an engaging felicity and charm to the art of the short study, whilst in his travel essays he emerged as a writer possessing unusual descriptive powers. The overall effect of his essays is of an acutely literate and shrewd intelligence revelling in the sheer pleasure of the craft of writing. Whether one is reading a literary study, an essay of travel, a philosophical reflection or a reminiscence of childhood one has a sense of a recognisable personality bringing to bear a fascination with the diversity of life and attitudes. Continually one is aware of a challenging of accepted ideas, an implied questioning of received assumptions and an ability to identify fresh approaches to familiar sights and situations.

It cannot be stressed too often that each of his essays is an experiment in statement, an attempt to define a particular theme or idea and to compel the reader to examine afresh his own approaches to aspects of life and literature. The earlier essays, particularly some of those written in his twenties, are open to criticism on the grounds of their superficiality and self-absorption, their contrived rhetoric and narrowness of range. But for too long these weaknesses have been allowed to obscure the cumulative power of the essays as a whole. Through their illumination of numerous aspects of life and ideas, their discussion of problems and attitudes from contrasting points of view and their continual refinement of thought and language, his shorter studies represent an impressive literary achievement which merits careful study. In writing them he gained increasing self-confidence in the handling of ideas, in the shaping of materials and the introduction of lines of discussion and incident. The novels and short stories are the richer for this lengthy literary apprenticeship.

Part III
THE SHORT STORIES

The Short Stories

Stevenson published four volumes of short stories during his life-time: *New Arabian Nights* (1882), *More New Arabian Nights* (1885), *The Merry Men and Other Tales and Fables* (1887) and *Island Nights Entertainments* (1893). A final collection, *Tales and Fantasies*, was published posthumously in 1905.

He had graduated to writing short stories after a long apprenticeship of writing essays, literary criticism and book reviews. From the time of his earliest published story 'A Lodging for the Night', written when he was twenty-seven, to the closing years of his life he never lost his interest in the short story as an art form and continued to experiment in techniques of narration and the presentation of character. His stories are remarkably varied in style and theme. They range from tales of atmosphere and suspense to allegorical fantasies, from exciting narratives of adventure to profound studies of human character. Taken together his stories constitute an impressive body of work embracing many facets of his personality and interests and containing abundant evidence of the diversity of approach at his command.

New Arabian Nights consists of six short stories, all originally published in periodicals during the years 1877–80. As the title suggests, the tales were intended primarily to entertain (*The Arabian Nights Entertainments* had been among the favourite reading of his boyhood) and in some of them Stevenson strove consciously to achieve the mannered, artificial style of the original. 'The Suicide Club' and 'The Rajah's Diamond', though somewhat marred by their obvious artificiality of tone and manner, are notable for their economy of characterisation and incident. Already there is evidence of that selectiveness in the choice of material which was to become one of his distinguishing hallmarks.

Writing to William Archer in 1888 he commented:

> If there is anywhere a thing said in two sentences that could
> have been as clearly and as engagingly and as forcibly said in
> one, then it's amateur work . . . the story-teller's art of writing is
> to water out by continual invention, historical and technical,
> and yet not seem to water; seem on the other hand to practise
> that same wit of conspicuous and declaratory condensation
> which is the proper art of writing. That is one thing in which
> my stories fail: I am always cutting the flesh off their bones.[1]

The stories in *New Arabian Nights* are remarkable precisely
because of this quality of economy: though he was still feeling his
way as an artist he was rapidly becoming adept at techniques of
delineation and incident, at the presentation of character and
scene in the minimum number of words. One thinks, for example,
of the description of Major O'Rooke ('The Adventure of the
Hansom Cabs'), the dealing of the cards at the Suicide Club ('Story
of the Young Man with the Cream Tarts') or the pursuit of Denis
de Beaulieu through the streets of medieval Paris ('The Sire de
Maletroits' Door'). Each of these is written with that attention to
detail, that determination to achieve the utmost clarity of effect,
which he had imbibed from such masters as Poe and which he
used with such telling effect in the later stories and novels.

With changing tastes in literary fashion the bulk of the stories in
New Arabian Nights are probably little read today, but the collection
does contain two stories, 'The Pavilion on the Links' and 'A
Lodging for the Night', which are notable for their imaginative
qualities and will repay careful study because of their importance
as precursors of his mature style.

'The Pavilion on the Links', a long story of about the same
length as *The Strange Case of Dr. Jekyll and Mr. Hyde*, was written
between 1878–9 and completed at Monterey when Stevenson was
desperately short of money. It was the most elaborate work of
fiction he had attempted up to that time and he took great pains
over its composition. On its completion he forwarded it to W. E.
Henley, describing it as a 'grand carpentry story in nine chapters,
and I should hesitate to say how many tableaux. . . . It is not bad,
though I say it; carpentry of course, but not bad at that; and who
else can carpenter in England, now that Wilkie Collins is played
out?'[2]

The setting, a lonely stretch of the Scottish coast, was suggested by haunts of his boyhood – Dirleton in East Lothian, near North Berwick – and forms a sombre backcloth against which the exciting events of the story unfold. The scenery is described with unforgettable distinctness and with a palette which immediately evokes an atmosphere of foreboding:

> The country, I have said, was mixed sand-hill and links; *links* being a Scottish name for sand which has ceased drifting and become more or less solidly covered with turf. The pavilion stood on an even space; a little behind it, the wood began in a hedge of elders huddled together by the wind; in front, a few tumbled sand-hills stood between it and the sea. . . . On summer days the outlook was bright and even gladsome; but at sundown in September, with a high wind, and a heavy surf rolling in close along the links, the place told of nothing but dead mariners and sea disaster. A ship beating to windward on the horizon, and a huge truncheon of wreck half buried in the sands at my feet, completed the innuendo of the scene.

Such touches as 'a hedge of elders huddled together by the wind', 'a heavy surf rolling in close along the links', 'dead mariners and sea disaster' and 'a huge truncheon of wreck half buried in the sands' contribute significantly to the overall effect, whilst the whole passage achieves an impression of menace: a mood which pervades the chapters which follow. The skill with which Stevenson evokes this atmosphere with such particularity recalls the opening paragraphs of Poe's brilliant short story 'The Gold-Bug'; it is an atmosphere created through an accumulation of evocative detail and a deliberate use of oppressive imagery.

The *construction* of the story reveals a maturity and self-confidence unusual in such a young writer: though Stevenson had been writing for some years it has to be remembered that fiction was still a relatively new medium for him. The ease with which the narrator introduces the main elements of the story, deftly building up an atmosphere of suspense and intrigue, is impressive evidence of his powers as a storyteller and must have provided him with valuable experience in the art of assembling a long narrative. Moreover 'The Pavilion' is rich in episodes of excitement and tension which anticipate the pace and drama of *Treasure Island* and *Kidnapped*. The scene in which the narrator flees from his tent, having been awakened in the night by a flashing lantern,

is a striking example of Stevenson's gift of creating an air of
suspense:

> It required some nerve to issue forth into the black and intri-
> cate thicket which surrounded and overhung the den; but I
> groped my way to the links, drenched with rain, beaten upon
> and deafened by the gusts, and fearing at every step to lay my
> hand upon some lurking adversary.

Throughout the narrative the reader is held in suspense
through a skilfully contrived accumulation of tension. This
suspense intensifies as the story proceeds, culminating in a violent
climax with the destruction of the pavilion and the death of the
wily banker, Huddlestone, at the hands of his assassins. The rising
of the tension to an almost intolerable level as the unseen
assassins close in on the isolated pavilion is handled with complete
assurance and renders the story both an emotional and an aesthe-
tic experience.

But it is from the point of view of *characterisation* that 'The
Pavilion on the Links' is most remarkable, for it contains one
character, Northmour, who could be regarded as a trial sketch of
the figure later to be drawn as Long John Silver. Northmour, who
embodies in his personality both good and evil traits, is described
in terms which leave no room for doubt as to his ambivalence:

> He had the appearance of a finished gentleman; his face bore
> every mark of intelligence and courage; but you had only to
> look at him, even in his most amiable moment, to see that he
> had the temper of a slaver captain . . . he combined the vivacity
> of the south with the sustained and deadly hatreds of the north;
> and both traits were plainly written on his face, which was a
> sort of danger-signal.

Northmour is in fact one of the earliest examples of Stevenson's
fascination with moral ambivalence. In his combination of physical courage and unscrupulosity he anticipates such characters as
Hoseason in *Kidnapped*, James Durie in *The Master of Ballantrae* and
Attwater in *The Ebb-Tide*. The ambiguity of his personality, the
continual uncertainty concerning his motives and behaviour,
provides the story with much of its intrinsic interest and compels
the reader to acknowledge afresh the complexity of human

psychology. To the end the reader is kept in doubt as to whether or not Northmour is fundamentally evil.

'The Pavilion on the Links' has influenced many later writers, most notably Sir Arthur Conan Doyle. In his essay 'Mr. Stevenson's Methods in Fiction' (*National Review*, January 1890) Doyle observed: 'it is hardly conceivable that it should ever be allowed to drop out of the very first line of English literature', and in *Through the Magic Door* described it as 'the very model of dramatic narrative'.[3]

'A Lodging for the Night', the first of his stories to be printed (October 1877) is a slighter tale set in fifteenth-century Paris and stems from his studies of the life of François Villon. In common with 'The Pavilion on the Links' it is an *atmospheric* story in which a mood of suspense and fear is built up through the skilful use of language and incident. The story relates an episode in the life of Villon, an unscrupulous poet, who flees from the scene of a murder on a bitterly cold November night. The intense cold is described with such conviction that the reader experiences it almost as a physical emotion: 'The air was raw and pointed, but not far below freezing; and the flakes were large, damp, and adhesive. The whole city was sheeted up. An army might have marched from end to end, and not a footfall given the alarm.'

The thoughts and feelings of Villon as he hurries from the scene of the crime through the snow-clad streets are vividly described. Guilt, fear, panic and anger pass through his mind as he hastens on his way, intent on avoiding the passing patrols. In a particularly striking passage he shelters in a derelict building and stumbles on the body of a dead woman. The reader identifies with him as he recoils from the body in horror then stoops to examine it, reflecting on the pathos of her poor life. Unable to find shelter for the night and sensing increasing panic in case he is arrested for the murder he selects a house at random and begs food and shelter from the courteous old gentleman within. The stranger quickly senses Villon's true character, engaging him in conversation whilst forming his own assessment of his worth. The conversation between the two – Villon cautious and uncertain, the old gentleman shrewd and suspicious – is cleverly executed; the scene is one of the earliest examples of that fascination with human motivation which exercised Stevenson throughout his literary career. Each seeks to probe the philosophy and intentions of the other; each seeks to appraise the other's purpose whilst reluctant to declare his own attitude to life.

The story ends inconclusively with Villon, having resisted the temptation to rob his host, bidding him farewell and departing from the house as dawn breaks over the town. The old gentleman is left with a wider appreciation of the depths of human fallibility; Villon departs with a closer understanding of the courage and rectitude of his host. The antithesis between the contrasting personalities of the two characters provides the story with an interesting psychological dimension and raises questions of behaviour and morality which Stevenson explored more fully in his novels and romances. 'A Lodging for the Night', though clearly the work of a writer who is still feeling his way as a literary artist, is significant not only as his first published work of fiction, but as the forerunner of a lifelong preoccupation with the complexity of human character.

More New Arabian Nights, subtitled *The Dynamiter*, was commenced at Hyères in the spring of 1884 and completed at Bournemouth in the following year. The stories were originally devised as an enter-tainment while convalescing after a nearly fatal illness and, as with *New Arabian Nights*, were conceived primarily as a divertisse-ment. The book was written in collaboration with his wife: 'Zero's Tale of the Explosive Bomb' was the work of Stevenson alone; 'The Destroying Angel' and 'The Fair Cuban' were the work of Fanny Stevenson; the remaining stories were written jointly. In form the tales follow the pattern of *The Arabian Nights Entertain-ments* and *The Decameron* in introducing a series of narrators who each relates the story of his life. The thread which links the stories together is that of the futility and folly of dynamiters (anarchists). Stevenson had been outraged by the Fenian bombings of the 1880s and was anxious to express his loathing for the aims and methods of the anarchists. As with 'The Suicide Club' and 'The Rajah's Diamond' the weakness of the stories is their remoteness from reality, their mannered prose and forced comedy. *The Dynamiter* is probably one of the least read of his works today yet it is not without significance. Though the stories can be faulted on the grounds of their artificiality and imitativeness they represent a genuine attempt to find a satisfying literary direction. Through the medium of these tales Stevenson was feeling his way towards those techniques of narrative and characterisation which were to earn for him a world-wide reputation as a storyteller.

Stevenson had been anxious for some years to issue a further collection of his stories before publication of *The Merry Men and Other Tales and Fables* was finally agreed upon. The six stories included in the volume form an extremely heterogeneous collection, ranging from Poesque horror to gentle allegory, from the vivid descriptive writing of 'The Merry Men' to the haunting power of 'Thrawn Janet'. Each story possesses features of interest but three of the tales – 'Will o' the Mill', 'Markheim' and 'Olalla' – are of exceptional significance in the context of his life and his distinctive personal philosophy.

'Will o' the Mill' was the first of his stories to be accepted by Leslie Stephen's influential journal the *Cornhill Magazine* (January 1878) and provides interesting evidence of his growing mastery of style and willingness to experiment in a variety of literary forms. Strongly influenced by Hawthorne and Meredith, it is an allegory on the dichotomy in man's nature between the classical and the romantic: between the desire for security and order and the quest for emotional fulfilment. Will, the central character, has an intense desire to leave his home in the valley for the world which beckons beyond the mountains, yet despite this longing he opts for a safe, predictable life of quiet labour. At the age of thirty he becomes attracted to a parson's daughter, Marjory, but because of his quietism and gentle ways he loses the opportunity of marrying her. When she marries another man he congratulates himself on his prudence and settles down to a simple life alone. Before his death he experiences again the unsatisfied longings of his youth – he receives many invitations to leave his home and travel beyond the valley he has known since childhood – but resists all such temptations. He dies at last a hale old man, content in his philosophy of quiet resignation.

Whilst superficially the story would seem to contradict all that we know of Stevenson's approach to life it has to be borne in mind that 'Will o' the Mill' was written as an experiment in statement: it was written, he confided to Graham Balfour, 'as an experiment, in order to see what could be said in support of the opposite theory'.[4] Will represents a type of person whom he deplored: the 'hanger-back', the person who continually forfeits opportunities, who resists all appeals to the romantic, adventurous side of his nature and opts always for stability and safety. He felt very strongly that there could be no escape from man's secret longings, no matter how securely one tried to shield oneself from distracting forces. In his own life he had abandoned security and certainty in the shape of a legal career and instead had thrown all his energies into a romantic but uncertain future in the world of literature. Respectable Edinburgh no doubt found such a decision incomprehensible (as did Thomas Stevenson) but Louis never regretted the choice he had made.

The story reveals a growing preoccupation with time and with the passage of time, as if his chronic ill-health had made him unusually sensitive to the passing of the years. At one stage Will, lying awake at night after a thunderstorm, is 'besieged by tumultuous and crying memories':

> His boyhood, the night with the fat young man, the death of his adopted parents, the summer days with Marjory, and many of those small circumstances, which seem nothing to another, and are yet the very gist of a man's own life to himself – things seen, words heard, books misconstrued – arose from their forgotten corners and usurped his attention.

This acute awareness of the past, this ability to recall those small incidents which are 'the very gist of a man's own life to himself', is unusual in a man who was aged twenty-seven at the time. It is indicative of an attitude of mind which was determined to live life to the full, of a man who was resolved to overcome all obstacles of health and parental opposition in order to follow his chosen career. Though the allegory is imperfectly realised – the publisher in accepting it drew attention to its 'indeterminate hovering between realism and allegory'[5] – it remains one of his most interesting and gracefully written fables.

'Markheim', in common with 'Will o' the Mill', is a story rich in allegorical undertones but probing far deeper levels of psychology. Strongly influenced by Dostoevsky's *Crime and Punishment* (he remarked to a friend that the latter was 'easily the greatest book I have read in ten years'[6]), it is one of his most carefully executed tales and is a fascinating example of that preoccupation with man's dual personality which found its fullest and most dramatic expression in *Dr. Jekyll and Mr. Hyde*. On first reading, the story appears to be a study in terror after the manner of Poe or Algernon Blackwood. Markheim schemes to murder an antique dealer and rob him of his money. He enters the antique shop on the pretext of being a customer wishing to purchase a present for a lady. Engaging the dealer in conversation he waits for a suitable opportunity and then stabs his victim from behind. Stricken with fear and guilt at his action, Markheim wanders through the premises in search of the dealer's hidden wealth. He is still search-ing the building when a strange visitor enters the house, purporting to know the murderer's innermost thoughts and to understand his intentions. The visitor converses with Markheim for some time, reviewing his past life and the motives for his actions. When the dealer's maid enters the building the visitor tempts Markheim with the prospect of killing her also, ransacking the house at his leisure and making good his escape. Markheim rejects this counsel, dismisses the stranger and confesses his crime to the maid, urging her to summon the police. In confessing to the murder he thus forfeits his own life.

One of the most remarkable aspects of the story is the manner in which an atmosphere of tension is built up through a steady accumulation of detail. A candle on the counter flickers, casting weird shadows; faces on paintings change and waver 'like images in water'; a multitude of clocks tick and chime; strange reflections stare back at the murderer from mirrors; heavy rain outside causes unnerving echoes and a sound 'like some dripping cavern'; odd sounds and creaking floorboards cause paroxysms of fear and suspense. The steady accretion of atmospheric detail continues with such relentless force that at last Markheim fears for his own sanity: 'on every side he was haunted and begirt by presences'. The suspense mounts to an unbearable intensity as Markheim's nervousness increases. It -is almost a physical relief when the tension is burst by the sound of a stranger slowly and steadily mounting the stairs. The murderer's presentiment that he is not alone, that he is being watched by unseen eyes, is communicated in a series of powerful images. Rarely has a writer depicted so forcefully the combination of guilt and terror which afflict a criminal in the immediate aftermath of his deed.

Critical opinion is sharply divided as to the identity of Markheim's strange visitor. Some commentators regard the stranger as the devil; some insist that he has no objective reality, that he is simply a figment of Markheim's disordered imagination; some, including Colvin, regard the conversation between the two as 'the dialogue of Markheim with his other self'.[7] My own reading supports the latter view. There can be no question that Stevenson was fascinated with the idea of the *doppelganger* (literally 'double-goer' — a mirror-image) which figures so prominently in English literature and which exercised him throughout his life. This can be seen in his portrayal of Janet McClour in 'Thrawn Janet', of the brothers in *The Master of Ballantrae*, of Hoseason in *Kidnapped* and, most strikingly of all, in *Dr. Jekyll and Mr. Hyde*. His attitude to morality, the influence of his Calvinist background and his obsession with evil and with moral ambiguity found its most profound expression in the idea of the duality of man, the divided self which affects every human action.

Seen in these terms the stranger is a mirror in which Markheim is made to see his own soul and debate his own weaknesses. The description of the visitant is revealing:

> Perhaps there was a film upon his sight, but the outlines of the newcomer seemed to change and waver like those of the idols in the wavering candlelight of the shop; and at times he thought he knew him; and at times he thought he bore a likeness to himself; and always, like a lump of living terror, there lay in his bosom the conviction that this thing was not of the earth and not of God. And yet the creature had a strange air of the commonplace, as he stood looking on Markheim with a smile.

The language of this passage needs to be approached with some care. The use of such terms as 'the creature' and 'this thing' suggests a supernatural presence, while the phrase 'like a lump of living terror' powerfully evokes the fear and misgiving with which Markheim regards the man. Yet the effect of the passage as a whole strongly reinforces the notion of a *doppelganger*, a second self confronting the murderer with a reminder of his shortcomings. 'at times he thought he knew him'; 'at times he thought he bore a likeness to himself'; 'the creature had a strange air of commonplace' — the cumulative effect of these phrases is striking. In surveying his interlocutor Markheim is uncomfortably aware that he is face to face at last with the evil within him, with those aspects of his personality most susceptible to greed and corruption. (It should be noted that the confrontation between them is the opposite of that depicted in Poe's short story 'William Wilson'. Whereas the narrator in that story is confronted by his better self, Markheim is faced with his *worst* self, by a personification of his inherent propensity to selfishness.) It seems clear that Stevenson recognised in Markheim not simply a representative human being with a propensity to both disinterested and selfish actions, but a surrogate for himself. Markheim is thirty-six years of age: Stevenson's own age at the time of publication. Moreover, in the conversation between Markheim and the stranger can be discerned numerous echoes of the author's preoccupation with good and evil, of his lifelong concern with the mainsprings of human behaviour. It is as if Stevenson is debating with himself on the conflict between vice and virtue, on the continual tensions within the human make-up which shape our actions.

Particularly suggestive is the stranger's comment : 'Do I say that I follow sins? I follow virtues also; they differ not by the thickness of a nail. . . . Evil, for which I live, consists not in action but in character.' To which Markheim replies: 'I prize love, I love honest laughter, there is no good thing nor true thing on earth but I love it from my heart. And are my vices only to direct my life, and my virtues to lie without effect, like some passive lumber of the mind? Not so; good, also, is a spring of acts.'

In this insistence that evil consists not in action but in *character*, this awareness of the continual interplay between altruism and the pursuit of self-interest, can be recognised the author's distinctive approach to human conduct. As a description of murder and its aftermath 'Markheim' could have been written by any of a dozen writers; only Stevenson could have transformed such an apparently simple plot into a profound allegory of the duality of man.

'Olalla', written at Bournemouth in the autumn of 1885, is a sustained study in horror which owes much in both style and conception to the tales of Edgar Allan Poe. Told in the first person, it relates the experiences of a wounded soldier who journeys to a remote house in the Spanish mountains to convalesce. His hosts are a strange, taciturn family: an ageing, once beautiful mother; a son, Felipe, a bestial half-wit; and a mysterious, enigmatic daughter, Olalla, to whom the narrator is drawn by an irresistible attraction. Obsessed with his fascination for the strange Olalla, he is drawn closer and closer towards her but is repelled by the family's atavistic cruelty – Felipe is caught in the act of torturing a squirrel, the mother attempts to suck the narrator's blood in an apparent act of vampirism –– and at last departs from the house, convinced that the family is irretrievably lost to animalism. He leaves Olalla to her life of resigned penitence, concluding that he is powerless to arrest the ancestral forces which dominate the household.

The story, which bears all the hallmarks of having been most carefully written, came to Stevenson in a dream. In his essay 'A Chapter on Dreams' he wrote: 'Here the court, the mother, the mother's niche, Olalla, Olalla's chamber, the meetings on the stair, the broken window, the ugly scene of the bite, were all given me in bulk and detail as I have tried to write them.'

The fact that the main outlines of the tale came to him in a nightmare (as had happened with *Dr. Jekyll and Mr. Hyde* shortly before) may account in part for the haunting atmosphere of the piece, though it should be noted that the Spanish setting is wholly imaginary. The long journey through the wild mountainous terrain, the arrival at the lonely and forbidding residencia, the first encounters with the strange household, the air of brooding suspense which hangs over all – each element contributes to the unforgettable aura which pervades the story as a whole. Again and again the reader is struck with the force of writing, so reminiscent of Poe:

> She cast a dark shadow on my fancy; and . . . it was often a glad thought to me that my enchantress was safe in the grave, her wand of beauty broken, her lips closed in silence, her philtre spilt. And yet I had a half-lingering terror that she might not be dead after all, but re-arisen in the body of some descendant.

> All morning I went from one door to another, and encountered spacious and faded chambers, some rudely shuttered, some receiving their full charge of daylight, all empty and unhomely. It was a rich house, on which Time had breathed his tarnish and dust had scattered disillusion.

> As I turned from the window, my eyes alighted on the portrait. It had fallen dead, like a candle after sunrise; it followed me with eyes of paint. I knew it to be like, and marvelled at the tenacity of type in that declining race

These passages, which recall so vividly the atmosphere of such tales as 'The Fall of the House of Usher' and 'The Oval Portrait', are convincing evidence of Stevenson's gift for creating a mood appropriate to his theme and his unusual ability to subordinate language, style and approach to this end. The deliberate use of such words as 'shadow', 'grave', 'tarnish' and 'disillusion' adds appreciably to the aura of decay he is striving to achieve, whilst such phrases as 'I had a half-lingering terror' and 'it followed me with eyes of paint' contribute to the atmosphere of menace which accumulates with disturbing force throughout the story. 'Olalla' is one of his most impressive stories, not least because of its carefully controlled tension and the pervasiveness of its ambience of horror.

The story is of particular significance in relation to its apparently quietistic philosophy. The narrator, despite the powerful physical attraction he feels towards Olalla, concludes that he must leave her to pursue her own life and departs from the scene, reflecting that 'pleasure is not an end, but an accident; that pain is the choice of the magnanimous; that it is best to suffer all things and do well'. In turning his back on Olalla and the strange household he appears to be opting out of life : he is renouncing a potentially challenging situation – the possibility of returning to the family and seeking to reform them from their atavistic ways – and choosing instead the path of stoicism.[8] Olalla, in rejecting him, is similarly renouncing the prospect of a fuller life and retreating to a world of resignation and piety. Both retreat from the challenge of uncertainty in favour of a life of known and familiar boundaries: he to return to his soldiering and she to bury herself in religious devotion. On this strangely passive note, so at odds with Stevenson's approach to life, the story ends.

One concludes the tale with an uneasy sense of ambiguity, aware that the fascination with moral ambivalence which was so characteristic of his fiction underlies much of its power. Though he himself was dissatisfied with the story – he commented to Lady Taylor that 'the trouble with "Olalla" is that it somehow sounds false . . . "Markheim" is true; "Olalla" false; and I don't know why, nor did I feel it when I worked on them'[9] – it occupies an important place in the canon of his work not only for its intrinsic literary qualities but because its themes came increasingly to exercise his imagination. The motivations which govern human behaviour, the ancestral forces which shape personality, the conflict between man's yearning for security and his quest for adventure – these are the themes which dominate his novels and stories. 'Olalla' is also important because it is one of his few stories treating realistically the passion between a man and a woman. For these reasons it merits careful study as one of his most consistently rewarding tales.

Island Nights Entertainments consists of two short stories, 'The Bottle Imp' and 'The Isle of Voices', and a novella, 'The Beach of Falesa'. The short stories, both with a Hawaiian setting, are slight tales in Stevenson's most whimsical vein. Each was conceived during his extensive South Seas cruise in 1888–9 and was intended to illustrate aspects of life and belief in the Pacific islands. The novella is in a far more serious vein, an elaborately structured story which occupied his imagination over a period of many months.

'The Beach of Falesa', begun in November 1890 but not completed until October 1891 – characteristically the story was abandoned and resumed on a number of occasions – is one of his most sustained attempts to capture the spirit and atmosphere of the South Seas. The idea came to him in a flash of inspiration while clearing the woods behind his house on Samoa. He confided to Colvin: 'I have taken refuge in a new story, which just shot through me like a bullet in one of my moments of awe, alone in that tragic jungle.'[10] Writing to him a year later, after the story had been thoroughly reshaped, he observed:

> It is the first realistic South Sea story; I mean with real South Sea character and details of life. Everybody else who has tried, that I have seen, got carried away by the romance. . . . Now I have got the smell and look of the thing a good deal. You will know more about the South Seas after you have read my little tale than if you have read a library.[11]

The story, which is told throughout in the first person, is narrated by John Wiltshire, a white trader. Wiltshire is one of Stevenson's most remarkable creations. Insensitive, uncouth, unprincipled, he embodies all those characteristics which Stevenson himself found abhorrent, and yet he remains a wholly consistent personality. Unlike Henry Jekyll, Markheim, or the Durie brothers in *The Master of Ballantrae* he is not divided within himself and acts throughout in accordance with his own conceptions of right and wrong. The device of telling the story through the eyes of an invented and alien personality is a difficult one, fraught with technical difficulties but in 'Falesa' the method is employed with total conviction. It is largely for this reason – that the reader enters wholly into the mood and atmosphere evoked by the narrator – that 'Falesa' remains one of his most realistic and convincing tales. There is no attempt to present a romanticised picture of life in the South Seas but rather a distillation of the *feel* of the Pacific islands in the closing years of the nineteenth century. The illusion that the narrator is not Stevenson but Wiltshire, a semi-illiterate man with attitudes typical of his type, is so effectively carried forward that the story differs in mood from any of his other works. (It is interesting to compare the story with *The Ebb-Tide,* a tale which raises similar moral issues but is told in the third person.)

The central episode of the story is Wiltshire's illicit 'marriage' to Uma, a lovely and innocent native girl, his gradual realisation of her inherent worth, and his final decision to commit himself to her and to their children. In its original version the wording of the marriage certificate was considered too outspoken for the readers of 1892: 'This is to certify that Uma, daughter of Faavao, of Falesa, island of ——, is illegally married to Mr. John Wiltshire for one night, and Mr. John Wiltshire is at liberty to send her to hell next morning.'

On its publication in the *Illustrated London News* the editor, Clement Shorter, omitted this sentence altogether. The first edition in book form (and all book editions until 1979)[12] included the sentence but bowdlerised the crucial passage to read: 'is illegally married to Mr. John Wiltshire for one week, and Mr. John Wiltshire is at liberty to send her to hell when he pleases'. The alteration blurs Stevenson's intention, for it is central to an understanding of the story to grasp that Wiltshire originally agreed to take Uma as his wife for the most cynical and selfish of reasons and that he comes to feel genuine affection for the woman he had at first taken simply as a concubine. His slow recognition of her intrinsic goodness, his awareness that he is bound to her by ties of enduring emotion, forms one of the central themes of the narrative.

Wiltshire's rival on the island is Case, an unscrupulous trader who seeks to terrorise the natives and exploit their ignorance to his own advantage. Case, like Wiltshire, is not merely a caricature, a stock villain, but a complex character, a man possessed of both courage and guile. On first acquaintance with him Wiltshire admires Case for his air of civilisation: 'No man knew his country, beyond he was of English speech; and it was clear he came of a good family and was splendidly educated.' As the story proceeds, however, it becomes apparent that the urbanity is simply a veneer; continually a contrast is drawn between the innocence of the native population and the corruption of the 'civilised' Case. Realising that the natives are terrified of evil spirits, Case exploits this fear by constructing masks coated with luminous paint and placing Aeolian harps in the trees in order to produce unnerving wailing sounds. Through these methods he plays on the fear of devils and strengthens his hold on the islanders.

An underlying element throughout the narrative is Stevenson's awareness of the insidious effects of European domination. Case, who embodies in his own person the values and attitudes of Western civilisation, relies on superstition and ignorance in order to exercise power over the islanders. This debasement of European values distressed and angered Stevenson and compelled him to recognise the inherent injustice of white domination. (An interesting comparison is with H. G. Wells's *The Island of Doctor Moreau* (1896), a story which is also rich in imagery presaging the end of white dominion.)[13] The thin dividing line between 'civilisation' – as exemplified by Wiltshire and Case – and 'barbarism' – as represented by Uma and the other natives – is strikingly presented. As the tale unfolds one is increasingly aware of the veneer separating urbanity and primitiveness, and the manner in which behaviour is affected by environment: themes which frequently recur in Stevenson's work.

The story moves to a climax in the final chapter, 'Night in the Bush', in which Case and Wiltshire confront one another in the forest, each determined to outwit and slay the other. This confrontation is preceded by a tense passage describing Wiltshire's lonely, fearful journey through the dark trees:

> The light of the lantern, striking among all these trunks and forked branches and twisted rope-ends of lianas, made the whole place, or all that you could see of it, a kind of a puzzle of turning shadows. They came to meet you, solid and quick like giants, and then span off and vanished; they hove up over your head like clubs, and flew away into the night like birds. . . . Big, cold drops fell on me from the branches overhead like sweat. There was no wind to mention; only a little icy breath of a land-breeze that stirred nothing; and the harps were silent.

The tension of this chapter recalls the suppressed excitement prior to the midnight duel in *The Master of Ballantrae*. An atmosphere of intolerable suspense is built up through an accretion of significant detail: the light of the lantern illuminates a weird pattern of shadows which 'hove up over your head like clubs, and flew away into the night like birds'; 'Big, cold drops' of water fall on him from the trees above; there is no wind 'only a little icy breath of a land-breeze that stirred nothing'; even the harps planted by the wily Case are silent. The cumulative effect of the darkness, the silence, the cold and the shadows is such as to create a *physical* sensation: the reader does not simply share vicariously in Wiltshire's emotions – he experiences them himself as a tangible feeling.

The duel which culminates in Case being stabbed to death is one of Stevenson's most dramatic set-pieces, rising to a climax in a passage of memorable starkness; 'The blood came over my hands, I remember, hot as tea; and with that I fainted clean away, and fell with my head on the man's mouth.'[14] With Case's death there is no sense of right triumphing over wrong or of a villain having been despatched by one who is demonstrably worthy, for the two traders are not *fundamentally* different. Both men are selfish and both are willing to take advantage of gullible islanders for their own aggrandisement. But circumstances conspire to bring out the best in Wiltshire. Realising his love for Uma, realising her total loyalty to him, he resolves to legalise their union and to risk his life for her sake. Case, in his eyes, is despicable because by exploiting the natives' fear of devils and dominating them by means of their own taboos he has violated the white man's code. Case is beyond the pale precisely because he has abandoned the accepted code and sought to exercise power through the use of the natives' own superstitions.

'The Beach of Falesa' is not an allegory yet it contains within it a number of images which are capable of an allegorical interpreta-tion. The island itself can be seen as a microcosm of paradise:

The world was like all new painted; my foot went along to music; Falesa might have been Fiddler's Green, if there is such a place, and more's the pity if there isn't! It was good to foot the grass, to look aloft at the green mountains, to see the men with their green wreaths and the women in their bright dresses, red and blue.

A dominant theme in the story is the implied contrast between the unspoilt beauty of this island paradise and its gullible people and the corrupting influence of white civilisation. Uma and her fellow-islanders are presented as superstitious and illogical, yet fundamentally innocent, loyal and trusting. Their simplicity and devotion are in the sharpest contrast to the deviousness of Case and his like. In this sense the island is a paradigm of the tainting effects of imperialism, of the impact of European behaviour and attitudes on an unsophisticated, taboo-ridden society. There can also be identified in the story an explicit reference to religious imagery which had exercised Stevenson since childhood. The gullibility of Case's 'disciples' in accepting a belief in evil spirits may be likened to the fanaticism of the zealots Stevenson had known in Edinburgh who believed firmly in the existence of the devil, hell-fire and eternal damnation. The taboos and fears of the natives, their rituals and belief in devilry are demonstrated to be false: empty superstitions based on fear and ignorance. In the same way, Stevenson suggests, the religious fanaticism he had experienced as a young man was irrational and empty, a dogma without intellectual foundation.

'The Beach of Falesá' is open to criticism on the grounds that its occult element – a significant ingredient within its overall design – proves to have a perfectly natural explanation, and that the atmosphere of suspense and mystery, so carefully built up in the narration, peters out in a conventional happy ending with the story-teller settling down to a life of domesticity with his wife and children. There is some substance in both these comments: Stevenson himself may well have been aware of them, for there is evidence that the revision of the story occupied his mind over a long period and raised many problems of balance and characterisation. Yet the weaknesses of the novella are far outweighed by its strengths. Taken together with *The Ebb-Tide* it represents his most elaborate attempt to portray the reality of life in the Pacific islands at the nadir of empire and a remarkable attempt to reach inside the mind of an alien personality. In its uncompromising presentation of the corrupting influence of European domination it anticipates such works as Conrad's *Heart of Darkness* and Orwell's *Burmese Days*. Perhaps most significant of all, it is one of the few stories from his pen set in a contemporary location of time and place and treating of themes stemming directly from his own experience. In its starkness and realism it is one of his most rewarding tales. Though far removed from the romanticism his admirers wished to remember it may yet prove to be among his most enduring works.

Tales and Fantasies, though the last collection to be published, contains three of his earliest short stories: 'The Story of a Lie' (1879), 'The Body-Snatcher' (1881) and 'The Misadventures of John Nicholson' (1885). The latter, one of his least known works – after its original publication it was not reprinted during his lifetime – is remarkable for its anticipation of themes he was to explore more fully in *The Wrong Box* and *Weir of Hermiston* and for its affectionate recapitulation of the Edinburgh he had known and loved as a young man.

The story, related in his most engaging and humorous style, recounts the adventures of a young law student, John Varey Nicholson, whose well-intentioned actions invariably culminate in disaster. His father, a strict, upright puritan, is described in terms which inevitably recall Adam Weir and Stevenson's own father, Thomas:

> His father – that iron gentleman – had long ago enthroned himself on the heights of the Disruption Principles. What these are (and in spite of their grim name they are quite innocent) no array of terms would render thinkable to the merely English intelligence; but to the Scot they often prove unctiously nourishing, and Mr. Nicholson found in them the milk of lions. . . .
> Here was a family where prayers came at the same hour, where the Sabbath literature was unimpeachably selected, where the guest who should have leaned to any false opinion was instantly set down, and over which there reigned all week, and grew denser on Sundays, a silence that was agreeable to his ear, and a gloom that he found comfortable.

The theological, Calvinistic flavour of Stevenson's home background is vividly conveyed in the introductory chapters. These chapters, so fluently written, are remarkable for their circumstantiality and their striking evocation of the Edinburgh milieu at the height of the Victorian era. Mr. Nicholson is presented as a dour man, not without humour (his humour was 'of the Scots order – intellectual, turning on the observation of men'), totally immersed in the world of religion and polite society and utterly convinced of his own probity. John, a well-meaning, gauche young man, falls foul of his father by becoming involved in a series of mishaps: he is robbed of four hundred pounds while on his way to the bank; the robbery takes place in an area of the city his father had forbidden him to enter; and to compound his predicament he had pawned his mother's watch and been seen in a billiard room – unpardonable crimes in his father's eyes. The scene in which John, summoning all his courage, enters Mr. Nicholson's study and confesses his misdeeds (Ch. 3, 'In Which John Enjoys the Harvest Home') perfectly encapsulates the difficult relationship between father and son which played such a decisive part in Stevenson's own life and which he later elaborated on a fuller canvas in the portrayal of Adam and Archie Weir in *Weir of Hermiston*. In John's eyes his behaviour, though foolish, has been a series of unfortunate accidents; in his father's eyes his conduct has been a reprehensible catalogue of disobediences, a series of wilful wrongs which cannot be condoned. This central relationship between the stern, unrelenting father and the wayward son underlies all John's subsequent adventures – his flight from home, his sojourn in America, his return to Scotland and ultimate reconciliation – and represents one of Stevenson's few attempts to express in fictional form the basic emotional tension of his own life. For Mr. Nicholson embodies a range of characteristics and attitudes which Thomas Stevenson had also embodied and which Louis as a young man had found puzzling and alien: excessive religious fervour, undemonstrativeness, undeviating adherence to a strict code of behaviour, and an intolerance of such personal qualities as imagination and initiative. This rigid, puritanical stance denies any overt expression of the emotions and finds solace in an intolerant self-righteousness. The tragedy of the situation is that Mr. Nicholson does not understand his own son. Looking at John he can only see foolishness, laziness and gullibility: he cannot see beyond to discern the essential worth of the personality beneath. It is not until the very end of the story that he can bring himself to forgive John for his misdemeanours:

> Of the contention of feeling that ran high in Mr. Nicholson's starched bosom, no outward sign was visible; nor did he delay long to make a choice of conduct. Yet in that interval he had reviewed a great field of possibilities both past and future; whether it was possible he had not been perfectly wise in his

treatment of John; whether it was possible that John was innocent; whether, if he turned John out a second time, as his outraged authority suggested, it was possible to avoid a scandal.

The phrase 'outraged authority' is revealing in this context and demonstrates that his decision to forgive has only been arrived at after a long period of hesitation and misgiving. This reluctance to concede an error of judgement, this unwillingness to admit the possibility of codes of behaviour other than one's own, are characteristic of that inflexible Protestantism symbolised by Mr. Nicholson and his circle. Rarely in his work did Stevenson present so convincingly the atmosphere of orthodox, professional Edinburgh in the 1870s and the harshness of the prevailing moral framework. Both Stevenson and his father were in reality far more complex personalities than the father and son in 'The Misadventures of John Nicholson' but the story will repay careful study for its insight into the mental and emotional background of his youth and its detailed recreation of an ethos which both fascinated and repelled him.

A second main strand in the story is its firm topographical basis in the streets and scenes of Edinburgh and its surrounding suburbs. Written when Stevenson was living in Bournemouth, having reluctantly concluded that the climate of Scotland was too harsh for his health, its predominant tone is one of nostalgia in looking back on the scenes of his childhood:

> Meanwhile he walked familiar streets, merry reminiscences crowding round him, sad ones also, both with the same surprising pathos. The keen frosty air; the low, rosy, wintry sun; the castle, hailing him like an old acquaintance; the names of friends on door-plates . . . and the gutters where he had learned to slide, and the shop where he had bought his skates, and the stones on which he had trod, and the railings in which he had rattled his clachan as he went to school; and all those thousand and one nameless particulars, which the eye sees without noting, which the memory keeps indeed yet without knowing, and which, taken one with another, build up for us the aspect of the place that we call home: all these besieged him, as he went, with both delight and sadness.

This blending of 'delight and sadness' is evident at many points in the narrative. The description of John wandering on Princes Street, his adventures on Calton Hill, his visit to Regent Terrace, his memorable journey to the house at Murrayfield (then a largely rural area): all these are depicted with a total recall of detail borne of close knowledge and deep attachment. Moreover, in describing the shebeens and pawnshops of the Edinburgh backstreets Stevenson was writing from his own acquaintance with the less respectable aspects of the city: an acquaintance he recalled with mingled feelings of pride and regret. There is ample evidence in his life and work to suggest that he never fully assimilated the Edinburgh experience, never fully came to terms with all that Edinburgh meant to him. 'The Misadventures of John Nicholson' is unusual in that it is the only story from his pen set in the Scotland of his lifetime. Whereas his other Scottish tales – Kidnapped, The Master of Ballantrae, Weir of Hermiston – are placed in the historical past, 'John Nicholson' is set recognisably in the age of hansom-cabs and gas-lamps. The affection with which the city is recalled, both as the scene of his childhood escapades and his youthful indiscretions, forms one of the most moving elements in the story. Though he returned to this theme at the end of his life – in passages in St. Ives, for example, and in Weir of Hermiston – he rarely conveyed with such deep feeling the intensity of his emotions concerning 'the aspects of the place that we call home'.

The central chapters, in which John visits his old friend Alan Houston at Murrayfield (for this purpose Stevenson 'borrowed' the home of his schoolfriend H. B. Baildon) only to become involved in a series of farcical adventures with a corpse, are written with that high spirited enthusiasm, that delight in storytelling for its own sake, he was later to employ in The Wrong Box. Though John's adventures are undeniably humorous and are narrated with relish there is an element of grim pathos in his increasingly desperate attempts to extricate himself from a quagmire of incriminating situations. The reader experiences a deep feeling of relief when John succeeds at last in escaping from the house containing the body of the murdered man for, despite his foolishness, the hero engages the reader's sympathy to the end.

At the age of thirty-five Stevenson was still a relatively untried novelist, his most sustained achievements up to that time being Treasure Island, Kidnapped and Dr. Jekyll and Mr. Hyde. It is fascinating therefore to see in 'John Nicholson' numerous indications of those literary powers which were already in the ascendant. Thus, in the scene in Mr. Nicholson's study when John is confessing his misdemeanours the following passage occurs: 'The lad panted out these phrases, one after another, like minute guns; but at the last word, which rang in that stately chamber like an oath, his heart failed him utterly; and the dreaded silence settled on father and son.'

The phrase 'like minute guns' is a masterly touch, conveying in an apt simile the tension and nervousness with which John recites his list of crimes; he is clearly in an explosive state of emotion as he confesses to one offence after another against the family code; 'the dreaded silence settled on father and son' is an equally telling phrase, redolent of the painful encounters which must have occurred on previous occasions in that forbidding room. The description of the study as 'that stately chamber' perfectly conveys its intimidating, formal atmosphere and the awe with which John entered it.

A further instance is the scene in the closing chapter when John returns home, a prodigal son seeking reconciliation. There is an awkward moment as the family sit down to a meal: 'And then, in an embarrassed silence, all took their places; and even the paper — from which it was the old gentleman's habit to suck mortification daily, as he marked the decline of our institutions – even the paper lay furled by his side.'

There are several indications here of the novelist Stevenson was to become. It was the old gentleman's habit 'to suck mortification daily' from the newspaper: a peculiarly apposite comment, bearing in mind all we have learned of Mr. Nicholson's temperament. As he read the paper 'he marked the decline of our institutions': a characteristic touch which might have been added by Dickens or Wells. Notice that each word, each phrase in the sentence has been chosen with care: 'in an embarrassed silence'; 'all took their places'; 'lay furled by his side' – each passage is designed to contribute to the overall effect. Already in this short tale, which Stevenson seems to have regarded as little more than a 'potboiler', there is evidence of that eye for detail, that gift for telling phrase which reveals the hand of the novelist in the making.

It was entirely in keeping with his character that, having commenced work on the tale in November 1885 he broke it off to write 'Olalla', not returning to it until almost a year later. He confided to Colvin that he was writing 'a damn tale to order, which will be what it will be: I don't love it, but some of it is pass-able in its mouldy way'.[15] Later critical opinion has not shared this disparaging judgement but has discerned in 'John Nicholson' significant evidence that Stevenson was no longer a tiro but a writer of considerable promise. Each of his short stories can be regarded as an experiment in which he tested out varying approaches towards narration and structure. The importance of this tale lies in the fact that it marks a watershed between the self-conscious, artificial style of his early stories and essays and the mature style of his finest achievements. It is also one of the very few stories in which he tried to come to terms with the emotional traumas of his past.

In his review of the collected short stories of Edgar Allan Poe,[16] Stevenson observed:

> Pointlessness is, indeed, the very last charge that could be brought reasonably against them. He has the true storyteller's instinct. He knows the little nothings that make stories or mar them. He knows how to enhance the significance of any situa-tion, and give colour and life to seeming irrelevant particulars.

These words were written in 1874, three years before the publi-cation of his own first story, yet they could be taken as a summa-tion of his achievement in the field of the short story. The range of his endeavour in this field was remarkably wide. In form his tales range from the gripping narrative of adventure ('The Pavilion on the Links') to the subtle allegory or fable ('Will o' the Mill' and 'The Merry Men'), from the psychological study of 'Markheim' to the sustained horror of 'Olalla' and 'The Body Snatcher', from the realistic comedy of 'John Nicholson' to the profound imagery of 'The Beach of Falesá'. Within these stories Stevenson experi-mented in methods of presenting character and incident and in approaches to narration and construction. He perfected techni-ques of storytelling which came to full fruition in the novels but which are none the less effective for being wrought on a smaller canvas. Above all he excelled at the 'little nothings that make stories or mar them', those literary touches which make the read-ing of his shorter works of fiction such a rewarding experience. Whilst he was deeply influenced by Poe and Hawthorne, he in turn exercised a profound influence on later practitioners of the short story and novella including Wells, Conrad and Conan Doyle. His tales will continue to be read not simply for their artistic merit and the force of their narrative power but for their illumination of the darker facets of human personality and continuing relevance to twentieth-century concerns.

Part IV
NOVELS AND ROMANCES

Treasure Island

Treasure Island, originally entitled *The Sea Cook: A Story for Boys*, was begun at Braemar in the summer of 1881. Stevenson, accompanied by his wife and parents, had rented a cottage for August and September; here they were joined from time to time by several of their friends, including Sidney Colvin, Charles Baxter and Edmund Gosse. His stepson, Lloyd Osbourne, was toying one day with a box of paints and Stevenson amused himself by drawing a map of an imaginary island. This was the germ of an idea which rapidly seized his imagination.

> as I paused upon my map of 'Treasure Island', the future character of the book began to appear there visibly among imaginary woods; and their brown faces and bright weapons peeped out upon me from unexpected quarters, as they passed to and fro, fighting and hunting treasure, on these few square inches of a flat projection. The next thing I knew I had some papers before me and was writing out a list of chapters. . . . On a chill September morning, by the cheek of a brisk fire, and the rain drumming on the window, I began *The Sea Cook*, for that was the original title.[1]

Such was his enthusiasm for his new tale that he succeeded in writing fifteen chapters in fifteen days, reading each instalment aloud to his family as the work proceeded. Early in the sixteenth chapter, however, inspiration temporarily failed him and he came to a halt. As the weather at Braemar had by this time deteriorated he hurried to Davos (where he had arranged to spend the winter) and here inspiration returned. He completed the book in a further two weeks of 'delighted industry' in which, as he later recorded,

the writing 'flowed from me like small talk'.[2] The story was published as a serial in the magazine *Young Folks* (October
1881–January 1882) and appeared in book form in December
1883.

The story has always been regarded as one of Stevenson's finest
achievements and has been described by Henry James as being
perfect of its kind. Whilst its stature as a boys' adventure story has
earned for it a continuing readership and reputation – it seems
destined to be one of that handful of romances by which Stevenson will be permanently remembered – its very success has
militated against its acceptance as a serious work of art. In recent
years, however, *Treasure Island* has begun to receive critical attention not simply because of its significance as a watershed in his
career but for its intrinsic literary and imaginative qualities.[3] It is
now acknowledged to be one of the finest examples of its genre in
the English language.

The genre to which *Treasure Island* belongs is that of the
romance. If one defines a romance as 'a work of prose fiction in
which the scenes and incidents are more or less removed from
common life and are surrounded by a halo of mystery, an atmosphere of strangeness and adventure' (William Rose Benet, *The
Reader's Encyclopaedia*, 1965) it is at once apparent that Stevenson
was thoroughly at home in this medium and that *Treasure Island*
complies in all respects to the conventions of the form. (There is a
delightful letter from Stevenson to Henley in which Stevenson
expresses his 'sighings after romance'; he quotes specimen opening sentences from romances he would wish to read and concludes: 'That is how stories should begin. And I am offered HUSKS
instead.'[4])

In his essay 'My First Book' Stevenson gives the impression that
the story was almost wholly derived from literary materials: 'A
few reminiscences of Poe, Defoe, and Washington Irving, a copy of
Johnson's *Buccaneers*, the name of the Dead Man's Chest from
Kingsley's *At Last*, some recollections of canoeing on the high
seas, and the map itself, with its infinite, eloquent suggestion,
made up the whole of my materials.' It is clear that some details
are taken from Poe's ingenious short story 'The Gold-Bug' (most
notably the tall tree and the skeleton pointer) and from his *Narrative of Arthur Gordon Pym*; that some features of the island are
derived from *Robinson Crusoe*; and that Captain Johnson's *History of
Notorious Pirates* provided him with information concerning pirate

lore. These elements alone, however, whilst they may have provided the seeds from which the story germinated, are insufficient
in themselves to account for the extraordinary conviction of the
narrative and for the immense popularity of the book as a tale of
adventure.

Readers have rightly praised Stevenson's mastery of narrative,
his skill in pacing the details of the story and the apparent ease
with which the reader is drawn on from each exciting episode to
the next. The opening scenes at the Admiral Benbow inn, the discovery of the sea chest and the treasure chart, the voyage to the
island on board the *Hispaniola*, the mutiny and the adventures on
the island: all are handled with consummate skill and with a narrative power the author never excelled.

But the book is notable not only for its excellence as an example
of the art of the storyteller but also for its peculiar insight into the
mind of a child. The bulk of the story is narrated by a boy, Jim
Hawkins, who both describes his adventures and comments upon
them as they unfold. Thus the story is at once a gripping narrative
and an extremely interesting example of a child's vision of the
world.

At an early stage in the story Jim reveals the terror of his boyhood nightmares:

> How that personage haunted my dreams, I need scarcely tell
> you. On stormy nights, when the wind shook the four corners
> of the house, and the surf roared along the cove and up the
> cliffs, I would see him in a thousand forms, and with a thousand
> diabolical expressions. Now the leg would be cut off at the
> knee, now at the hip; now he was a monstrous kind of a crea-
> ture who had never had but the one leg, and that in the middle
> of his body. To see him leap and run and pursue me over hedge
> and ditch was the worst of nightmares.

This dream, so reminiscent of Pip's waking nightmare in *Great
Expectations* in which he is pursued by a young man 'who wanted
my heart and liver',[5] reveals an acute understanding of a child's
outlook on the adult world. Not the least of the reasons why the
opening chapters make such a deep impression on the reader is
that they are written with the freshness and innocence of a young
person seeking to convey a coherent picture of his world. One is
reminded of both Pip and David Copperfield: a naïve yet engaging

child trying to come to grips with forces beyond his understanding – cruelty, duplicity and hatred – and to relate these to his limited experience of life. In the course of the story Jim's role is transformed from that of onlooker to principal character; there is a gradual change from simply narrating events which have happened to him to actively *determining* the course of action; he becomes the 'hero' in the sense that he plays a decisive role in thwarting the designs of the pirates. Thus, the story is not simply a record of the quest for the treasure but of Jim's progress towards maturity.

The characterisation in *Treasure Island* is assured and convincing. Whilst Stevenson follows the conventions of the romance in describing each character in the minimum of words, he succeeds in conveying the idiosyncrasies of each personality with admirable succinctness. For example, whilst almost no information is given concerning the physical appearance of Captain Smollett the reader has a vivid sense of his sharpness and decisiveness and his ability to form shrewd judgements in times of crisis. Similarly, both Dr. Livesey and Squire Trelawney are described with that gift for pen-portrayal which became Stevenson's hallmark and their neatness and urbanity are contrasted vividly with the rough uncouthness of the pirates.

Three of the characters – Billy Bones, Israel Hands and Long John Silver – are drawn with that ambiguity which so fascinated Stevenson; each is a composite of good and evil. Bones, for all his drunkenness and temper, retains a good deal of Jim's pity and sympathy, and on his death Jim bursts into 'a flood of tears'. Israel Hands, a more complex character, is described at first as a wily man 'who could be trusted at a pinch with almost anything'. At the crucial point in the story when Hands and Jim are alone on board the *Hispaniola* Jim comments on the odd smile which appears continually on Hands' face:

> It was a smile that had in it something both of pain and weakness – a haggard, old man's smile; but there was, besides that, a grain of derision, a shadow of treachery, in his expression as he craftily watched, and watched, and watched me at my work.

Such adjectives as 'pain', 'weakness' and 'haggard' are calculated to arouse the reader's sympathy; the juxtaposition of these terms with 'derision' and 'treachery' considerably dilutes the force of that

sympathy; the result is a deliberate ambivalence entirely characteristic of Stevenson's approach to human character.

One of the great strengths of the story, and one which lingers in
the mind long after the book has been laid aside, is the character
of Long John Silver, surely one of Stevenson's most powerful
creations. Stevenson himself, discussing the book many years
later, commented: 'I liked the tale myself, for much the same
reason as my father liked the beginning; it was my kind of
picturesque. I was not a little proud of John Silver, also; and to this
day rather admire that smooth and formidable adventurer.'[6] That
Silver was intended from the outset to play a significant role in the
narrative, if not to be the principal character, is clear from the
original title, *The Sea Cook*. (It was Henderson, the proprietor of
Young Folks, who selected *Treasure Island* as the title in preference to
this.)

On his first appearance Silver is presented with considerable
economy of words and yet with those touches of verisimilitude for
which Stevenson has become renowned:

His left leg was cut off close by the hip, and under the left
shoulder he carried a crutch, which he managed with wonderful dexterity, hopping about upon it like a bird. He was very tall
and strong, with a face as big as a ham – plain and pale, but
intelligent and smiling. Indeed, he seemed in the most cheerful
spirits, whistling as he moved about among the tables, with a
merry word or a slap on the shoulder for the more favoured of
his guests.

Not only is Silver himself drawn with real conviction – such
phrases as 'wonderful dexterity', 'a face as big as a ham', 'whistling
as he moved about among the tables' add solidity and depth to the
portrait – but the ambiguity which is inseparable from his personality is present from the outset. He was 'plain and pale' but also
'intelligent and smiling'. Jim Hawkins, deeply suspicious of him, is
soon convinced of his innocence: 'My suspicions had been
thoroughly reawakened on finding Black Dog at the "Spy-glass",
and I watched the cook narrowly. But he was too deep, and too
ready, and too clever for me, and . . . I would have gone bail for
the innocence of Long John Silver.'

As the narrative proceeds it becomes clear that this naïve trust
is quite unfounded and that Silver is capable of treachery,

violence, deceit and murder. But he is also capable of loyalty – at one point he is instrumental in saving Jim's life – and of displaying qualities of leadership, good humour and companionship. He is in fact a case-study in that duality of man which was later to become the theme of a powerful allegory, *The Strange Case of Dr. Jekyll and Mr. Hyde*. Despite his treachery, Silver retains to the end the affection of the reader and it is significant that at the conclusion of the narrative he is not punished for his crimes but succeeds in making good his escape. Stevenson was clearly reluctant to have him executed, and his disappearance with a portion of the treasure neatly solved the technical problem of removing him from the narrative whilst hinting at his further adventures. 'I daresay he met his old Negress', Jim comments, 'and perhaps still lives in comfort with her and Captain F

The importance of Silver li⸻⸻⸻⸻ation as a character but in the continu⸻⸻⸻⸻⸻een himself and Jim Hawkins. H⸻⸻⸻⸻after veering sharply from compl⸻⸻⸻⸻com ing aware for the first time ⸻⸻⸻⸻think, if I had been able, that I wo⸻⸻⸻⸻barrel' – fluctuates between disli⸻⸻⸻⸻ion. In recording the shifts of this rei⸻⸻⸻⸻s stages the narrative is also displaying Jim's grow⸻⸻⸻ he transition from immaturity to adulthood reaches its culm⸻⸻ on in the scene in which Hawkins, having promised Silver that he will not attempt to escape, is persuaded to do so by Doctor Livesey: ' "No," I replied, "you know right well you wouldn't do the thing yourself; neither you, nor squire, nor captain; and no more will I. Silver trusted me; I passed my word, and back I go." '

Hawkins, then, despite his mistrust of Silver, feels that having given his word he is bound to honour it; Silver, overhearing the conversation, behaves towards him with renewed respect. This relationship between the two, so innocent on the one hand, so calculated on the other, forms one of the dominant strands of the story and elevates it beyond the level of the conventional romance.

Stevenson confessed to his friend W. E. Henley that 'It was the sight of your maimed strength and masterfulness that begot John Silver in *Treasure Island*.'[7] It seems clear that the combination of a dominating personality and a crippled body held for him a powerful emotional appeal: an appeal which is also evident in the haunt/

ing quality of the deformed Black Dog and the eyeless Blind Pew.

Reviewing the book in the *Saturday Review* (8 December 1883), Henley perceptively observed: 'but Long John, called Barbecue, is incomparably the best of all. He, and not Jim Hawkins, nor Flint's treasure, is Mr. Stevenson's real hero.'

The island itself is described with such particularity that it is a significant contribution to the 'desert island' myth which has haunted English literature since the publication of *Robinson Crusoe* in 1719. It has the fascination of all such islands; remote, mysterious, virginal, isolated from human contact. When Hawkins first sets eyes on the land he has the distinct impression that it has not been explored before: 'From the ship, we could see nothing of the house or stockade, for they were quite buried among trees; and if it had not been for the chart on the companion, we might have been the first that had ever anchored there since the island arose out of the seas.' *Treasure Island* shares with other 'desert island' narratives – notable examples in our literature include R. M. Ballantyne's *The Coral Island*, H. G. Wells's *The Island of Doctor Moreau*, William Golding's *Lord of the Flies* and John Fowles's *The Magus* –the ability to provide a setting, an amphitheatre, in which the characters can be seen in isolation: 'a stage from which superfluous characters have been cleared'. This has the effect of focusing the reader's attention on to a limited number of individualities confined within a finite geographical area; all extraneous influences are removed. It is as if, during the experience of reading the book, one is removed from conventional notions of space and time and is peering into another world, remote from the present and yet evoked with extraordinary solidity.

It should be noted in passing that the verisimilitude of the island owes much to the accuracy with which it is described: an accuracy which extends to the smallest topographical details. In his youth Stevenson had studied engineering and surveying, and he well knew the importance of exactness in geographical matters: 'The author must know his countryside, whether real or imaginary, like his hand; the distances, the points of the compass, the place of the sun's rising, the behaviour of the moon, should all be beyond cavil.'[8]

Much of the realism of the story stems from the precision with which the landscape is described; one has the impression that the writer knows every inch of his territory and is describing scenes and features etched permanently on his memory. So vividly is this achieved that the physical details of the island remain in the mind long after the book has been read; its colours, terrain, trees – even its smell – linger persistently in the imagination:

> There was not a breath of air moving, nor a sound but that of the surf booming half a mile away along the beaches and against the rocks outside. A peculiar stagnant smell hung over the anchorage – a smell of sodden leaves and rotting tree trunks.

Stevenson had not in fact visited the West Indies at the time of writing the story; he relied for the details of the scenery on his memories of California, together with his literary sources and his own imagination. The result is an extraordinary exercise in precision: it is with an effort – and not a little reluctance – that the adult reader is compelled to the realisation that the island has no existence outside the author's imagination.

Each of Stevenson's novels contains insights and reflections on the moral ambiguity of human actions and *Treasure Island* is no exception to this rule. Silver himself, as we have seen, encapsulates that inherent duality of man which so fascinated his creator and which infuses the character with such vitality. There are in addition a number of incidents which raise interesting moral questions and possess implications of which Stevenson must have been aware. Hawkins's action in deliberately running away from the stockade, thereby deserting his friends, is in a sense an act of treachery; yet his action proves to be decisive in routing the pirates. Thus, whilst morally he was wrong, tactically he was right. Again, Ben Gunn assists Silver to escape but 'he assured us he had only done so to preserve our lives'. Stevenson deliberately leaves unanswered the question whether Gunn was right or wrong to take the action he did, but implicit in this incident is the difficulty of adopting unambivalent courses of action. A further example is the decision to leave behind on the island three of the mutineers. This seems to Hawkins a painful but unavoidable decision: 'It went to all our hearts, I think, to leave them in that wretched state; but we could not risk another mutiny; and to take them home for the gibbet would have been a cruel sort of kindness.' In each of these instances there is a careful balancing of competing considerations but the reader is aware that inherent in each set of circumstances is the impossibility of arriving at a wholly judicious course of action.

This dimension of ambiguity, whilst not detracting from the excitement of the story as a romance, adds considerably to its stature as a microcosm of human behaviour. Flowing behind and through the surface narrative is a continual shifting of focus, a blurring of identity, which compels the reader to acknowledge the duality of human nature. (The device of changing narrators mid-way through the story is an interesting example of the technique: this permits the reader to observe the same sequence of events from two different points of view and thus to form contrasting impressions. A further example is Chapter 28, 'In the Enemy's Camp', where the description of the mutineers' stronghold *seen from the inside* permits a different vantage point from that of the preceding chapters.) Continually, then, Stevenson invites his readers to view his characters in the round; to acknowledge that none of his villains, however corrupt, is wholly evil and that behaviour which seems reprehensible from one point of view may be justified when seen from a fresh perspective.

In a perceptive essay on *Treasure Island* W. W. Robson has observed that 'on its own plane it fulfils the primary purpose of all fiction: to provide the reader with imaginative understanding of human nature, in ideal conditions for the existence of that understanding'.[9] Whilst it was conceived primarily as a boys' adventure story its status as a children's classic has diverted attention from its deeper qualities and its importance to Stevenson's own approach to his art. He entitled his essay on it 'My First Book'. In fact, it was very far from being his first book for he had previously published *An Inland Voyage, Travels with a Donkey, Virginibus Puerisque, Familiar Studies of Men and Books* and *New Arabian Nights*. It was, however, his first full-length novel and the first book in which he had been called upon to apply his talents in a sustained way to the techniques of characterisation and narrative. *Treasure Island* is significant not simply because it was his first full-length work of imagination, nor the first of his works to become widely known, but because it marks a departure from the preoccupations (and occasional immaturities) of his early essays and short stories and a move towards his true concerns as a novelist.

In this tale of pirates and buried treasure Stevenson faced and surmounted many problems of narration, style and characterisation and in so doing found himself as a creative writer.

Prince Otto

Writing to his friend W. H. Low in December 1883 Stevenson confided:

> My brief romance *Prince Otto* – far my most difficult adventure up to now – is near an end . . . . There is a good deal of stuff in it, both dramatic and, I think, poetic; and the story is not like these purposeless fables of today, but is, at least, intended to stand firm upon a basis of philosophy – or morals – as you please. It has been long gestated, and is wrought with care.

This story, his 'most difficult adventure up to now' and one on which he lavished great pains, had been begun as early as 1880 under the title *The Forest State* or *The Greenwood State: A Romance*. Much of this was written in San Francisco and then laid aside, characteristically, whilst he pursued other projects. It was not taken up again until April 1883 when he set to work and rewrote it from the beginning, completing it at Hyères in the spring of 1884. The book was serialised in *Longman's Magazine* from April–October 1885 and published in book form in November of that year.

Prince Otto, which Stevenson described as 'my chief o' works; hence probably not so for others, since it only means that I have here attacked the greatest difficulties',[10] is very different in form and style from *Treasure Island*. Written whilst strongly under the influence of George Meredith, it is cast in the form of a romance set in the imaginary European state of Grünewald. Otto, Prince of Grünewald, a sincere but ineffectual ruler, neglectful of his duties, is the victim of a conspiracy to overthrow him and declare a republic. The leading conspirators are his estranged wife, Princess

110

Seraphina, and Baron Gondremark, who schemes to usurp Otto's power. The story concerns the unmasking of the plot by the Prince, his realisation of his own inadequacies as ruler and husband, and his eventual reunification with the Princess and decision to abandon the throne.

The interest of the book lies less in the rather artificial plot than in the strength of the characterisation, some of which was drawn from life. Otto himself, while based partly on the character of Stevenson's cousin R. A. M. Stevenson, is given the physical appearance of the author himself:

> He is not ill looking; he has hair of ruddy gold, which naturally curls, and his eyes are dark, a combination which I always regard as the mark of some congenital deficiency, physical or moral; his features are irregular, but pleasing; the nose perhaps a little short, and the mouth a little womanish; his address is excellent, and he can express himself with point.

What led Stevenson to describe his own characteristics with such candour is not known. One is reminded of Poe's description of himself in 'The Fall of the House of Usher' and Wells's account of his own personality in *Mr. Britling*. It is clear that he was attracted by Otto and by the moral dilemma in which the Prince finds himself and that in describing Otto's quest for imaginative and personal fulfilment he was expressing some of his own concerns in the guise of fiction.

Seraphina, based in part on his wife Fanny, is perhaps less successful as a rounded portrait, if only because she is presented less sympathetically. Whether Fanny recognised herself in the portrait is doubtful, for it is in some respects unflattering, but Seraphina is a person of considerable strength of will, with a mind and outlook of her own.

The relationship between Seraphina and the Prime Minister, Gondremark, her alleged lover, is handled with great skill and one has a vivid sense of the in-fighting and intrigue inseparable from nineteenth-century principalities.

Most critics are agreed that the most convincing portrayal is that of the Countess von Rosen, by common consent one of Stevenson's few successful female characters. Suggested by the personality of one of two Russian sisters he had befriended at Menton, she possesses a life and vivacity which makes her one of his most memorable creations. Anthony Hope drew on her in describing Antoinette de Mauban in *The Prisoner of Zenda*, and she is clearly the exemplar for many similar *femmes fatale* in romantic fiction. There are in addition a number of well-drawn minor characters – Killian Gottesheim, a farmer who befriends the Prince whilst unaware of his identity; Gondremark, the scheming Prime Minister; Sir John Crabtree, an English baronet who visits the Court and forms a shrewd assessment of it; and Gotthold, the Palace librarian. Though none of these, including the principal characters, is drawn with the vitality and conviction of Long John Silver in *Treasure Island*, each is presented with honesty and provided the author with valuable experience in the depicting of personality and temperament.

The writing itself has been much criticised on the grounds of its over-elaborateness and it remains true that much of the book is too florid and mannered for modern taste. It does, however, contain some powerful passages over which Stevenson obviously devoted great care (Book 2, Ch. XI, for example, was rewritten eight times before he was satisfied). The dissolution of the Council by the Prince; the midnight conversation between Otto and the Countess; the confrontation between the Princess and Gondremark – all are described with that mastery of incident and nuance which earned for him a deserved reputation as a master storyteller. Finest of all is the chapter entitled 'Princess Cinderella', a very carefully written account of the journey of the Princess through a lonely forest. This contains some admirable descriptive passages which reveal Stevenson's deep love of natural beauty and his power of evoking moods through the adroit use of language.

In insisting that the story was 'intended to stand firm upon a basis of philosophy – or morals',[11] Stevenson seems to have intended that the story should be interpreted as a parable on the theme of marriage. A marriage of minds, he suggests, cannot work whilst surrounded by the machinations of Court intrigue; it is only when Otto and the Princess flee from the trappings of Court life and become anonymous citizens in another land that they rediscover their love for one another. Artificiality and convention could all too easily stifle affection; a marriage can only work effectively in an atmosphere of complete mutual trust in which each partner sees the other without illusions. Interwoven with this main theme are a number of subsidiary motifs including the conflict between duty and the yearning for domesticity, between strength of character and sensitivity. Stevenson had been compelled to grapple with these dilemmas in his own life and was acutely aware of the dichotomy between following one's duty on the one hand and pursuing one's inclinations on the other. Beneath the complicated net of intrigue which forms the substance of the novel can be discerned a preoccupation with issues and themes close to his own life and to his struggle to achieve artistic and emotional consummation.

During Stevenson's lifetime *Prince Otto* was warmly praised by Andrew Lang, W. E. Henley and George Meredith[12] but in our own century the book has fallen into disfavour. Technically, no doubt it is an impressive achievement but the reader has the impression that stylistic competence has been achieved at the expense of narrative power. The book altogether lacks the drama-tic qualities of *Treasure Island* and *Kidnapped*, although some critics have commented favourably on the romantic comedy of the chapters describing Countess von Rosen and her attempts to entice the Prince. The principal weakness of the story stems from Stevenson's own indecision concerning his intentions. Writing to Henley in May 1883 he observed: 'the whole thing is not a romance, nor yet a comedy; nor yet a romantic comedy; but a kind of preparation of some of the elements of all three in a glass jar'. It is precisely this ambiguity of purpose which militates against the artistic unity of the work as a whole. Neither a novel of adventure in the vein of *Treasure Island* nor a comedy of manners in the vein of Meredith's romances *Prince Otto* is an uneasy hybrid between the two. Moreover the book suffers from a number of structural weaknesses which his friends were not slow to point out. Whilst the marriage between Otto and Seraphina has clearly broken down, the reader is given no indication of how they came to be married or of the nature of their original attraction for one another. There is, in fact, no account of their marriage except by hearsay – in the 'On the Court of Grunewald' chapter written by Sir John Crabtree, and in the conversations at the River Farm. Thus, the relationship between the Prince and Princess, a crucial element within the plot, is seen from the outside but rarely glimpsed from the vantage point of the two participants. It was this omission which led Meredith to complain that Otto was insufficiently 'humanised' and that he was 'morally limp'.

Stevenson himself, whilst confident that he had written a work possessing intrinsic literary merit, sensed its limitations. To Sidney

Colvin (9 March 1884) he confessed: 'But, mind, it is very likely that the big effort, instead of being the masterpiece, may be the blotted copy, the gymnastic exercise.' It is significant that whilst other writers sought to emulate his example – most notably Anthony Hope in *The Prisoner of Zenda* (1894) and *Rupert of Hentzau* (1898) – he himself did not repeat the experiment. His later achievements lay in the historical adventure story or in the novel *per se* rather than the Ruritanian romance.

The Strange Case of Dr. Jekyll and Mr. Hyde

Dr. Jekyll and Mr. Hyde, one of Stevenson's most celebrated tales, was written at Bournemouth in 1885 where he was convalescing after one of his recurrent haemorrhages. The germ of the idea came to him in a nightmare, from which he was awoken by his wife Fanny. Stevenson protested that she had broken off 'a fine bogy-tale' and developed the idea into a full-length narrative. As originally conceived the tale was apparently a straightforward horror story with no allegorical undertones. When he read this first draft to his wife she suggested that it would be better if it were recast as an allegory. Stevenson protested strongly but eventually relented, burning the original version and rewriting it from beginning to end. The idea so obsessed him that the rewriting occupied a period of only three days.[13]

On its publication in January 1886 it was immediately recognised as a work of unusual stature. An anonymous review in *The Times* praised the book highly, observing that 'Nothing Mr. Stevenson has written as yet has so strongly impressed us with the versatility of his very original genius', and concluding with the plea that the story 'should be read as a finished study in the art of fantastic literature'. In an influential article in the *Saturday Review* Andrew Lang commented: 'while one is thrilled and possessed by the horror of the central fancy, one may fail, at first reading, to recognise the delicate and restrained skill of the treatment of accessories, details, and character'. Both reviewers and the reading public responded enthusiastically to a story which possessed so obviously a single dominant motive and one which was recognisably of universal application.

Neither Stevenson's previous romances, *Treasure Island* and *Prince Otto*, nor his volumes of essays and short stories had prepared his readers for a work of such sombre dramatic power or seriousness of intent. In such tales as 'Thrawn Janet' and 'The Body-Snatcher' he had demonstrated his ability to create an atmosphere of brooding horror and suspense, but in *Dr. Jekyll* he evinced for the first time a capacity to sustain a full-length narrative which was not only an exciting and well-composed story but also a powerfully wrought parable.

In our own century successive film adaptations have so popularised the story that many thousands are familiar with the basic plot who have never read the book and who probably could not name the author. Famous in both Stevenson's time and in ours, its very popularity has served to militate against its acceptance as a serious work of art and against the literary reputation of its author. The phrase 'Jekyll and Hyde' has become part of English folk-lore and the story has tended to be grouped with those luridly written tales described by George Orwell as 'good bad books': such stories as *Dracula, Dr. Fu Manchu* and *The Phantom of the Opera*. A careful reading of Stevenson's tale, however, will demonstrate that *Dr. Jekyll and Mr. Hyde* is in a different category from these; that it is a skilfully executed work possessing considerable literary and imaginative power and moreover that it is rich in symbolisms of continuing relevance to the twentieth century. Before turning to a discussion of the thematic and allegorical elements within the tale it is necessary to examine closely its structure and language.

The *structure* of the story is of exceptional interest. It would have been possible to have cast the entire narrative in first-person form, and to have told the story in the manner of a confession seen from Jekyll's point of view. Stevenson deliberately chose not to adopt this device. Instead, he opted for a more discursive treatment in three distinct parts: first, a leisurely account of the two characters, Dr. Jekyll and Mr. Hyde, described from several different standpoints (in the course of which it is established that there is some mysterious link between the two); secondly, a narrative written by Dr. Lanyon, a colleague and former school companion of Henry Jekyll's in which is revealed for the first time the physical metamorphosis from Hyde to Jekyll; lastly, a full and detailed confession from Jekyll himself, including an account of the experiments leading up to the transformation, his emotional torments and his regrets at all that has transpired under the influence of the drug. At first sight this method of presenting the story seems rather clumsy: it is akin to the unusual structure adopted by Wells in *The Invisible Man*, a tale which contains a number of thematic similarities to *Dr. Jekyll*. On a second reading, however, it can be seen that the method chosen by Stevenson, discursive though it is, has the effect of gaining sympathy for Jekyll and of adding depth to what would otherwise be simply an interesting experiment in the novella form. It enables the reader to see Jekyll through several different eyes and in this way to form a composite picture of the central character which would not have been possible had the story been told in the first-person. Moreover it makes possible a *gradual* unfolding of the solution to the mystery and a slow building up of tension which add considerably to the emotional impact of the story.

It should be noted that Jekyll does not speak for himself until the final chapter; until this point he has been described *from the outside*, first by Enfield, then by Utterson, then by Dr. Lanyon. It is not until the concluding section that Jekyll gives his own account of all that has occurred; his narrative supplements those of the others and *inter alia* provides solutions to some of the problems posed by them. Thus his confession imposes a unity and a symmetry on what would otherwise be a series of disparate incidents: it provides the story with both a literal and a symbolic ending since it concludes with his own suicide.

Structurally, then, *Dr. Jekyll and Mr. Hyde* marks a departure from the more conventional patterns of *Treasure Island* and *Prince Otto* and in this sense represents a significant innovation in his work. It reveals Stevenson's growing mastery of the long short story as a literary genre and his increasing self-confidence in handling narrative and style.

The story also affords an extremely interesting case-study in literary technique when examined from the point of view of the linguistic devices employed by the author to achieve the effects he desires. The opening chapter, intriguingly entitled 'Story of the Door', begins without preamble with a description of one of the central characters: 'Mr. Utterson the lawyer was a man of a rugged countenance, that was never lighted by a smile; cold, scanty and embarrassed in discourse; backward in sentiment; lean, long, dusty, dreary, and yet somehow lovable.'

This description succeeds, with considerable economy of words, in conveying a skilful word-picture of Utterson. The technique clearly owes something to Dickens in its manner and its emphasis on physical characteristics, but it is the *Stevensonian* touches – such phrases as 'backward in sentiment', 'yet somehow lovable' and 'embarrassed in discourse' – which at once reveal the hand of a literary craftsman thoroughly acquainted with his medium. Within the compass of this one sentence we learn much about the lawyer: that he is a man without humour, that he is undemonstrative and taciturn, that he is tall and lean, and that, for all his shortcomings, he is an attractive man. Utterson is indeed one of Stevenson's most engaging characters; and whilst the limitations of the novella form (as in 'The Beach of Falesá') preclude the full development of the character in all its facets, nevertheless he is within these constraints a rounded and solid individuality.

Throughout this first chapter the language and style merit careful attention: with a deft touch the narrator describes Utterson and his friend Richard Enfield wandering through a busy quarter of London on one of their Sunday rambles. It is immediately apparent that this is no ordinary friendship: 'It was reported by those who encountered them in their Sunday walks, that they said nothing, looked singularly dull, and would hail with obvious relief the appearance of a friend.' This then is a friendship between two kindred spirits: the silent companionship of two men who do not need to converse, but find sufficient pleasure in the proximity of one another. A relationship of this kind is a rare thing and has satisfactions of its own: Stevenson unobtrusively draws this to the reader's attention before moving on to a description of the London by-way.

These paragraphs form the prelude to the Poesque description of Hyde's sinister residence:

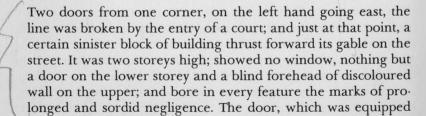

Two doors from one corner, on the left hand going east, the line was broken by the entry of a court; and just at that point, a certain sinister block of building thrust forward its gable on the street. It was two storeys high; showed no window, nothing but a door on the lower storey and a blind forehead of discoloured wall on the upper; and bore in every feature the marks of prolonged and sordid negligence. The door, which was equipped with neither bell nor knocker, was blistered and distrained. Tramps slouched into the recess and struck matches on the panels; children kept shop upon the steps; the schoolboy had tried his knife on the mouldings; and for close on a generation, no one had appeared to drive away these random visitors or to repair their ravages.

This is by any standards a powerful piece of writing and it succeeds admirably in achieving the author's intention. The language, firstly, is such as to convey an atmosphere of decay and foreboding: notice particularly the use of such adjectives as 'sinister', 'sordid negligence', 'discoloured 'and 'blistered'. There is set before us a mental picture of a building in an advanced stage of degradation. Then the passage has the effect of arousing the reader's curiosity: the building has no windows, it is apparently untenanted, and it is clear from its context that it is to play an important role in the story about to unfold. This is confirmed when Enfield poses the question 'Did you ever remark that door?' and adds immediately 'It is connected in my mind with a very odd story.' This is one of many touches in the narrative which reveal the hand of the master storyteller and which indicate that Stevenson was moving away from the occasional immaturity of the early romances and towards the full development of his powers as a novelist. His biographer J. C. Furnas has rightly observed: 'though sweepingly popular, _Jekyll_ was by no means a cheap piece of work'.[14]

Examples of Stevenson's care and artistry in the use of language occur throughout the narrative. In Chapter 3, for instance, we learn more of Utterson's companionable qualities: 'Hosts loved to detain the dry lawyer, when the light-hearted and the loose-tongued had already their foot on the threshold; they liked to sit awhile in his unobtrusive company, practising for solitude, sobering their minds in the man's rich silence, after the expense and strain of gaiety.' It could be argued that passages such as this are, strictly speaking, unnecessary within the context of a tale of this nature; that they do not contribute towards the development of the plot and would be more appropriate in a full-length novel. Against this it can be asserted that, on the contrary, their very presence indicates that Stevenson intended much more than merely a vividly written horror story, that he was consciously setting out to produce a work of literature and was therefore determined to introduce the incidents, nuances and descriptive passages essential to that end. Phrases such as 'unobtrusive company' and 'the man's rich silence' tell us much concerning the quiet lawyer: they add an element of solidity to his portrait and leave us with the feeling that if it were possible for Utterson to step out of the confines of the story it would be rewarding to make his acquaintance.

Similar touches can be found at numerous stages in the tale. Here, for example, is a reference to the London fog:

> The fog still slept on the wing above the drowned city, where the lamps glimmered like carbuncles; and through the muffle and smother of these fallen clouds, the procession of the town's life was still rolling in through the great arteries with a sound as of a mighty wind.

Here again may be discerned the hand of a highly skilled practitioner. 'The fog still slept on the wing'; 'the lamps glimmered like carbuncles'; 'the muffle and smother of these fallen clouds'; these are the strokes of an accomplished writer with a keen eye and ear for the telling phrase. Stevenson is particularly adept at the powerful visual image:

> The street shone out in contrast to its dingy neighbourhood like a fire in a forest   (Ch. 1)

> Mr. Enfield's tale went before his mind in a scroll of lighted pictures.   (Ch. 2)

> A great chocolate-coloured pall lowered over heaven, but the wind was continually charging and routing these embattled vapours.   (Ch. 4)

> It was a wild, cold, seasonable night of March, with a pale moon, lying on her back as though the wind had tilted her, and a flying wrack of the most diaphanous and lawny texture.   (Ch. 8)

The vividness of his images and similes is such as to etch them indelibly on the imagination and to remain in the memory long after the tale has been completed. The reason why the story is read and remembered today a century after it was written, when so much of its period is forgotten, must lie to a large degree in this very factor: the extraordinary power of its narration and the intensity of its descriptive framework. It shares with such tales as (has) *The Time Machine* and 'The Fall of the House of Usher' the capacity to provide an extra-literary experience: to sustain, by means of a brilliantly conceived series of descriptive images, the illusion of having witnessed *and participated in* a graphic sequence of events.

The structural and linguistic devices employed by Stevenson each contribute to the unusual atmosphere of the story. This atmosphere – one of controlled suspense, a gradual building up of a sense of horror and destruction – is achieved through a slow accumulation of unemotional detail, a relentless accretion of incident and mood. It owes much to the curiously *static* quality of the narrative. Though set in late nineteenth-century London there is little sense of movement; though the story depicts a number of characters there is little real intimacy between them. The effect of this deliberate exclusion of activity is to heighten the sinister undertones of the story and concentrate the reader's attention on its prevailing mood.

It is perhaps in the concluding chapter that Stevenson's natural gifts as a novelist are most in evidence. This chapter, 'Henry Jekyll's Full Statement of the Case', commences in the solid, novelistic manner of a narrative by Poe or Wells:

> I was born in the year 18– to a large fortune, endowed besides with excellent parts, inclined by nature to industry, fond of the respect of the wise and good among my fellow-men, and thus, as might have been supposed, with every guarantee of an honourable and distinguished future.

It is interesting to compare this passage with the opening paragraph of Poe's short story 'M.S. Found in a Bottle':

> Of my country and of my family I have little to say. Ill usage and length of years have driven me from the one, and estranged me from the other. Hereditary wealth afforded me an education of no common order, and a contemplative turn of mind enabled me to methodise the stores which early study very diligently garnered up.

The effect of such an opening is to arouse the interest and curiosity of the reader and to set the scene for the detailed explication
which follows. Jekyll proceeds to lay bare the profound dichotomy
in his own temperament:

> And it chanced that the direction of my scientific studies, which
> led wholly towards the mystic and the transcendental, reacted
> and shed a light on this consciousness of the perennial war
> among my members. With every day, and from both sides of
> my intelligence, the moral and the intellectual, I thus drew
> steadily nearer to that truth, by whose partial discovery I have
> been doomed to such a dreadful shipwreck: that man is not
> truly one, but truly two.

The narrative goes on to describe with unforgettable clarity the
agonies of indecision which Jekyll experienced as he continued
with his experiments and his emotions on assuming for the first
time the character and appearance of his other self, Edward Hyde.
Hyde, he notes, causes revulsion in the eyes of all he meets, since
'all human beings, as we meet them, are commingled out of good
and evil' but 'Hyde, alone in the ranks of mankind, was pure evil'.

The weakest element in the story is the physical means of transformation from Jekyll to Hyde and vice versa. Jekyll explains in his
statement that 'Certain agents I have found to have the power to
shake and to pluck back that fleshy vestment, even as a wind
might toss the curtains of a pavilion.' That a drug could cause a
mental transformation seems plausible but that it could also
achieve a *physical* metamorphosis – including a marked difference
in stature – seems incongruous. A number of critics drew
attention to this point on publication but were compelled to
acknowledge that the power and conviction of the narrative were
such as to override this technical weakness. Jekyll's confession is
written with such circumstantiality as to suspend disbelief; the
reader overlooks its implausibilities and is borne along with the
matter-of-fact narration and with its underlying emotion.

At first reluctantly but then with mounting eagerness, as the
character of Hyde becomes more and more dominant, Jekyll
embarks in his new guise on a career of depravity and crime,
culminating in the wanton murder of an innocent man, Sir
Danvers Carew. At each stage in his retrogression Jekyll is at pains
to include in his confession a full statement of his emotions and

reactions, as he is drawn irresistably into a life of duplicity. His is the horrible torment of a man who, whilst fully aware of his degeneration and consumed with remorse at his wrongdoing, is powerless to resist the 'insensate readiness to evil' which with mounting frequency invades his being. There are few more powerful passages in the entire canon of Stevenson's writings than those depicting Jekyll's gradual transformation under the pernicious influence of his own darker character. The reader shares with Jekyll his slow awareness of his moral decline, his initial curiosity on assuming the persona of Hyde, giving way to feelings of fascinated terror, his deeper and deeper enmeshment in a life of unbridled depravity. Stevenson was above all things a consummate storyteller and in this tale of a respected English gentleman possessed by a recrudescence of evil, he brought to bear his very considerable prowess as a narrator.

In his awareness that 'man is not truly one, but truly two' Jekyll is by no means alone. As early as the second chapter, Utterson the lawyer reflects upon the iniquities of his own past:

His past was fairly blameless; few men could read the rolls of their life with less apprehension; yet he was humbled to the dust by the many ill things he had done, and raised up again into a sober and fearful gratitude by the many that he had come so near to doing, yet avoided.

Throughout his life Stevenson was fascinated by man's double being, by 'those provinces of good and ill which divide and compound man's dual nature'. He had been intrigued by the career of William Brodie (1741–88), a respected Edinburgh businessman who was simultaneously an unscrupulous thief. Moreover his own character and imagination were irrevocably marked by the strict Calvinism of his early environment and by his rebellion against the narrow morality of Victorian Scotland. In his essay 'The Works of Edgar Allan Poe' (1875) he had expressed his admiration of Poe's works and drawn attention to their 'important contribution to morbid psychology'. It seems certain, then, that he had read Poe's powerful short story 'William Wilson' and had reflected on its theme of man's duality. The broodings and reflections of many years, then, combined in *Dr. Jekyll and Mr. Hyde* to create a haunting fable: a fable which he described as 'a dreadful thing, I own; but the only thing I feel dreadful about is that damned old business of the war in the members. This time it came out; I hope it will stay in, in future.'[15]

Yet the story is much more than a simple allegory of good versus evil; it is a profound study of hypocrisy. Part of Jekyll's ambivalence lies in his attitude to evil, in the fact that he regards the throwing off of moral control as a liberation. It is not so much that he *wishes* to embark on an orgy of lust and violence as that he cannot tolerate the notion that certain forms of behaviour are not permissible. In this ambivalence Jekyll embodies that hypocrisy which Stevenson sought to expose and criticise. Moreover Jekyll at first feels no remorse for Hyde's crimes: his attitude is rather one of satisfaction at his supposed immunity from justice:

> I had but to drink the cup, to doff at once the body of the noted professor, and to assume, like a thick cloak, that of Edward Hyde. . . . And thus fortified, as I supposed, on every side, I began to profit by the strange immunities of my position.

Thus, by adopting the guise of Hyde he is enabled both to pursue a career of 'vicarious depravity' and to escape the consequences of his actions. In this way he can maintain a façade of respectability and sobriety whilst simultaneously indulging in a career of crime. The story is then a parable both on the dual nature of man and on the double standards man applies to his own behaviour.

The story has been seen by many critics as a variation on the *Frankenstein* myth: that of the misguided scientist who is ultimately destroyed by his own creation. It should be noted, however, that in committing suicide Jekyll destroys not only himself but also Hyde; the two personalities are inseparably bound together. Jekyll is fully aware that he can remove Hyde at any time he chooses by ending his own life: this is made explicit towards the end of his confession when he observes

> But his love of life is wonderful . . . I, who sicken and freeze at the mere thought of him, when I recall the abjection and passion of this attachment, and when I know how he fears my power to cut him off by suicide, I find it in my heart to pity him.

Thus, a further dimension of self-awareness is an escapable part of Jekyll's tragedy – his recognition that the only way in which he can put a conclusive end to Hyde and his crimes is to end his own existence. He is not faced with a simple choice between good and evil; he is compelled to accept that either both exist or neither. It is from this recognition, this central dilemma, that so much of the tale's force as an allegory is generated.

It is not difficult to see why *Dr. Jekyll and Mr. Hyde* became on publication an immediate success nor why so distinguished a novelist as John Fowles has described it as 'very possibly the best guidebook to the [Victorian] age'.[16] The book encapsulates as no other nineteenth-century novel does the fundamental dichotomy which lay at the heart of Victorian man: that between outward respectability and inward lust, between a veneer of decorum and a raging inferno of evil. This theme preoccupied Stevenson throughout his life and can be traced in such short stories as 'Markheim' and 'Thrawn Janet' and in the novels of his maturity. He was not only one of the first writers to examine this dichotomy but to identify the good and evil elements within man as 'spiritual' and 'animal'. This identification is made explicit at the point where Jekyll, sitting on a bench in Regent's Park, muses on his life and character: 'I sat in the sun on a bench; the animal within me licking the chaps of memory; the spiritual side a little drowsed, promising subsequent penitence, but not yet moved to begin'.

This was a theme which H. G. Wells was to elaborate in *The Island of Doctor Moreau* (1896), an allegorical tale which in both its published and draft versions owed much to Stevenson's conception.[17]

Dr. Jekyll and Mr. Hyde has exercised a profound impact on our literature, most notably on such tales as Oscar Wilde's *The Picture of Dorian Gray* (1891) and Wells's *The Invisible Man* (1897). It is to Stevenson's recognition of 'the thorough and primitive duality of man' that we owe one of the most powerful myths of our age, the twentieth-century obsession with the sudden metamorphosis from good to evil. The Gothic melodrama of the outwardly upright but inwardly tormented Jekyll and the brutal, selfish Hyde has spawned a multitude of lesser imitations ranging from wolf-men to vampires, from possession by evil and alien forces to the story of the man with the head of a fly.

That Stevenson had unerringly identified a previously unspoken truth there can be little doubt: that the human psyche consists of a complex of competing forces, some with benign tendencies and others with immense potentiality for harm, and that the unleashing of the latter is fraught with incalculable consequences. The theme of the coexistence within the same person of altruistic and selfish motives was later to be treated on a broader canvas in *The Master of Ballantrae* and *Weir of Hermiston*, but in this short allegory Stevenson pared down to essentials his awareness of man's ineradicably dual nature and in so doing created a unique distillation of his art.

Kidnapped and *Catriona*

Kidnapped (originally entitled *David Balfour*) was commissioned by the magazine *Young Folks* and begun in March 1885. Stevenson worked enthusiastically on the story, commenting in a letter to his father:

> But as far as I have got . . . I think David is on his feet, and (to my mind) a far better story and far sounder at heart than *Treasure Island*. I have no earthly news, living entirely in my story, and only coming out of it to play patience.[18]

Characteristically he abandoned the book when inspiration momentarily failed him, resuming it with renewed enthusiasm in January 1886 and completing it in the spring of that year. Ill health compelled him to truncate his original design and he accepted Sidney Colvin's suggestion of bringing the story to a conclusion with the narrator's return to Edinburgh and to relate the remaining adventures in a sequel. This sequel was duly published in 1893 under the title *Catriona*.

Kidnapped, set in the year 1751 (i.e. six years after the Jacobite Rebellion, and in a period when Scotland was in a state of turmoil) relates the story of David Balfour, a country boy who embarks on a journey to Edinburgh in search of his inheritance. His scheming uncle seeks to deprive him of his inheritance by arranging for David to be kidnapped aboard a brig bound for the Carolinas. The bulk of the story consists of David's subsequent adventures; his escape from his captors, his journey across Scotland, his suspected involvement in the murder of Campbell of Glenure, and the final confrontation with his uncle and the claiming of his rightful possessions.

The book falls naturally into four parts: Chapters 1–6 describing David Balfour's journey to the House of Shaws and his meeting with Uncle Ebenezer; Chapters 7–13 describing his kidnapping and the journey on board the brig *Covenant*; Chapters 14–26 relating his journeyings through Scotland in the company of Alan Breck; and Chapters 27–30 relating his return to Shaws, his claiming of his inheritance and his parting from Alan.

The opening chapters, describing David Balfour's journey from his home at Essenden to the mysterious House of Shaws, contain some of his finest writing. Stevenson carefully builds up an atmosphere of suspense as David approaches closer and closer to the house he has sought for so long. His impression of the building vividly recalls the description of the ruined House of Usher in Poe's short story:

> the house itself appeared to be a kind of ruin; no road led up to it; no smoke arose from any of the chimneys; nor was there any semblance of a garden. My heart sank. 'That!' I cried. . . . The nearer I got to that, the drearier it appeared. It seemed like the one wing of a house that had never been finished. What should have been the inner end stood open on the upper floors, and showed against the sky with steps and stairs of uncompleted masonry. Many of the windows were unglazed, and bats flew in and out like doves out of a dovecot.

This suspense is skilfully maintained throughout the House of Shaws sequence, as the reader enters into a complex web of gothic incident and melodrama. These introductory chapters, so circumstantial and gripping, are written with a conviction and veracity which Stevenson rarely equalled.

David is a boy of sixteen who becomes involved in a complicated snare of intrigue and pursuit at the hands of adults and yet retains throughout his child-like vision of the world. His first encounter with his miserly uncle, so reminiscent of the early chapters of *David Copperfield*, owes much to Dickens and yet possesses certain touches entirely characteristic of Stevenson:

> Presently there came a great rattling of chains and bolts, and the door was cautiously opened, and shut to again behind me as soon as I had passed.
> 'Go into the kitchen and touch naething,' said the voice; and

while the person of the house set himself to replacing the defences of the door, I groped my way forward and entered the kitchen.

The fire had burned up fairly bright, and showed me the barest room I think I ever put my eyes on. Half-a-dozen dishes stood upon the shelves; the table was laid for supper with a bowl of porridge, a horn spoon, and a cup of small beer. Besides what I have named, there was not another thing in that great, stone-vaulted, empty chamber but lockfast chests arranged along the wall and a corner cupboard with a padlock.

As soon as the last chain was up, the man rejoined me. He was a mean, stooping, narrow-shouldered, clay-faced creature; and his age might have been anything between fifty and seventy. His nightcap was of flannel, and so was the nightgown that he wore, instead of coat and waistcoat, over his ragged shirt. He was long unshaved; but what most distressed and even daunted me, he would neither take his eyes away from me nor look me fairly in the face. What he was, whether by trade or birth, was more than I could fathom; but he seemed most like an old, unprofitable serving-man, who should have been left in charge of that big house upon board wages.

The interest of this passage lies in its combination of acute observation and the sense of wonder inseparable from the mind of an imaginative boy. There is, first, the cumulative effect of David's immediate impressions: the rattling of chains and bolts, the bare room, the frugal supper, the stooping uncle in his nightcap. Beyond this there is the fact that the detail impressed most strongly on David's memory is of Ebenezer's shiftiness: 'what most distressed and even daunted me, he would neither take his eyes away from me nor look me fairly in the face'. It is entirely in harmony with the mind of a boy to note such a trait, and even more apposite when he adds the homely afterthought 'he seemed most like an old, unprofitable serving-man, who should have been left in charge of that big house upon board wages'. It is this ability to reach inside the mind of a child, to describe scenes, incidents and relationships from the vantage point of a narrator with but a limited experience of life, which provides both *Treasure Island* and *Kidnapped* with much of their interest and accounts in large measure for their continuing popularity with young readers.

The chapters describing the imprisonment aboard ship and the

journey round the coast of Scotland, culminating in the loss of the
brig and David's sojourn on the island of Earraid, are written with
all Stevenson's affection for the sea. The highlight of this section,
'The Siege of the Round-House', a spirited account of a battle
between Alan Breck and David on the one hand and the captain
and crew on the other, is a masterly piece of writing strongly
reminiscent of the most exciting scenes in *Treasure Island*. This is
closely followed by a fascinating account of David's adventures on
an uninhabited island, an episode containing much of the charm
(albeit in miniature) of *Robinson Crusoe* and *The Coral Island*. As a boy
Stevenson had accompanied his father on journeys to remote
parts of the coast whilst Thomas Stevenson supervised the construction of lighthouses and he knew Mull and Earraid well from
his three-week visit there in August 1870.[19] This detailed knowledge of the topography of the Hebrides adds much to the interest
of the story and lends an element of authenticity to an already
realistic narrative.

Stevenson's affinity with Defoe is plain at numerous points in
the story. A comparison of the title-page of *Kidnapped* with that of
Robinson Crusoe reveals at once his implicit debt to Defoe and his
intention to follow in the steps of a distinguished literary tradition:

*The Life and Strange Surprising Adventures of Robinson Crusoe of York,
Mariner*: Who lived Eight and Twenty Years, all alone in an
uninhabited Island on the Coast of America, near the Mouth of
the Great River of Oroonoque; Having been cast on Shore by
Shipwreck, wherein all the Men perished but himself. With An
Account how he was at last as strangely delivered by Pirates.
Written by Himself.

Kidnapped, being Memoirs of the Adventures of David Balfour
in the Year 1751: how he was kidnapped and cast away; his
sufferings in a desert isle; his journey in the West Highlands; his
acquaintance with Alan Breck Stewart and other notorious
Highland Jacobites; with all that he suffered at the hands of his
Uncle, Ebenezer Balfour of Shaws, falsely so-called; Written by
Himself.

Stevenson, in common with Poe before him, owed much to
Defoe's terse, matter-of-fact, documentary style: his technique of
narrating events with the circumstantiality of a factual account.

The verisimilitude of the central chapters stems precisely from this Defoe-like technique of accumulating detail upon detail until the reader is compelled to suspend disbelief. The following passage from the 'Flight in the Heather' sequence illustrates the point:

This was a dreadful time, rendered the more dreadful by the gloom of the weather and the country. I was never warm; my teeth chattered in my head; I was troubled with a very sore throat, such as I had on the isle; I had a painful stitch in my side, which never left me; and when I slept in my wet bed, with the rain beating above and the mud oozing below me, it was to live over again in fancy the worst part of my adventures – to see the tower of Shaws lit by lightning, Ransome carried below on the men's backs, Shuan dying on the round-house floor, or Colin Campbell grasping at the bosom of his coat. From such broken slumbers, I would be aroused in the gloaming, to sit up in the same puddle where I had slept, and sup cold drammach; the rain driving sharp in my face or running down my back in icy trickles; the mist enfolding us like as in a gloomy chamber – or perhaps if the wind blew, falling suddenly apart and showing us the gulf of some dark valley where the streams were crying aloud.

The conviction of the paragraph is markedly heightened through the addition of such details as 'my teeth chattered in my head', 'I was troubled with a very sore throat', 'I had a painful stitch in my side'. Moreover the account is strengthened by the vivid impression of physical discomfort; the reader has an uncomfortable sense of 'the rain beating above and the mud oozing below me', of 'the mist enfolding us like as in a gloomy chamber', of the miserable combination of wet, cold and damp. Few writers have excelled Stevenson in the realistic narrative of adventure. The journey across the moors and valleys of Scotland could so easily have been depicted as a summer idyll; instead he is at pains to present the reality as a saga of discomfort and of continual tribulation at the mercy of the elements.

Kidnapped can be seen as a 'condition of Scotland' novel in the same sense that *Middlemarch* and *Sybil* are 'condition of England' novels.[20] Stevenson had made a close study of the history of the Highlands in the eighteenth century (he had even projected writing a *History of the Highlands*) and in the central chapters he sought to convey a vivid impression of Scotland in the years following the 1745 rebellion. In doing so he was emulating the tradition of Scott; indeed *Kidnapped* and *Catriona* represent his most ambitious and most carefully researched attempt to write a full-scale eighteenth-century novel.

After the excitement of 'The Flight in the Heather' chapters the remainder of the story, in which the narrative is brought to an abrupt conclusion, is perhaps an anti-climax. Careful examination of the concluding chapters reveals however an artistry and sense of timing which compel admiration. The whole of Chapter 27, 'I Come to Mr. Rankeillor', is an excellent example of Stevenson's technique. David's emotions on anticipating the long-awaited encounter with the lawyer are described with complete conviction and the final denouement and defeat of Uncle Ebenezer form a fitting conclusion to his adventures.

Whilst superficially *Kidnapped* belongs to the same genre as *Treasure Island* – both are fast moving, skilfully written romances of adventure – there are a number of respects in which *Kidnapped* represents a development of Stevenson's powers as a novelist. First, whilst it contains all the elements of excitement and suspense one associates with the genre, it is in addition a novel of character. In particular the relationship between David Balfour (a Whig Lowlander) and Alan Breck (a Tory Highlander) is handled with maturity and insight; the account of their friendship, their quarrel and eventual reconciliation provides the story with an interesting counterbalance to the rather complex plot and permits the weaving of an intricate web of nuances which adds considerably to the depth of the story. There are few more telling moments in the novel than David's reluctant admission of his surliness towards Alan:

> During all these horrid wanderings we had no familiarity, scarcely even that of speech. The truth is that I was sickening for my grave, which is my best excuse. But besides that I was of an unforgiving disposition from my birth, slow to take offence, slower to forget it, and now incensed both against my companion and myself. For the best part of two days he was unweariedly kind; silent, indeed, but always ready to help, and always hoping (as I could very well see) that my displeasure would blow by. For the same length of time I stayed in myself,

nursing my anger, roughly refusing his services, and passing
him over with my eyes as if he had been a bush or a stone.

It is this quarrel sequence which was praised so highly by Henry
James. James commented that the quarrel

has the very logic and rhythm of life . . . such a passage as the
one I speak of is in fact a signal proof of what the novel can do
at its best and what nothing else can do so well. . . . It is capable
of a rare transparency – it can illustrate human affairs in cases
so delicate and complicated that any other vehicle would be
clumsy.[21]

In elaborating the relationship between Alan and David,
Stevenson was drawing on qualities of observation and understanding on which he drew more fully in *The Master of Ballantrae*
and *Weir of Hermiston*: he was gaining increasing self-confidence in
the handling of narrative and conversation. Moreover, the novel
is rich in minor characters, conveyed with impressive conviction.
Hoseason, the Captain of the *Covenant*; Rankeillor, the cautious
lawyer; Cluny Macpherson, one of the leaders of the '45 rebellion;
Robin Oig, one of the sons of Rob Roy: all are depicted with that
amalgam of realism and economy which became his hallmark.
Second, the plot reveals a growing mastery of construction. The
story is not simply of a struggle between David and Uncle
Ebenezer for his rightful inheritance, but is simultaneously an
account of the pursuit of David and Alan by the King's redcoats
and the outraged Campbells. Superimposed on the story of the
kidnapping engineered by the wily Ebenezer is a graphic account
of a manhunt across the wilds of Scotland in which is interwoven
the historical rivalry between Whig and Jacobite. It is therefore a
novel on several different levels, each balancing the other; yet it is
possible to read the book with great enjoyment, as many generations have done, without any close understanding of the complexities of Scottish history. In *Kidnapped* Stevenson displayed his ability
to sustain a diffuse plot without sacrifice of suspense or interest. It
is for this reason that the book has been described as 'the sort of
bridge by which Stevenson passed from the story of adventure to
the serious historical novel'.[22]
Third, in David Balfour Stevenson created a wholly convincing

narrator who recounts the story with considerable verve and yet is aware throughout of his own faults. When he and Alan disagree due to a combination of misunderstandings and temperamental differences, David is honest enough to confess that the onus of blame lies upon himself: 'I knew it was my own doing, and no one else's; but I was too miserable to repent. . . . So I went like a sick, silly and bad-hearted schoolboy, feeding my anger against a fellow-man, when I would have been better on my knees, crying on God for mercy.' At numerous points in the story he displays an engaging honesty and innocence; he is in some ways a more mature character than Jim Hawkins and possesses a shrewd ability to assess human nature — including an acknowledgement of his own weaknesses — and to weigh the merits of alternative courses of behaviour.

Andrew Lang described *Kidnapped* as 'a volume containing more of the spirit of Scott than any other in English fiction.'[23] Stevenson himself was quietly confident of its literary merits. Writing to T. Watts-Dunton, who had reviewed the book in the *Athenaeum*, he observed:

> What you say of the two parts in *Kidnapped* was felt by no one more painfully than by myself. I began it partly as a lark, partly as a pot-boiler; and suddenly it moved, David and Alan stepped out from the canvas, and I found I was in another world.[24]

Approaching the book afresh it is not difficult to see why it was praised with such enthusiasm by some of the leading writers and critics of the day, including Henry James, Edmund Gosse and Matthew Arnold, nor why, unlike *Prince Otto*, it has stood the test of time. It has achieved the status of a classic because of its unusual combination of narrative power with depth of characterisation and because the reader's attention is sustained throughout the vicissitudes of a many-faceted story. *Kidnapped* confirmed Stevenson's reputation as an imaginative writer of real talent for it demonstrated once again his ability to fashion a convincing story based on realistic yet *imagined* episodes and to create a range of characters drawn with the solidity of an accomplished novelist. It remains a classic of romance, a book fulfilling all his expectations of the genre whilst possessing at the same time a hint of the novelist yet to come.

He himself wrote in the dedication: 'This is no furniture for the scholar's library, but a book for the winter evening school-room when the tasks are over and the hour for bed draws near.'

Catriona, written in 1892 whilst Stevenson was living at Samoa, is a more diffuse story than *Kidnapped* and falls into two distinct parts, comparable to two movements of a symphony. Part One, 'The Lord Advocate', describes David's pursuit across Scotland, partly in the company of Alan Breck, and his imprisonment on the Bass Rock to prevent his giving vital evidence at a murder trial. Part Two, 'Father and Daughter', relates his encounters with the unscrupulous James More Drummond (the son of Rob Roy) and his daughter Catriona, and the final resolution of his adventures with his marriage to Catriona and the escape of Alan Breck to France. The two parts do not jell easily together, and since much of the action hinges on an understanding of Scottish political history (particularly inter-clan rivalries) the overall effect is of a convoluted plot in the sharpest contrast to the comparative simplicity of its predecessor. Nevertheless, it is a powerful work on which Stevenson undoubtedly set great store and which was warmly praised by many of his friends. The novel is primarily of interest today for the evidence it affords of his growing literary self-confidence, and in particular for its convincing demonstration of his strengths as an imaginative writer and a creator of memorable and well-drawn characters.

As in *Kidnapped*, the vividness of the narrative is heightened through the skilful use of circumstantial detail, a technique Stevenson had derived from his close study of the works of Defoe. The following passage from Chapter 8, 'Gillane Sands', illustrates his mastery of the gripping documentary style:

I stood where he had left me, with my hands behind my back; Alan sat with his head turned, watching me; and the boat drew smoothly away. Of a sudden I came the nearest hand to shedding tears, and seemed to myself the most deserted, solitary lad in Scotland. With that I turned my back upon the sea and faced the sandhills. There was no sight or sound of man; the sun shone on the wet sand and the dry, the wind blew in the bents, the gulls made a dreary piping. As I passed higher up the beach, the sand-lice were hopping nimbly about the stranded tangles. The devil any other sight or sound in that unchancy place. And yet I knew there were folk there, observing me, upon some secret purpose. They were no soldiers, or they would have fallen on and taken us ere now; doubtless they were some common rogues hired for my undoing, perhaps to kidnap, perhaps to murder me outright. From the position of those engaged, the first was the more likely; from what I knew of their character and ardency in this business, I thought the second very possible; and the blood ran cold about my heart.

The inclusion of such details as 'the sun shone on the wet sand and the dry', 'the gulls made a dreary piping', 'the sand-lice were hopping nimbly about the stranded tangles' add impressively to the effectiveness of the paragraph and help to fix the scene in the mind of the reader. The loneliness and tension of the scene are also powerfully suggested through the use of such phrases as 'There was no sight or sound of man', 'The devil any other sight or sound in that unchancy place', 'the blood ran cold about my heart'. Though *Catriona* is by no means free of defects the danger with Stevenson is always to underestimate him; here and in other works he demonstrates an uncommon ability to achieve precisely the effects he desires through the deployment of deceptively simple literary techniques.

Stevenson excelled in the narrative of adventure and was particularly adept at describing a manhunt through a lonely or wild terrain. The 'My Shore Adventure' chapters in *Treasure Island* and 'The Flight in the Heather' chapters in *Kidnapped* both illustrate an accomplished ability to convey the excitement of a pursuit without minimising any of its dangers. A similar technique is employed in *Catriona* in the description of David's journey across Scotland in search of his old companion Alan Breck:

This brought my face to Silvermills; the path came past the village with a crook, but all plainly visible; and, Highland or Lowland, there was nobody stirring. Here was my advantage, here was just such a conjuncture as Stewart had counselled me to profit by, and I ran by the side of the mill-lade, fetched about beyond the east corner of the wood, threaded through the midst of it, and returned to the west selvage, whence I could again command the path, and yet be myself unseen. Again it was all empty, and my heart began to rise.
For more than an hour I sat close in the border of the trees,

and no hare or eagle could have kept a more particular watch. When that hour began the sun was already set, but the sky still all golden and the daylight clear; before the hour was done it had fallen to be half mirk, the images and distances of things were mingled, and observation began to be difficult. All that time not a foot of man had come east from Silvermills, and the few that had gone west were honest countryfolk and their wives upon the road to bed. If I were tracked by the most cunning spies in Europe, I judged it was beyond the course of nature they could have any jealousy of where I was; and going a little further home into the wood I lay down to wait for Alan.

Rarely has the suppressed emotion and suspense of a pursuit across lonely country been conveyed with such power. The characteristic Stevensonian touches such as 'For more than an hour I sat close in the border of trees, and no hare or eagle could have kept a more particular watch' and 'The strain of my attention had been great, for I had watched not the path only, but every bush and field within my vision' vividly impart the sense of tension and excitement which David clearly feels. At the same time the reader has the conviction that this is no imaginary tract of countryside but a real wood: phrases such as 'I ran by the side of the mill-lade', 'the east corner of the wood', 'returned to the west selvage' confirm the impression that what is being described is an actual location, depicted with the familiarity borne of intimate knowledge. It is a device which has been brilliantly employed by a number of later writers, most notably John Buchan in *The Thirty Nine Steps* and Geoffrey Household in *Rogue Male*, and provides impressive evidence of Stevenson's unusual powers as a story-teller.

His gift of describing a scene with the utmost vividness and the maximum economy of words is nowhere better illustrated than in the description of the Bass Rock (which he had visited as a boy):

There began to fall a greyness on the face of the sea; little dabs of pink and red, like coals of slow fire, came in the east; and at the same time the geese awakened, and began crying about the top of the Bass. It is just the one crag of rock, as everybody knows, but great enough to carve a city from. The sea was extremely little, but there went a hollow plowter round the base of it. With the growing of the dawn I could see it clearer and clearer; the straight crags painted with sea-birds' droppings like a morning frost, the sloping top of it green with grass, the clan of white geese that cried about the sides, and the black, broken buildings of the prison sitting close on the sea's edge.

The effectiveness of the description is considerably strengthened by the vivid use of metaphor: 'little daps of pink and red, like coals of slow fire'; 'great enough to carve a city from'; 'the straight crags painted with sea-birds' droppings like a morning frost'. The effect is such that a reader who had never seen the Rock would have a clear picture of it impressed on the mind, stark and distinct. Scattered through the novel are a number of word-pictures of this kind, witnessing to his ability to convey striking mental images based upon his recollections of Scottish scenes. Indeed there is discernible at many points in the story the longing of the expatriate for the Scotland he had known and loved as a child. By the time he came to write *Catriona* he well knew that he could never return to his homeland again[25] – to do so would mean almost certain death from a lung haemorrhage – but his mind dwelt continually on Scottish themes and memories. The description of David's wanderings in the neighbourhood of Edinburgh, for example (Ch. 3, 'I Go to Pilrig'), is imbued with a warm affection for the scenes described; one senses an intimate topographical knowledge borne of close and loving acquaintance. It is as if Stevenson is following David's path at each stage of the journey, renewing his familiarity with a countryside embedded in his imagination.

Catriona possesses a wealth of major and minor characters, of which the most impressive is William Grant of Prestongrange, the Lord Advocate for Scotland. The description of David's first meeting with him (Ch. 4), David's courageous admission of his own presence at the scene of the Glenure murder and the Advocate's gradual realisation of the importance of this evidence is one of the most memorable scenes in the novel. The Advocate's dilemma in deciding to suppress this evidence – a course of action which is judicially indefensible yet politically expedient – is admirably presented and its execution forms one of the dominant strands of the story. His daughter, Barbara Grant, who has been described as 'perhaps the most successful of Stevenson's not very numerous feminine creations',[26] is one of the most living and vital of his female characters.

The Advocate is such a commanding figure and so powerfully drawn, and the murder trial occupies such a prominent part in the novel, that the relationship between Grant and David underlies much of the action. The interweaving of this relationship into the plot structure of the story permits Stevenson to contrast David's innocence, his inability to appreciate the moral dilemmas which may lie behind political decisions, with the Advocate's shrewdness and understanding of human character. From David's standpoint the evidence he has to offer – that the accused man, James Stewart, is innocent – is of cardinal importance and, since he has a deep respect for legalities, he feels it is his duty to present his testimony regardless of its political implications. From Grant's standpoint any evidence which tends to cast doubt on Stewart's guilt cannot be admitted; the accused man is to be tried before a Campbell jury in the heart of Campbell territory; the result must be a foregone conclusion. The resulting battle of wits is a struggle between David's determination to do what is right and the Advocate's equally strong determination to do what is expedient. Since the Advocate is a man with a vast experience of life and affairs David, with his political *naïveté*, is no match for him and is inevitably the loser. Grant, however, is by no means an evil man and David retains an acute respect for his shrewdness and kindliness. This tension between practicality on the one hand and well-intentioned guilelessness on the other forms a continual backcloth to the story.

Catriona Drummond, with whom David Balfour falls in love, was much praised by contemporary critics but seems less successful to twentieth-century readers. Despite her evident spirit and willpower she lacks the vivacity of Barbara Grant and seems curiously wooden by comparison with the portrayal of her father, James Drummond, or Alan Breck. The love affair between David and Catriona is presented in a decidedly coy, muted fashion and, although its underlying emotion is hinted at – e.g. 'She kissed my hand, as she had kissed Prince Charlie's, with a higher passion than the common kind of clay has any sense of' – nowhere does the relationship come to life. The reader sympathises with David's innocence and gaucherie throughout his courtship of Catriona, yet the relationship as a whole appears peculiarly Victorian in its sedateness. Other Victorian novelists – Gissing, for example, in *The Odd Women* (1893) and George Meredith in *Diana of the Crossways* (1885) – were simultaneously exploring problems of sexual relationships, yet Stevenson's attempt to present a convincing relationship between a young man and woman has to be acknowledged as a valiant failure. In attempting to fuse together a boys' adventure story in the manner of *Kidnapped* with a full-dress novel with an adult heroine he was blending two genres which are difficult to combine in one volume. The earlier adventures of David Balfour are satisfying because the reader identifies himself with the hero and sympathises with him through his changing fortunes. In *Catriona* one is aware of a diminution of sympathy. Despite episodes of vivid interest – the journey through the heather and the woods, the imprisonment on Bass Rock, the encounter with James More, the exciting scenes at Dunkirk – David seems a less mature personality, a figure less at the centre of action, a narrator controlled by events rather than shaping the course of his adventures. The change represents a loss of innocence on the part of the author, a movement away from the romance of adventure to the more sophisticated canvas of the novel. His finest achievements still lay ahead of him.

Stevenson himself thought highly of the book; in a letter to Mrs. Sitwell (April 1894) he commented: 'I shall never do a better book than *Catriona*, that is my high-water mark.' The book was also praised by his contemporaries. Henry James observed that it 'so reeks and hums with genius that there is no refuge for the desperate reader but in straightforward prostration'; Vernon Lee described it as 'a masterpiece of constructive craft'.[27] Later critical opinion has failed to confirm the enthusiasm of his friends and it is significant that whereas *Kidnapped* shows no signs of losing its popularity with readers of all ages, *Catriona* seems unlikely to survive in this sense. Henry James made a perceptive comment when he drew attention to its comparative lack of imaginative incident : 'The one thing I miss in the book is the note of *visibility* – it subjects my visual sense, my *seeing* imagination, to an almost painful underfeeding.'[28]

The total effect is of a book composed of a series of vivid incidents, a story different in kind from *Kidnapped* since it lacks the inner unity and pace of action of its predecessor. Between the Stevenson of thirty-five writing at Bournemouth and the Stevenson of forty-one writing in voluntary exile on Samoa there lay a significant difference. It is the difference between a man respond-

ing enthusiastically to an invitation to write a boys' adventure
story in the vein of *Treasure Island* and a man who, in the interven-
ing years, has thought out his approach to life and art and is
feeling his way towards a fuller and more complex means of
expression. Sensing perhaps that his readers would find the sequel
less satisfying he wrote in the preface : 'It is the fate of sequels to
disappoint those who have waited for them.'

Yet it is possible to detect in *Catriona* a continuing preoccupation
with that moral ambiguity which lies at the heart of so much of
Stevenson's work. As with Silver in *Treasure Island* and Hoseason in
Kidnapped, the reader is reminded again and again of the ambivalence of human character; he is presented with situations and
problems involving choices between alternative courses of action,
each beset with difficulties. In reflecting on the characters he has
met in the course of his adventures David observes: 'It must be
owned the view I had taken of the world in these last months was
fit to cast a gloom upon my character. I had met many men, some
of them leaders in Israel whether by their birth or talents; and
who among them all had shown clean hands?' In reflecting on the
integrity of the Advocate, Prestongrange, whom he has deeply
mistrusted, he comments ruefully: 'Here I did him, as events have
proved, the most grave injustice; and I think he was at once far
more sincere, and a far more artful performer, than I supposed.'
Even when reviewing the character of the rascally James Drummond, David finds it in his heart to add some mitigation: 'I saw
him to be perfectly selfish, with a perfect innocency in the same.
. . . I think he was so false all through that he scarce knew when he
was lying; and for one thing, his moments of dejection must have
been wholly genuine.' Throughout the novel there is an emphasis
on 'the duplicity of life and men',[29] on the conflict of motives
which determine human behaviour, on the impossibility of
judging a man solely on the evidence of his conduct. This insistence that no person is wholly good or wholly evil, that each
person he has met – including the most outwardly corrupt – is an
amalgam of altruistic and selfish motives, is a recurring theme in
his novels and is a theme never far from the surface of *Kidnapped*
and *Catriona*.

The Black Arrow

The Black Arrow: A Tale of the Two Roses, published in 1888 but written five years previously while Stevenson was living at Hyères, had originally been commissioned by the magazine *Young Folks* whose editor, James Henderson, wished to publish a serial to follow *Treasure Island*. Stevenson set to work with enthusiasm, completing the book within two months. *The Paston Letters* had been among the favourite reading of his childhood, and he immersed himself with boyish zeal in the England of the fifteenth century. 'It's great sport to write tushery', he confided to Sidney Colvin apropos the book.[30] His wife disapproved of the project and refused even to read it, a point he noted in his dedication 'To the Critic on the Hearth'.

The story was serialised in *Young Folks* in seventeen weekly instalments and thus provided him with valuable experience in the demands of periodical publication. The task of satisfying his young readers by writing an exciting adventure story replete with incident and sustained by a consistent plot proved to be a challenging one which Stevenson enjoyed, though he seems to have found it difficult in practice to organise his material. When Henderson's proofreader pointed out a number of omissions in the final instalment he candidly replied: 'Nowhere do I send worse copy than to *Young Folks*, for, with this sort of story, I rarely rewrite; yet nowhere am I so well used.'[31]

Set in the reign of Henry VI during the troubled years of the Wars of the Roses, *The Black Arrow* was intended as a pastiche of the adventure stories of Alfred R. Phillips, whose serial 'Don Zalva the Brave' appeared in *Young Folks* simultaneously with *Treasure Island*. The magazine's readers greatly preferred Stevenson's new tale to his first novel (both were serialised under the pseudonym

142

'Captain George North') and the circulation increased considerably as a result. The story had a strong appeal for readers who
demanded a fast-moving narrative with a minimum of characterisation and a maximum of exciting episodes and for some years it
enjoyed a vogue. With the passage of time, however, Stevenson
became less confident of its merits and came to dislike it. In the
year of his death he confided to his friend William Archer: 'I find
few greater pleasures than reading my own works, but I never, O I
never read The Black Arrow.'[32] Though it is a slighter work than
Treasure Island or Kidnapped and lacks their depth of characterisation and psychological insight, it is by no means the hack-work
which the circumstances of its writing would suggest. No book
could survive for almost a century which did not possess some
intrinsic qualities. Whilst it has received remarkably little critical
attention it bears upon it the stamp of Stevenson's personality and
embodies a number of his most characteristic preoccupations.

The characterisation, whilst nowhere complex, is competently
handled and provides fresh evidence of the author's facility in
sketching realistic portraits. The book contains no personality as
finely drawn as Long John Silver or Alan Breck yet it possesses a
range of figures described with deftness and economy. The central
figure, Richard Shelton, shares with Jim Hawkins and David
Balfour a capacity to learn from his mistakes and to reflect on the
consequences of his own actions. As the book proceeds he gains in
sagacity, having witnessed in the course of his adventures human
nature at its finest and most ignoble and been chastened by all he
has experienced. The girl he loves, Joanna Sedley, is engagingly
drawn and whilst their courtship strikes a modern reader as coy it
represents one of Stevenson's earliest attempts to describe a love
affair and was highly praised by contemporary critics. The most
convincing portrayal is that of Richard III, who emerges as a
formidable and charismatic figure, consumed by his ambitions
and yet loyal to those who serve him. Stevenson follows Shakespeare in presenting him as a cruel hunchback and could not have
been aware that later scholarship would present Richard in a very
different light;[33] nevertheless the portrait has depth and Stevenson was satisfied with it even if the book as a whole displeased
him.

The story permitted him full rein for his powers of description.
Here is a characteristic scene from Book 1, Chapter 4: 'A Greenwood Company':

Right in the corner of the ruin, two rafters had fallen crosswise, and protected a clear space no larger than a pew in church. Into this the lads silently lowered themselves. There they were perfectly concealed, and through an arrow loophole com-manded a view upon the farther side.

Peering through this, they were struck stiff with terror at their predicament. To retreat was impossible; they scarce dared to breathe. Upon the very margin of the ditch, not thirty feet from where they crouched, an iron cauldron bubbled and steamed above a glowing fire; and close by, in an attitude of listening, as though he had caught some sound of their clam-bering among the ruins, a tall, red-faced, battered-looking man stood poised, an iron spoon in his right hand, a horn and a formidable dagger at his belt. Plainly this was the singer; plainly he had been stirring the cauldron, when some incautious step among the lumber had fallen upon his ear. A little further off another man lay slumbering, rolled in a brown cloak, with a butterfly hovering above his face. All this was in a clearing white with daisies; and at the extreme verge a bow, a sheaf of arrows, and part of a deer's carcase hung upon a flowering hawthorn.

The circumstantial touches — 'two rafters had fallen crosswise, and protected a clear space no larger than a pew in church', 'an iron spoon in his right hand', 'a clearing white with daisies', 'part of a deer's carcase hung upon a flowering hawthorn' — add a strong element of conviction to the scene. The reader has a clear sense of the 'battered-looking man' and of the other man 'with a butterfly hovering above his face'. The entire vignette is depicted with the clarity of a painting by Holman Hunt. The addition of such phrases as 'To retreat was impossible; they scarce dared to breathe', and 'in an attitude of listening, as though he had caught some sound of their clambering among the ruins' add a hint of menace to an otherwise pastoral spectacle. In numerous scenes — the underground passage beneath the Moat House, the journey aboard the ship *Good Hope*, the entry in disguise into Sir Daniel's residence at Shoreby, the battle of Shoreby, the pursuit through the forest in search of Joanna Sedley — Stevenson demonstrates his gifts as a storyteller: his ability to convey vivid word-pictures which compel attention by their descriptive power.

An interesting example of his technique is the scene in which

Shelton succeeds in escaping from the Moat House where he has
been held prisoner:

> The cord was knotted, which made it the easier to descend; but
> so furious was Dick's hurry, and so small his experience of such
> gymnastics, that he span round and round in mid-air like a
> criminal upon a gibbet, and now beat his head, and now
> bruised his hands, against the rugged stonework of the wall.
> The air roared in his ears; he saw the stars overhead, and the
> reflected stars below him in the moat, whirling like dead leaves
> before the tempest. And then he lost hold and fell, and soused
> head over ears into the icy water.

In the hands of a lesser writer the hero would simply have
climbed down the rope and made good his escape but Stevenson
has him spinning 'round and round in mid-air like a criminal upon
a gibbet' and beating his head and hands on the rough stones. The
description of the reflected stars 'whirling like dead leaves before
the tempest' as he makes his descent is a striking image which
could only have come from an experienced writer with a strong
sense of metaphor.

Yet *The Black Arrow* is rather more than a boys' adventure story
and beneath its apparently simple structure there is evidence of a
continuing concern with problems of conduct and motive. There
can be no question that the underlying theme of the book – the
effects of civil war on the lives of ordinary men and women – was
one which interested him deeply. At numerous points in the
narrative he is at pains to point out the indiscriminate horror of
war and violence and the misery caused by a conflict involving
civilians. In the opening chapter a woman, on hearing the news of
an impending battle, remarks 'It is the ruin of this kind land. If the
barons live at war, ploughfolk must eat roots.' This emphasis on
the destructive effects of the war on the homes and livelihoods of
the poor reaches its culmination in the chapter entitled 'The Sack
of Shoreby': a vivid and circumstantial account of the rapine and
savagery which follow in the wake of battle. Though the story
follows the conventions of the adventure narrative in its general
construction, it is significant that the conflict between York and
Lancaster is not presented as a simple confrontation between
right and wrong. The hero, Richard Shelton, chooses his side
almost by accident and changes his allegiance mid-way through

the book. Though he fights on the side of York, the courage and integrity of the Lancastrians are evident throughout: neither side possess a monopoly of virtue. Interwoven through the narrative one is aware of a continual emphasis on the complexity of human character. Thus, the Duke of Gloucester (later Richard III) is presented as a wily and dangerous man yet loyal in his allegiances and extremely courageous in battle; Risingham, though of the opposite political persuasion to the hero, is a man of obvious integrity; Lawless, whom Shelton has trusted as a loyal companion, confesses that he is 'a thief by trade and birth and habit'; Sir Daniel Brackley, an unscrupulous and wicked man, is murdered by an archer who then prays over his victim 'like one in a great disorder or distress of mind'. It is as if Stevenson is continually questioning stereotyped judgements of personality. No man, he reminds us, is wholly right or wholly wrong. Even the most deceitful and cunning man may still possess qualities of bravery or compassion.

The point is well illustrated in the relationship between Richard Shelton and Arblaster. Shelton steals Arblaster's ship in a well-intentioned attempt to outwit his enemies but his plans go awry and the ship is wrecked. Later in the story he is instrumental in saving Arblaster's life and hopes that by doing so he has made amends for his former wrongdoing. But Arblaster has lost his livelihood and will never forgive Shelton:

> Dick was seized with unavailing penitence and pity; he sought to take the skipper's hand; but Arblaster avoided his touch. 'Nay', said he, 'let be. Y' have played the devil with me, and let that content you'. The words died in Richard's throat. He saw, through tears, the poor old man, bemused with liquor and sorrow, go shambling away, with bowed head, across the snow, and the unnoticed dog whimpering at his heels; and for the first time began to understand the desperate game that we play in life, and how a thing once done is not to be changed or remedied by any penitence.

This theme, that 'a thing once done is not to be changed or remedied by any penitence', underlies much of the action of *The Black Arrow*. Richard finally achieves happiness and is reunited with his heroine but at a cost of much travail and bloodshed. The reader identifies with the hero and sympathises with him in his changing fortunes yet is simultaneously aware of the unhappiness and death which are the lot of others. It is a world in which moral judgements must be constantly weighed in the balance, a world where a course of action embarked upon for the loftiest motives can redound on the instigator and bring havoc in its train.

Many critics then and since have felt that Stevenson was out of his depth in the fifteenth century and that his attempt to write antique language mars an otherwise gripping tale. Other commentators disagree strongly with this view. The book was admired by Wyndham Lewis and G. M. Trevelyan, for example, the latter stating that it 'reproduces a real state of society in the past . . . like a good historical novel'.[34] Though the story was written in haste and without the subtlety of his finest work he undoubtedly had a genuine feel for the period and sought to present a realistic picture of England torn by internecine conflict. The story is not only an exciting tale of adventure and intrigue but a paradigm of the manner in which war evokes the finest and basest of which the human spirit is capable. It also raises questions of judgement and human worth which underlie all his fiction, from the major novels to the short stories.

It is these qualities which will ensure a continuing readership for *The Black Arrow*. Despite its manifest weaknesses – a too frequent reliance on a *deus ex machina* to extricate the hero from difficult situations, and a rather contrived plot – it remains a highly readable and exciting romance which conveys a memorable impression of medieval England.

The Master of Ballantrae

The idea for a new novel, *The Master of Ballantrae*, came to Stevenson in December 1887 while pacing the verandah of the house where he was staying near Saranac Lake in the Adirondack mountains. He had been re-reading Marryat's *The Phantom Ship* and was 'moved with the spirit of emulation'. 'Come,' he said to himself, 'let us make a tale, a story of many years and countries, of the sea and the land, savagery and civilisation.'[35] He embarked on the project with characteristic enthusiasm, confiding to Sidney Colvin that he had 'fallen head over heels into a new tale. . . . It is to me a most seizing tale: there are some fantastic elements; the most is a dead genuine human problem – human tragedy, I should say rather.'[36] He completed the first part of the book at Saranac, abandoning it to work on *The Wrong Box*, then resumed work on it in the autumn of 1888 while staying at Tahiti. The novel was not completed until May 1889, the final chapters causing him particular difficulty. It was published in book form in September 1889, having first been serialised in twelve monthly instalments in *Scribner's Magazine*.

Readers and critics were almost unanimous in their admiration for the new work. Henry James described it as 'a pure hard crystal, a work of ineffable and exquisite art', whilst W. E. Henley referred to its 'sombre fascination'.[37] What so impressed reviewers was its evidence of Stevenson's growing maturity and versatility as an imaginative writer. Hitherto he had been widely regarded as an author of considerable promise who excelled at the writing of short stories, essays and romances but whose forte lay in these directions rather than the novel *per se*. With the publication of *The Master* critics were compelled to look at his work afresh, for here was an unmistakable departure from his previous range. The new

148

work was clearly more than an adventure story in the vein of
Treasure Island or *Kidnapped*, and more complex than *Jekyll and
Hyde*. It was an amalgam of these genres: a fusion of the tale of
adventure with the allegory of human psychology to form a
profound and haunting tragedy on the theme of intolerance.

Contemporary critics were not slow to point out, however, that
the book is marred by certain weaknesses, of which the most
obvious is its unevenness of construction – the opening chapters,
set in Kirkcudbright, do not blend easily with the chapters describing the Master's exploits on the high seas or in India. Stevenson
himself felt that the defects of the book were not so much structural as emotional. Writing to Colvin on 15 September 1892 (i.e.
three years after its completion) he commented that *Catriona* and
'The Beach of Falesa' 'seem to me to be nearer what I mean than
anything I have ever done; nearer what I mean by fiction; the
nearest thing before was *Kidnapped*. I am not forgetting the *Master
of Ballantrae*, but that lacked all pleasurableness, and hence was
imperfect in essence.' In drawing attention to its lack of 'pleasurableness' he was highlighting its dominant mood of melancholia.
Partly due to the austere personality of Mackellar, through whose
eyes much of the story is told, and partly due to the absence of any
fully attractive characters, the overriding mood of the story is one
of gloom. Moreover, so intense is the narrative and so obsessive
the antagonism between the brothers that the reader experiences
a sense of claustrophobia. It is as if one is peering into an enclosed,
nightmare world – a world governed by its own logic and ruled by
its own immutable laws. (Some readers have experienced a similar
claustrophobic sense on reading *Wuthering Heights*: both novels
depict an elemental tragedy unfolding between a comparatively
narrow range of characters.) In commenting that in his view the
novel was 'imperfect in essence' Stevenson was taking himself to
task for its overriding pessimism. He was aware that a novel in the
Jamesian sense must have a governing view of life; the view of life
which dominates *The Master of Ballantrae* is a profoundly depressing
one, an implication that human nature is inherently perverse, that
it is at its best unreliable, at its worst evil. Significantly this is a
conception of human character which does not recur in his fiction.
Neither in the novels which preceded *Ballantrae* nor in those
which followed it is there any comparable implication. It remains
his only novel which can be interpreted in wholly pessimistic
terms: a darkly tragic tale which stands alone.

Yet despite its fundamental pessimism it occupies an important place in the conspectus of his work and it is clear that Stevenson himself, despite his awareness of its weaknesses, sensed its overall haunting power. In its characterisation, its inherent literary qualities and its powerful sense of exile it occupies a central place in the canon and helped to lay the foundations on which his later achievements, most notably *Weir of Hermiston*, were built.

The Master of Ballantrae marks unquestionably a perceptible advance in Stevenson's powers of characterisation. This may be seen in the deliberate employment of two different narrators; in the portrayal of the brothers themselves; in their interaction upon one another; and in the depiction of the *evolution* of character. In each of these respects there is impressive evidence of his growing mastery of the craft of the novelist.

One of the many interesting features of the novel is that Stevenson employs the device of two different narrators (he had previously made use of such a device in *Treasure Island*, but in *Ballantrae* it is used with much more subtlety and insight). The bulk of the story is narrated by Ephraim Mackellar, for many years land steward on the Durrisdeer estates, whilst the adventures of the Master of Ballantrae aboard the pirate ship are related by Francis Burke, an Irish colonel in the service of the Pretender. The significance of the two narrators is that each has his own idiosyncrasies and prejudices which become increasingly evident as the story proceeds. Mackellar in particular, a dour, cautious, astute Scot, tinges the story with so much of his own personality that it is largely reflected through his mind. He becomes a character in his own right, both participating in the events and commenting on them as they unfold. His prosaicness and sombre disposition are in the sharpest contrast to the chilling narrative he relates – a tale of murder, revenge, jealousy, greed and persecution – and throw into vivid relief the haunting power of Stevenson's demonic tale. Moreover the very fact that Mackellar is a subjective witness (he states his loyalties plainly on the first page: 'I served him [Henry Durie] and loved him near twenty years') compels the reader to take this into account in all that follows. Mackellar's dryness, his dogged loyalty and marked self-righteousness make him one of Stevenson's most interesting creations, drawn with an apparent effortlessness which reveals his growing assurance as a creative writer. The employment of more than one narrator also permits the author to view his characters from a number of vantage points. The device had been employed with considerable effect by Wilkie Collins in *The Moonstone* (1868) – a novel Stevenson knew well – and is one which lends itself to the tale of mystery and detection. As employed in *The Master of Ballantrae* it reveals an impressive ability to handle characterisation, dialogue and narration from differing standpoints and to weave together a coherent story from a variety of sources including memoirs and letters.

But it is in the portrayal of the two principal characters, James and Henry Durie, and the interaction of their lives and personalities, that the enduring interest of the novel lies. James Durie, the Master of Ballantrae, is one of Stevenson's most powerful creations. Malign, virile, satanic, elemental, he dominates the novel from beginning to end. The character is drawn with such vigour that it is he who remains in the mind long after the book has been read. It is clear that Stevenson was fascinated by his combination of rascality and charm. Writing to Colvin he confided: 'the Master is all I know of the devil. I have known hints of him, in the world, but always cowards; he is as bold as a lion, but with the same deadly, causeless duplicity I have watched with so much surprise in my two cowards.'[38] This 'deadly, causeless duplicity' which so much intrigued him is drawn with far more depth than Long John Silver in *Treasure Island* or the Lord Advocate in *Catriona*. It is a rounded, solid portrait, depicted with an insight into the complexities of the human character unequalled in his fiction. Despite Stevenson's comment that 'the Master is all I know of the devil' James is not wholly evil. There is a revealing conversation between James and Mackellar in which the steward observes: 'I do not think you could be so bad a man if you had not all the machinery to be a good one.' There are numerous instances in the story of the Master's humour, wit and charm, and his indomitable spirit is in the sharpest contrast to the ineffectual passivity of his brother. (It should be noted that James is presented throughout through the eyes of the puritanical narrator, Mackellar: at no point does he narrate an incident for himself. Mackellar's loyalty to Henry and his detestation of James are such as to act as a distorting mirror.)

Perhaps the closest Mackellar approaches to an understanding of the Master's character is in a striking passage during the voyage to New York in which he comments on the duality of his nature:

This outer sensibility and inner toughness set me against him; it seemed of a piece with that impudent grossness which I knew to underlie the veneer of his fine manners; and sometimes my gorge rose against him as though he were deformed – and sometimes I would draw away as though from something partly spectral. I had moments when I thought of him as of a man of pasteboard – as though, if one should strike smartly through the buckram of his countenance, there would be found a mere vacuity within.

The deliberate use of such words as 'deformed 'and 'spectral' underlines the demonic nature of the Master and strengthens the parallel with *Dr. Jekyll and Mr. Hyde*, whilst the reference to 'a man of pasteboard' and 'a mere vacuity within' is an attempt on Mackellar's part to define James's inhumanity. Clearly a man of James's unscrupulosity is outside the range of the narrator's experience; in seeking to convey his larger than life quality he is compelled to make use of metaphor and analogy. The image which remains in the mind is of a combination of 'outer sensibility and inner toughness', of a devilish power which haunts the imagination and infuses the novel with an elemental quality consonant with its essentially tragic theme.

The younger brother, Henry, is by contrast patient, inactive and unemotional. He harbours his feelings inwardly, enduring the Master's taunts and threats with a veneer of calm whilst secretly consumed with jealousy and anger. His scrupulosity and mildness prove to be ineffective virtues in the face of James's perfidy and at each crucial stage in the story one senses that it is James who possesses the upper hand.

The antagonism between the two brothers is vividly portrayed. It is not simply that each hates and despises the other, but that each is *obsessed* by the other: each is both fascinated and repelled by his counterpart. This mutual fascination and complementality provides the novel with a powerful sense of equipoise and suggests the influence (perhaps unconscious) of Poe's short story 'William Wilson'. The fact that each brother possesses qualities which balance those of the other is made explicit in the fourth chapter:

It was during this time that I perceived most clearly the effect of manner, and was led to lament most deeply the plainness of my

own. Mr. Henry had the essence of a gentleman; when he was
moved, when there was any call of circumstance, he could play
his part with dignity and spirit; but in the day's commerce (it is
idle to deny it) he fell short of the ornamental. The Master (on
the other hand) had never a movement but it commended him.
So it befell that when the one appeared gracious and the other
ungracious, every trick of their bodies seemed to call out confirmation. Not that alone: but the more deeply Mr. Henry floun-
dered in his brother's toils, the more clownish he grew; and the
more the Master enjoyed his spiteful entertainment, the more
engagingly, the more smilingly, he went! So that the plot, by its
own scope and progress, furthered and confirmed itself.

Despite their mutual hatred each recognises that he cannot
achieve fulfilment in the absence of the other. Thus, the Master
returns to the ancestral home to torment Henry; he returns again
years later to resume his persecution; when he leaves in order to
pursue his quest for buried treasure he is followd in turn by
Henry. When, at one stage in the narrative, Mackellar seeks to
assure Henry that there is no likelihood of James appearing,
Henry immediately contradicts him: ' "He will not show face here
again", said I. "Oh yes he will", said Mr. Henry. "Wherever I am,
there will he be". And again he looked all about him.'
The interaction between the two protagonists is described with
such intensity and depth as to render the entire novel a profound
study of the duality of human nature: a theme to which Stevenson
recurred again and again in his work.
The contrast between Henry's passivity, loyalty and humility
with the insidiousness and amorality of the Master is a continual
theme, underlying each stage in the narrative. In one sense it can
be said to represent the dichotomy between the two sides of
Stevenson's own nature – the one intellectual, undemonstrative,
orderly; the other worldly, emotional, adventurous. In a document
not published until many years after his death he admitted: 'For
the Master I had no original, which is perhaps another way of
confessing that the original was no other than myself.'[39] In portraying the masterful, vigorous and charismatic James Durie he
was projecting the qualities of an unrealised aspect of his own
personality onto a fictional creation. Due to his wretched health
his personal life over a long period was inactive, sedentary and
retiring; an unfulfilled part of his make-up yearned for adventure,

action and romance. In a deeper sense the Master, in common with Edward Hyde, represents a reaction against the rigid, Calvinistic puritanism of his childhood and a release into the world of emotion and excitement. The interplay between the brothers may be seen then as a parable on the irresolvable diversity of human nature, on the coexistence of opposing forces which corrode man's propensity for good. It can also be regarded as a fantasia on the struggle between order and chaos, on that conflict between classical and romantic elements which Stevenson never satisfactorily resolved within his own temperament. On either interpretation the novel remains a profound study of the psychology of evil, arguably the most fully drawn study of its kind in the entire canon of his work.

At the heart of *The Master of Ballantrae* lies an ambiguity which is central to Stevenson's art and to his conception of human morality. The conventional interpretation of the story, as presented by Mackellar, is of the wickedness of the Master compared with the innocence of Henry. Yet the book is capable of a less dogmatic interpretation, a reading which poses the question: which of the brothers is predator and which is prey? It is this ambivalence which prevents the novel from being simply a gothic romance and raises it to the stature of a tragedy worthy of comparison with *Wuthering Heights* or *The Mayor of Casterbridge*.

The strength of the story resides not simply on the description of the brothers and the complexity of their relationship – impressive though this is – but on the manner in which human character *changes* under the influence of powerful emotions. One of the most fascinating strands within the intricate web of *Ballantrae* is the reader's awareness of Henry's gradual deterioration as a result of his consuming hatred for James. Henry, a gentle, kindly man, becomes increasingly morose and obsessed as the story proceeds. At last his determination to humiliate and impoverish James becomes his overriding mission in life; he neglects family and friends and violates his true nature in his *idée fixe* of inflicting harm on his brother. When Mackellar grasps the depth of this obsession he remonstrates with Henry, to no avail:

> 'My lord, my lord,' said I, 'this is no manner of behaviour.'
> 'I grow fat upon it', he replied; and not merely the words, which were strange enough, but the whole character of his expression shocked me.
> 'I warn you, my lord, against this indulgency of evil feeling,'

said I. 'I know not to which it is more perilous, the soul or the reason; but you go the way to murder both.'

'You cannot understand', said he. 'You had never such mountains of bitterness upon your heart.'

'And if it were no more,' I added, 'you will surely goad the man to some extremity.'

'To the contrary; I am breaking his spirit', says my lord.

Slowly and insidiously Henry becomes enslaved by his mania for revenge. The deterioration in his character parallel with the reversal of James's fortunes is such that in the concluding chapters, when James is outnumbered by unscrupulous men intent on murdering him, the elder brother regains much of the reader's sympathy. There is an awareness that Henry, for all his basic goodness, has tarnished his personality through his mono-maniacal desire for retribution; there is an equal recognition that James, despite his inherent evilness, possesses qualities of courage and pertinacity and that he deserves better than his ignominious fate. In his obsession with meting justice to James, Henry assumes more and more of his brother's attributes until at last it is difficult to assert which is the more selfish; once again Jekyll has been consumed by Hyde. The story of the two brothers becomes more than a study of human relationships and assumes the quality of a parable on the nature of man: more precisely, on the corrupting influence of jealousy and intolerance.

The novel confirmed the growing literary reputation Stevenson enjoyed following the success of *Dr. Jekyll and Mr. Hyde* and *Kidnapped*. It demonstrated his ability to produce good writing despite his exile and spasmodic health and strengthened his own confidence in his powers. During the writing of it he confessed to a correspondent that it had 'bewitched' him, adding: 'If it is not good, well, mine will be the fault; for I believe it is a good tale.'[40] His use of the word 'bewitched' is significant for one of the most notable aspects of the story is its capacity to enthral and move the reader through a series of brilliantly conceived mental images. In common with *Wuthering Heights* it possesses a haunting quality; even those who dislike *Ballantrae* have testified to its impressive power and its capacity to grip the imagination through the force of its writing.

An interesting example of Stevenson's technique is the description of the duel and its aftermath which forms the substance of Chapter 5. The account is preceded by a memorable word-picture of bitter weather closing in on the House of Durrisdeer: 'It was unseasonable weather, a cast back into winter: windless, bitter cold, the world all white with rime, the sky low and grey: the sea black and silent like a quarry-hole.'

Slowly the atmosphere of suspense is built up until at last the brothers resolve to fight to the death. Grimly the narrator describes the scene:

> I took up the candlesticks and went before them, steps that I would give my hand to recall; but a coward is a slave at the best; and even as I went, my teeth smote each other in my mouth. It was as he had said: there was no breath stirring; a windless stricture of frost had bound the air; and as we went forth in the shrine of the candles, the blackness was like a roof over our heads. Never a word was said; there was never a sound but the creaking of our steps along the frozen path. The cold of the night fell about me like a bucket of water; I shook as I went with more than terror; but my companions, bareheaded like myself, and fresh from the warm hall, appeared not even conscious of the change.

The effect of such literary touches as 'my teeth smote each other in my mouth', 'there was no breath stirring', 'the blackness was like a roof over our heads', 'the cold of the night fell about me like a bucket of water' is to fix the scene indelibly on the reader's imagination. The scene is not only described, it is *felt* : there is an irresistible persuasion that here is an account of an episode actually experienced. The narrator, who is at pains to present himself as a dour, unemotional Scot, cannot conceal a sense of excitement and participation; his teeth chatter, his feet creak on the icy path, he is shaking with fear. The entire scene is embedded in the consciousness as forcefully as the apple-barrel incident in *Treasure Island* or the arrival at Uncle Ebenezer's house in *Kidnapped* – it has the clarity of an etching. The episode reaches a climax with the discovery that the body of James, who had been supposed killed in the duel, has disappeared:

> I groped my way downstairs, and out at the door. From quite a far way off a sheen was visible, making points of brightness in

the shrubbery; in so black a night it might have been remarked for miles; and I blamed myself bitterly for my incaution. How much more sharply when I reached the place! One of the candlesticks was overthrown, and that taper quenched. The other burned steadily by itself, and made a broad space of light upon the frosted ground. All within that circle seemed, by the force of contrast and the overhanging blackness, brighter than by day. And there was the bloodstain in the midst; and a little further off Mr. Henry's sword, the pommel of which was of silver; but of the body, not a trace.

One is again struck by the extraordinary visual quality of Stevenson's imagination. The scene has the brilliant illumination of a stage setting: 'From quite a far way off a sheen was visible', there is 'a broad space of light upon the frosted ground', 'All within that circle seemed . . . brighter than by day'. The theatrical nature of the scene emphasises the absence of the centre-piece, the Master's body: 'And there was the bloodstain in the midst; and a little farther off Mr. Henry's sword, the pommel of which was of silver; but of the body, not a trace.' This ability to involve both the narrator and the reader as the story unfolds was one of Stevenson's most remarkable gifts: the discovery that the body is missing is experienced almost as a physical shock.[41]

A further instance of Stevenson's descriptive powers is the unforgettable (almost ghoulish) scene at the final denouement in which it is revealed that the Master of Ballantrae has been buried alive. The narrator disturbs the Indian, Secundra Dass, in the act of digging up the grave, a sight which 'struck us into pillars of stone':

He had cast the main part of his raiment by, yet his frail arms and shoulders glistened in the moonlight with a copious sweat; his face was contracted with anxiety and expectation; his blows resounded on the grave, as thick as sobs; and behind him, strangely deformed and ink-black upon the frosty ground, the creature's shadow repeated and parodied his swift gesticulations. Some night birds arose from the boughs upon our coming, and then settled back; but Secundra, absorbed in his toil, heard or heeded not at all.

Such a passage, once read, cannot be erased from the memory. It has the nightmarish quality of the resuscitation of the monster in Mary Shelley's *Frankenstein* or the escape of the puma in H. G. Wells's *The Island of Doctor Moreau*. The resounding of the blows on the grave 'as thick as sobs' is a powerful metaphor, suggesting both Secundra's grief and the intensity of his labours. The fact that the Indian 'absorbed in his toil, heard or heeded not at all' the night birds which arose from the boughs reinforces the air of concentration suggested by the passage as a whole. But the real force of the passage lies in its central image: 'and behind him, strangely deformed and ink-black upon the frosty ground, the creature's shadow repeated and parodied his swift gesticulations'. Not only does the reference to a shadow add appreciably to the memorable quality of the scene but it strengthens the symbolic imagery of the antagonism of the two brothers. For it is precisely by repeating and parodying the actions of the other that each becomes enmeshed in a web of hatred which is mutually destruc-tive. In this sense each brother is the other's 'shadow': each is a reflection of the other's weaknesses and motives.

The ending of the novel, in which James is buried alive and then exhumed before the eyes of his terrified brother, has been much criticised on the grounds of its melodramatic and contrived quality. On first reading the climax vividly recalls the closing scene of Poe's 'The Fall of the House of Usher':[42]

> For a moment she remained trembling and reeling to and fro upon the threshold, then, with a low moaning cry, fell heavily inward upon the person of her brother, and in her violent and now final death-agonies, bore him to the floor a corpse, and a victim to the terrors he had anticipated.   ('Usher')

> The next moment I beheld his eyelids flutter; the next they rose entirely, and the week-old corpse looked me for a moment in the face . . . he visibly strove to speak, his teeth showed in his beard, his brow was contorted as with an agony of pain and effort . . . at that first disclosure of the dead man's eyes, my Lord Durrisdeer fell to the ground, and when I raised him up, he was a corpse.   (*Ballantrae*)

The conclusion certainly possesses the elements of melodrama and the final chapters are marred by weaknesses of which Steven-son himself was well aware, yet the ending should be seen in the context of his overall design. His intention from the outset was to

imbue the Master with the qualities of an incubus. (An early draft
of the novel has the title 'The Familiar Incubus'.) Writing to Henry
James while the book was still in process of composition he stated:
'The elder brother is an INCUBUS,' and commented, apropos his
apparent resuscitation from the dead, 'it leads up to the death of
the elder brother at the hands of the younger in a perfectly cold-
blooded murder, of which I wish (and mean) the reader to
approve.'[43] A recurring theme in *The Master of Ballantrae* is the
apparently indestructible nature of James. Supposed to have been
killed at the battle of Culloden, he reappears to torment his
brother afresh; believed to be mortally wounded after a sword-
fight he regains consciousness and returns years later to extract
his revenge; believed to be dead a third time he is momentarily
brought back to life and causes his brother to die of fright. Each
brother is the agent of the other's death: Henry is responsible for
James's demise since it is he who has hounded him to his grave
and engineered his persecution; yet James is simultaneously
responsible for Henry's extinction. This gothic conclusion strengthens the demonic, nightmarish atmosphere of the story as a
whole: hence the subtitle 'A Winter's Tale'.

Of all his works *The Master of Ballantrae* is most strongly imbued
with a sense of loss. The opening sentence of the Preface exudes
the atmosphere of an expatriate looking back with longing at his
native Edinburgh : 'Although an old, consistent exile, the editor of
the following pages revisits now and again the city of which he
exults to be a native; and there are few things more strange, more
painful, or more salutary, than such revisitations.' This sense of
exile, of detachment, is evident at many points in the story, not
least in the descriptions of natural beauty. The descriptions of the
moors and burns of Kirkcudbright which he knew so well are
characterised by a feeling of *distance*, a tone of separation which is
at once touching and revealing. Begun in the icy cold of Saranac
and completed in the heat of the Pacific islands, the novel breathes
the atmosphere of Scotland: yet it is an atmosphere tinged with a
perception of regret. This reaches its climax in the scene in which
Henry leaves Scotland for the last time, en route for America.
Mackellar comments ruefully:

The sense of isolation burned in my bowels like a fire. It seemed
that we who remained at home were the true exiles, and that
Durrisdeer and Solwayside, and all that made my country

native, its air good to me, and its language welcome, had gone forth and was far over the sea with my old masters.

Whereas *Treasure Island* and *Kidnapped* had been written whilst Stevenson was still resident in Britain, *Ballantrae* (and, later, *Weir of Hermiston*) was composed thousands of miles from the scenes he knew and loved. In exile he could view his native Scotland with detachment and longing; in doing so he sensed that he could produce his finest work against a setting which he knew intimately. One of the many reasons why *Ballantrae* remains embedded in the mind is that, for all its wanderings in time and distance, it remains essentially a novel of Scotland, imbued with the atmosphere of Scottish history and landscape. Had it been set in an imaginary location it would lose much of its force as a story set firmly against an identifiable background. It is precisely this sense of *place*, this awareness that the tragic story of the Durie brothers is placed in a context of actual scenes and events (as with *Kidnapped*) that gives to the entire work a powerful feeling of immediacy. Stevenson well knew that he had written one of his most memorable tales.

Whilst the book was still in process of composition he remarked in a revealing aside that *The Master of Ballantrae* 'contains more human work than anything of mine but *Kidnapped*'.[44] The phrase 'human work' is interesting and demonstrates his own awareness that its greatest strength lay in the depiction of human character. In the portrayal of the two brothers, of their father, of Mackellar, and of several minor characters – including the pirate captain, Teach – he enhanced his reputation as a major novelist and gained invaluable experience which he put to skilful use in the writing of *The Ebb-Tide* and *Weir of Hermiston*. In this sense it marks a watershed in his work, for these novels could hardly have been written without the insight into characterisation acquired during its preparation.

In a deeper sense *Ballantrae* may be regarded as the literary workshop in which the components which helped to create *Weir of Hermiston* were first honed and tested. For in writing his compelling tale of the Durie brothers he was not only gaining experience in the handling of character and in the interaction of one with another, but was acquiring growing assurance in other techniques

of the novelist including the treatment of time, place and change.
David Daiches has described *The Master of Ballantrae* as marking 'a
transition from the adventure story to a much more profound
form of fiction'.[45] Seen in these terms it can be seen as a bridge
between the adventure-romance as exemplified by *Kidnapped* and
the novel of character as exemplified by *Weir of Hermiston* and its
precursors. It was not so much that he was abandoning the
romance as a literary genre but was transmuting it into a more
demanding and more enduring form.

The Wrong Box

Writing to his lifelong friend Charles Baxter on 8 March 1889 Stevenson confided: 'Lloyd and I have finished a story, *The Wrong Box*. If it is not funny, I am sure I do not know what is. I have split over writing it.' The story, originally entitled 'The Finsbury Tontine' and later 'A Game of Bluff', had originally been written by Lloyd Osbourne, Stevenson's stepson, in 1887. Stevenson had thought highly of the story and felt it showed considerable promise; so much so that he offered to revise it for publication and, intermittently over the next two years, set to work on an extensive revision of the original draft. During this period he was simultaneously at work on *The Master of Ballantrae* and it would be difficult to conceive of two more strongly contrasted works than the sombre, demonic *Master* and the light-hearted extravaganza of *The Wrong Box*.

The extent of his contribution to the joint work may be seen from the fact that of the 128 pages of the original manuscript all but 23 are in his handwriting and the remaining pages are heavily revised by him.[46] Nevertheless, it is clear that Stevenson followed Lloyd's initial concept and characters as closely as possible, whilst feeling free to add scenes and incidents of his own. Lloyd Osbourne commented later: 'Louis had to follow the text very closely, being unable to break away without jeopardising the succeeding chapters. He breathed into it, of course, his own incomparable power, humour and vivacity, and forced the thing to live as it had never lived before.'[47]

The Wrong Box is one of the curiosities of literature. By-passed by many Stevenson scholars and devotees, it remains one of the few works by him which is almost completely unknown. One has only to compare the book with *Three Men in a Boat*, published in the

same year, to appreciate the extraordinarily hazardous nature of
literary fashion. Whereas Jerome K. Jerome's humorous novel
shows no signs of diminishing in popularity and has been filmed
and dramatised on numerous occasions, sales of *The Wrong Box*
were disappointing to a hopeful author and the book seems
unlikely to endure in the same sense as *Treasure Island* or *Kidnapped*.

The complex plot of the story hinges on a tontine, i.e. a scheme
of life annuity which increases in value as the subscribers die. Two
brothers, Joseph and Masterman Finsbury, are the last survivors
of a long-established tontine; their nephews become convinced
that Masterman is dead but that his son, Michael, is concealing the
fact in order to deprive them of their inheritance. When Joseph is
apparently killed in a railway accident the nephews decide to call
Michael's bluff by concealing the body and maintaining the pre-
tence that Joseph is alive. Due to a series of misunderstandings
and mishaps their efforts to hide the corpse are continually
frustrated and the story becomes a farcical struggle between their
attempts to locate and conceal the body and Michael's equally
determined efforts to expose their deception. What is so remarkable about the book is that in Stevenson's hands the farce becomes
more than a 'black comedy' and displays elements of characterisation and depth unusual in humorous works of this kind.

The character of Uncle Joseph, for example, is drawn with a
verisimilitude and conviction which could only be derived from
life. A supreme bore on a par with Miss Bates in Jane Austen's
Emma or Pyecraft in H. G. Wells's 'The Truth about Pyecraft',
Joseph wearies his friends and relations with discourses of excessive tedium on the minutiae of factual and financial information.
The ease with which he empties a room through his excrutiating
prolixity on the cost of living is vividly described:

> Whereupon the old gentleman, with less compassion that he
> would have had for brute beasts, delivered himself of all his
> tedious calculations. As he occasionally gave nine versions of a
> single income, placing the imaginary person in London, Paris,
> Bagdad, Spitzbergen, Bassorah, Heligoland, the Scilly Islands,
> Brighton, Cincinnati, and Nijni-Novgorod, with an appropriate
> outfit for each locality, it is no wonder that his hearers look
> back on that evening as the most tiresome they ever spent.
> Long before Mr. Finsbury had reached Nijni-Novgorod with

the income of one hundred and sixty pounds, the company had dwindled and faded away to a few old topers and the bored but affable Watts. There was a constant stream of customers from the outer world, but so soon as they were served they drank their liquor quickly, and departed with the utmost celerity for the next public-house.

Joseph is a memorable creation who, despite his innate tedious-ness, engages the reader's affection. The careful reader of Steven-son will have noted other characters in his works — Long John Silver and James Durie, for example — who, whilst possessing unsavoury or sinister traits, succeeded in engaging sympathy and understanding. Joseph Finsbury is a less complex figure than these and yet compels admiration since, for all his long-windedness, he is a genuine *character* reminiscent of the creations of Dickens or Wells.

The comparison with Dickens is equally apposite in relation to William Dent Pitman, artist and charlatan. The description of Pitman at home in his studio strikingly recalls the technique of minutely detailed portraiture employed in such works as *Little Dorrit*:

> At the moment when we must present him to our readers, Pitman was in his studio alone, by the dying light of the October day. He sat (sure enough with 'unaffected simplicity') in a Wind-sor chair, his low-crowned black felt hat by his side; a dark, weak, harmless, pathetic little man, clad in the hue of mourn-ing, his coat longer than is usual with the laity, his neck enclosed in a collar without a parting, his neckcloth pale in hue and simply tied; the whole outward man, except for a pointed beard, tentatively clerical. There was a thinning on the top of Pitman's head, there were silver hairs at Pitman's temple. Poor gentleman, he was no longer young; and years, and poverty, and humble ambition thwarted, make a cheerless lot.

The significance of such passages is that it is unusual to find a writer employing such care in setting a scene in a book widely regarded as little more than a light-hearted piece of buffoonery. It seems clear from this and numerous other instances that Steven-son took the rather slight framework of his stepson's story and transformed it into a full-scale picaresque novel allowing scope for characterisation, description and narrative technique on a broad canvas.

The novel provides many instances of his gift for creating powerful word-pictures of scenes and episodes. One thinks of the railway accident at Browndean; of the arrival of the luggage van at the home of Gideon Forsyth; of Morris's destruction of the statue of Hercules; of his attempt to cash a cheque bearing a forged signature. These and other incidents are described with the eye for detail and narrative skill of a born novelist.

The description of Waterloo station towards the end of the story contains a number of characteristic Stevensonian touches, as idiosyncratic in their own way as anything comparable in Dickens or Arnold Bennett:

> About twenty minutes after two, on this eventful day, the vast and gloomy shed of Waterloo lay, like the temple of a dead religion, silent and deserted. Here and there, at one of the platforms, a train lay becalmed; here and there a wandering footfall echoed; the cab-horses outside stamped with startling reverberations on the stones: or from the neighbouring wilderness of railway an engine snorted forth a whistle. The main-line departure platform slumbered like the rest; the booking-hutches closed; the backs of Mr. Haggard's novels, with which upon a week-day the bookstall shines emblazoned, discreetly hidden behind dingy shutters; the rare officials, undisguisedly somnambulant; and the customary loiterers, even to the middle-aged woman with the ulster and the handbag, fled to more congenial scenes. As in the inmost dells of some small tropic island the throbbing of the ocean lingers, so there a faint pervading hum and trepidation told in every corner of surrounding London.

Such phrases as 'like the temple of a dead religion', and 'the rare officials, undisguisedly somnambulant' are evidence of a critical intelligence assessing the scene before him with a detachment and circumstantiality borne of close observation; 'The cab-horses outside stamped with startling reverberations on the stones' is the kind of detail one associates with his romances: a consciously evocative phrase designed to create an atmosphere of suspense. Most revealing of all is the deliberate comparison of the 'faint pervading hum' of London with the 'throbbing of the ocean' heard on a tropical island. Writing many thousands of miles away from the scenes he is describing he felt impelled to heighten his account with a striking metaphor. The metaphor at once strengthens the effectiveness of the passage and is a reminder of his exile from urban civilisation.

The Wrong Box is, then, rather more than a comic farce and a careful reading reveals beneath the impasto of (at times contrived) humour a real attempt to create a solid work of imagination. Its precise stature today seems uncertain. Extravagantly praised by a minority of votaries, it is a rare example of a work by a major nineteenth-century novelist which has virtually escaped critical attention. The time would seem ripe for its reissue in a popular edition.

On its publication in June 1889 *The Wrong Box* received largely unfavourable treatment from reviewers. Most critics found the book vulgar or trite, whilst a common theme among the reviews was the tastelessness of its subject matter. To write a book which depended for its humour on attempts to conceal a corpse was, it was felt, in questionable taste and some commentators expressed surprise that Stevenson should have lent his name and reputation to such an enterprise. Not all reviews were hostile, however, and an unsigned article in the *Scotsman* (24 June 1889) drew attention to the enduring elements in the work: 'The rich fancy everywhere displayed in the work, the extraordinary dash and brilliancy of the style, and the curiously eccentric conduct of the narrative are all qualities already identified with former stories that bear the name of Mr. Stevenson alone.' Whilst such praise may seem to a modern reader to err on the side of fulsomeness, the reviewer was surely right to emphasise the *literary* qualities of the book rather than its subject matter alone.

Whilst it has been consistently underrated or ignored by admirers of Stevenson, *The Wrong Box* is significant for the evidence it affords of his versatility and sense of humour and of his ability to handle a complicated interlocking plot with assurance. Though he never attempted to repeat what is essentially an experiment in the comic novel, he gained from it valuable experience in the art of collaboration – experience which proved indispensable in the writing of *The Wrecker* and *The Ebb-Tide* – and in the art of creating memorable and life-like scenes based on an accumulation of homely detail. Most important of all, he gained renewed self-confidence in the delineation of character and in those human touches which are the hallmark of a novelist.

The Wrecker

Stevenson and Lloyd Osbourne commenced work on *The Wrecker* during their eight-week stay in the Gilbert Islands in the summer of 1889 and completed it in Samoa in November 1891. It was conceived as the first of a series of 'South Sea Yarns' (other projected titles in the series were 'The Pearl Fisher', later renamed *The Ebb-Tide*, and 'The Beachcombers', though the latter was never completed). The story owed its origin to the mysterious disappearance of the brigantine *Wandering Minstrel*, news of which reached the Stevensons as they were preparing to leave Honolulu on their long cruise among the Pacific islands. His imagination was fired by stories of wrecked and missing ships. 'On board the schooner *Equator*,' he wrote, 'almost within sight of the Johnstone Islands . . . and on a moonlit night when it was a joy to be alive, the authors were amused with several stories of the sale of wrecks. The subject tempted them; and they sat apart in the alley-way to discuss its possibilities.'[48]

Their collaboration on the project was of a much more sustained and intimate nature than on *The Wrong Box*. Whereas the latter had been largely a case of Stevenson rewriting a preliminary draft prepared by Osbourne, *The Wrecker* was envisaged from the outset as a fully joint work. The entire story was first plotted in outline and a list of chapters drawn up; chapters were then allocated between the two, some for individual responsibility and others to be jointly written. Of the chapters written individually, the scenes describing the visit to Edinburgh and student life in Paris are wholly Stevenson's; the storm during the voyage of the *Norah Creina* and the massacre by the crew of the *Currency Lass* are apparently wholly Osbourne's. For the rest, their method was for a draft of each chapter to be prepared by one of them, usually

Osbourne; this would then be thoroughly revised by Stevenson or by both and then further mulled over by both authors. The diverse strands of the story were welded together by Stevenson who intended the book to be not so much a novel as 'a long, tough yarn with some pictures of the manners of today in the greater world – not the shoddy, sham world of cities, clubs and colleges, but the world where men still live a man's life'.[49]

In *The Wrecker*, alone of all his works, he adopted the discursive method adopted by Dickens in *The Mystery of Edwin Drood* and by Wilkie Collins in *The Woman in White*: the long narrative 'in which the reader is carried forward by the incidents surrounding a secret which is kept to the last'.[50] Stevenson was attracted to this approach since he felt it would permit a greater measure of realism through a more gradual introduction to the substance of the story. In the Epilogue to the book he summed up his intention in these terms:

> We had long been at once attracted and repelled by that very modern form of the police novel or mystery story, which consists in beginning your yarn anywhere but at the beginning, and finishing it anywhere but at the end; attracted by its peculiar interest when done, and the peculiar difficulties that attend its execution; repelled by that appearance of insincerity and shallowness of tone, which seems its inevitable drawback. For the mind of the reader, always bent to pick up clues, receives no impression of reality or life, rather of an airless, elaborate mechanism; and the book remains enthralling, but insignificant, like a game of chess, not a work of human art. It seemed the cause might lie partly in the abrupt attack; and that if the tale were gradually approached, some of the characters introduced (as it were) beforehand, and the book started in the tone of a novel of manners and experience briefly treated, this defect might be lessened and our mystery seem to inhere in life.

On first perusal the book strikes the reader as unusual precisely because of this leisurely approach. Stevenson's previous romances had accustomed his followers to fast-moving narratives in which the reader is quickly introduced to the principal characters and themes. *The Wrecker* clearly does not fall into this category. Instead, there are seven chapters of preliminary storytelling before the substance of the underlying mystery is reached and it is not until the conclusion of Chapter 8 that the narrator observes: 'Little did I suppose that I was leaving Act 1, Scene 1, of the drama of my life.'

These introductory chapters, whilst in essence irrelevant to the subsequent development of the story, are not without interest in the context of Stevenson's life and art. Thus, the fifth chapter, 'In which I am down on my luck in Paris', contains a vivid account of the artist's life in the Latin Quarter which he had experienced for himself during the years 1874–7 but had not described elsewhere. (It is interesting to compare his account of poverty and starvation in Paris with that of Orwell forty years later in *Down and Out in Paris and London*.) Similarly, the passages describing the narrator's sojourn in Edinburgh and his journey to San Francisco are written with considerable insight and reveal a touching affection for the scenes of his youth and early manhood. The description of the slums and waterfront of San Francisco (Ch. 8), for example, is an entirely characteristic piece of writing redolent of his fascination with the sea and out-of-the-way places. In the description of the narrator listening with enchantment to the seamen's yarns it is not difficult to recognise an authentic glimpse of the young author fired by tales of romance in the South Seas:

> From their long tales, their traits of character and unpre-meditated landscape, there began to piece itself together in my head some image of the islands and the island life; precipitous shores, spired mountain-tops, and deep shade of hanging forests, the unresting surf upon the reef, and the unending peace of the lagoon; sun, moon, and stars of an imperial brightness; man moving in these scenes scarce fallen, and woman lovelier than Eve; the primal curse abrogated, the bed made ready for the stranger, life set to perpetual music, and the guest welcomed, the boat urged, and the long night beguiled with poetry and choral song. A man must have been an unsuccessful artist; he must have starved on the streets of Paris; he must have been yoked to a commerical force like Pinkerton, before he can conceive the longings that at times assailed me.

Even more significant are the descriptions of the narrator's grandfather, Alexander Loudon. Though he occupies only a minor role in the story he is described with the care and verisimilitude one associates with Dickens:

In his appearance, speech, and manners he bore broad
marks of his origin, which were gall and wormwood to my
Uncle Adam. His nails, in spite of anxious supervision, were
often in conspicuous mourning; his clothes hung about him in
bags and wrinkles, like a ploughman's Sunday coat; his accent
was rude, broad, and dragging. Take him at his best, and even
when he could be induced to hold his tongue, his mere presence in a corner of the drawing-room, with his open-air
wrinkles, his scanty hair, his battered hands, and the cheerful
craftiness of his expression, advertised the whole gang of us for
a self-made family. My aunt might mince and my cousins bridle,
but there was no getting over the solid, physical fact of the
stonemason in the chimney-corner.

Such touches as 'his nails . . . were often in conspicuous mourning', 'his clothes hung about him in bags and wrinkles, like a
ploughman's Sunday coat', 'the cheerful craftiness of his expression' are evidence of a novelist's gift of observation. Moreover the
conversations with the grandfather reveal a biting (and quintes-
sentially Scottish) sense of humour which Stevenson plainly
revelled in. It is clear from this and other indications in the early
chapters that his intention from the outset was wider than that of
a conventional romance and that he attached great importance to
those aspects of the book which displayed 'some pictures of the
manners of today in the greater world'. One cannot but regret
that he did not draw Alexander Loudon on a larger scale; as it is
he who provides a tantalising glimpse of Stevenson's powers as a
creative writer and a hint of the novelist he might have become
had he lived to his maturity.

Once the gist of the story is reached, with the discovery of the
wreck of the brig *Flying Scud* on Midway Island, the pace of the
narrative quickens considerably and from this point onwards the
story becomes an exciting tale of adventure and intrigue worthy
of comparison with *Treasure Island*. The journey to the island
contains some fine descriptive passages and rarely has Stevenson
communicated with such feeling his love of the open sea:

I love to recall the glad monotony of a Pacific voyage, when the
trades are not stinted, and the ship, day after day, goes free. The
mountain scenery of trade-wind clouds, watched (and in my
case painted) under every vicissitude of light − blotting stars,

withering in the moon's glory, barring the scarlet eve, lying
across the dawn collapsed into the unfeatured morning bank,
or at noon raising their snowy summits between the blue roof
of heaven and the blue floor of sea; the small, busy, and deliberate world of the schooner, with its unfamiliar scenes, the
spearing of dolphin from the bowsprit end, the holy war on
sharks, the cook making bread on the main hatch; reefing
down before a violent squall, with the men hanging out on the
foot-ropes; the squall itself, the catch at the heart, the opened
sluices of the sky; and the relief, the renewed loveliness of life,
when all is over, the sun forth again, and our out-fought enemy
only a blot upon the leeward sea. I love to recall, and would that
I could reproduce that life, the unforgettable, the unremember-
able.

He shared with Edgar Allan Poe a deep affection for the sea and
for seafaring yarns; he had read and absorbed Defoe's *Robinson
Crusoe*, Melville's *Typee* and Dana's *Two Years Before the Mast*. Now
he expressed his lifelong enthusiasm in a gripping description of a
journey across the Pacific, a storm, and a landing on a lonely coral
reef.

The narrative owes much of its pace and suspense to what
Stevenson termed 'the redeeming element of mystery'.[51] At each
crucial stage of the story a strong element of mystery is present : at
the auction of the *Flying Scud*, in the conversations with Bellairs, in
the sudden disappearance of the crew of the brig, in the arrival at
Midway Island and the search of the wreck, in the pursuit of
Bellairs and the determined attempts by Dodd to arrive at an
explanation for the riddle. This element of suspense is maintained
to the final chapter and it is not until the concluding paragraphs
that the riddle of the wrecked and abandoned ship is solved.

Yet *The Wrecker* is more than a mystery story; it is also a novel of
character in the vein of Conrad's *Lord Jim*. (Stevenson himself,
comparing the story with *The Ebb-Tide*, commented shrewdly:
'*The Wrecker* is the least good as a story, I think; but the characters seem to me good.') The two principal characters, Loudon
Dodd and James Pinkerton, are drawn with a conviction and
depth he rarely excelled and the relationship between them – a
complex amalgam of affection and chagrin – is conveyed with
subtlety. Dodd, the narrator (based on Stevenson's friend Will H.
Low) is an artistic, naive, cautious man who embodies much of his

creator's latent romanticism and admiration of virility.

Pinkerton (based on the magazine proprietor S. S. McClure) combines those qualities of brashness, generosity, romanticism and open-handedness which Stevenson so much admired in the American make-up. These characters, so fundamentally unlike and yet drawn to one another by a friendship which survives many vicissitudes, each admires qualities possessed by the other. Pinkerton admires Dodd's Scottish caution and thoroughness; Dodd is fascinated by Pinkerton's thrusting energy and drive. In a key passage, following a disagreement between them, Dodd attempts to define the essence of their mutual affection:

> The end of the matter was to bring myself and the journalist in a more close relation. If I know anything at all of human nature – and the if is no mere figure of speech, but stands for honest doubt – no series of benefits conferred, or even dangers shared, would have so rapidly confirmed our friendship as this quarrel avoided, this fundamental difference of taste and training accepted and condoned.

A recurring theme in Stevenson's work is this fascination with human psychology, with the motivations which compel individuals to adopt certain courses of behaviour or to display particular facets of personality. In this emphasis on *a fundamental difference of taste and training accepted and condoned* may be seen evidence of his continuing preoccupation with this theme. In the preliminary chapters he has been at pains to describe the early environment of his two protagonists and to present the reader with an account of the formative influences on their lives and personalities. Continually in his work – both in the novels and the short stories – one is aware that behind and through the ostensible narrative there is a continual questioning of the motives underlying human behaviour and a recurring emphasis on the ambivalence of outwardly straightforward actions. Why do men and women behave as they do? Is wholly disinterested behaviour possible? Is this character fundamentally evil? Are the dividing lines between good and evil always clear cut? It is the constant element of doubt, implicit at many points in *The Wrecker* and elsewhere, which adds a moral dimension to his fiction and anticipates the work of such writers as Conrad and Greene.

The story contains in addition to the principal figures a number of well-drawn secondary characters including most notably Nares, Captain of the *Norah Creina*, Bellairs, the dishonest lawyer, and Carthew, owner of the *Currency Lass*. These characters are drawn with conviction and display a solidity impressive in its light and shade. The passages describing the relationship between Nares and Dodd, for example, are written with a veracity borne of close observation and are a refutation of the commonly held view that Stevenson's minor characters are mere ciphers, devoid of human interest. Nares above all is a fully rounded personality ('had there been more Nares', he wrote, 'it would have been a better book')[52] and will repay careful study as an example of Stevenson's ability to draw characters from life. The figure is based on Captain Otis, skipper of the yacht *Casco* in which Stevenson and his family sailed to Hawaii from San Francisco (1888–9): a man who earned his friendship and respect. In his own way Nares is as living and substantial a character as Alan Breck; it is his personality which lingers in the mind when the book has been read.

The weaknesses of the book stem precisely from the discursive, episodic method of narration Stevenson chose to adopt. The mystery itself, occupying some two-thirds of the story, is grippingly told and could be regarded as an adventure-romance in its own right. But this does not blend easily with the remainder nor stem naturally from it: the result is a curious hybrid, a grafting of an exciting adventure story onto a fragment of a conventional novel. Stevenson sought to impose a unity on the manuscript by adding a Prologue explaining how and why the narrator came to relate the story, and an Epilogue (dedicated to Will Low) describing the genesis of the book and the intentions of the authors – but these are consciously literary devices which do not altogether succeed in their intention. Indeed it could be argued that he was attempting the impossible; that to attempt to fuse together a mystery story with 'some pictures of the manners of today in the greater world' was to invite failure since the two genres could not in the nature of things be made to combine harmoniously. *The Wrecker* could in a sense be regarded as *two* books: a novel (occupying Chs 1–8) which would be capable of development, tracing the autobiography of Loudon Dodd; and a romance (occupying Chs 9–25) concerning the wreck of the *Flying Scud* and the mystery surrounding its recovery and contents. Within these two parts one is impressed with the power of single episodes – the scenes in Paris, the encounter with Pinkerton, the central episodes on Midway Island – rather than the story as a whole. The overall impression is of a farrago, a disconnected array of scenes, each animated with colour and incident but lacking any sense of a dominant unifying theme.

In part this was deliberate, since the author was aiming to emulate the sprawling, digressionary manner of the novelists of an earlier generation. He acknowledged this intention in the Epilogue: 'After we had invented at some expense of time this method of approaching and fortifying our police novel, it occurred to us it had been invented previously by someone else, and was in fact – however painfully different the results may seem – the method of Charles Dickens in his later work.' The dominant effect is of a series of vivid incidents, a multiplicity of short stories enclosed within an autobiographical framework, rather than a novel *per se*. It is significant that Stevenson, 'the austere stylist who accused himself of being always too ready to cut the flesh off the bones',[53] did not continue in this form. After *The Wrecker* – which proved to be a successful and profitable book – he returned to the narrative forms he had been perfecting for a decade and more. Henceforth his most enduring achievements lay in the romance, the novella and the short story; he clearly sensed that the elaborate, discursive novel on a large canvas was not a form best suited to his talents.

On the other hand he felt a constant need to experiment in literary forms and *The Wrecker*, despite its lack of artistic unity, remains his most sustained and promising attempt in a form Conrad was later to make his own. Though weakened by its diffuse structure it illustrates as no other single book does his versatility: his ability to handle in one narrative a depth of characterisation, humour and romance unusual in his fiction. Above all, it exemplifies his fascination with the varieties of life and temperament and his increasing concern with the moral issues underlying human actions. It is as a study of human nature under stress, as a reminder of the corrupting influence of greed and envy, that the story will continue to be read.

The Ebb-Tide

In 1890 Stevenson and his stepson planned a long novel, originally entitled *The Pearl Fisher*, which they intended to be the second of a series of 'South Sea Yarns'. The story was begun by Osbourne, who drafted the first six chapters, and then laid aside when the idea was abandoned. In February 1893 Stevenson took up the discarded chapters and resumed the story, working on it enthusiastically for some five months of feverish activity. Having decided to truncate the original conception and to write instead a novella of some 70,000 words he found it difficult to achieve the effect he desired without constant revision. 'But O, it has been such a grind!' he told Colvin, 'I break down at every paragraph . . . and lie here and sweat, till I can get one sentence wrung out after another.'[54]

The story was completed in June 1893 after numerous revisions and rewritings. The final chapters caused him endless difficulties; 'Well, it's done', he wrote with relief, 'Those tragic 16 pp. are at last finished, and I . . . have spent thirteen days about as nearly in Hell as a man could expect to live through.'[55] Though he sensed that he had written a profound and important work, *The Ebb-Tide* was not popular during his lifetime and it remains today one of his least known stories.

The Ebb-Tide was the last of Stevenson's works to be published in his lifetime. On its publication in book form (September 1894) it was widely, though on the whole unsympathetically, reviewed. Most critics found its underlying theme distasteful and regretted his departure from the historical romance, the genre to which his talents were felt to be best fitted. Israel Zangwill, reviewing the book in the New York *Critic*, was alone in praising its symmetry and overall literary merit. Hailing it as a 'little masterpiece' he described it as 'not only an enthralling romance, but a subtle study of the psychology of blackguardism'.[56] Its real significance, he urged, was that Stevenson had 'fused character and adventure intimately from the first page to the last' and expressed the hope that the author would continue to experiment with realistic stories of this kind.

The story carries the subtitle 'A Trio and Quartette' – an extremely apt description, since the plot hinges on the relation-ship between a group of three individuals and a fourth, and the manner in which the lives of the trio are transformed as a result of their encounter with a fourth man. The first half of the book, 'The Trio', describes the lives and personalities of three renegades – Davis, a drunken American sea captain; Herrick, an exiled English-man who, though longing for reassurance and civilisation, is yet weak and divided; and Huish, an unprincipled and shiftless Cockney clerk. The three are stranded on Tahiti, without money and with no hope of any change in their drifting, hand-to-mouth existence. They are drawn together by a common bond of poverty and unemployment, regarding themselves as outcasts from civi-lised society. Suddenly their expectations are altered when they are offered the task of taking a ship carrying a cargo of cham-pagne to Australia. Davis persuades his companions to accept the offer since he senses that the mission could provide an oppor-tunity to enrich themselves. His real intention is to steal the ship, sail it to Peru, then sell it together with its cargo, dividing the proceeds among the three.

Once out at sea, in the enclosed world of the schooner, the characters of the trio begin to emerge in their true light. Huish breaks into the champagne and spends most of the voyage in a state of maudlin drunkenness. Davis at first reprimands him, then he too succumbs to the temptation of alcohol. Herrick is the only one to remain sober, though he has no experience of seamanship; the navigation is left in his hands and the schooner is soon badly off course. The deteriorating relationship between them comes to a head when an argument breaks out in the cabin. Each tries to fasten blame on the others for their predicament and an ugly situation is only averted by the sighting of land in the distance. At the climax of the argument a state of extreme tension is reached which almost erupts into violence: 'Here at least was the gage thrown down, and battle offered; he who should speak next would bring the matter to an issue there and then; all knew it to be so and hung back; and for many seconds by the cabin clock, the trio sat motionless and silent.'

The interest of the story thus far lies in the skilful way in which Stevenson has built up a web of interlocking relationships between these three disparate characters. Both on Tahiti and on the schooner they are dependent wholly on one another, since they possess few if any inner resources. Herrick is a man who recognises his own limitations and respects leadership; he recognises in Davis a captain possessing 'sterling qualities of tenderness and resolution; he was one whose hand you could take without a blush'. Huish, though weak and feckless, is a man not wholly without loyalty and possesses courage and humour – qualities which his companions lack. As for Davis, he sees himself as a man of authority but in moments of crisis has shown himself to be ineffective and vacillating. He comes increasingly to depend on Herrick's judgement in practical matters and is shrewd enough to realise that his schemes are unlikely to succeed without the Englishman's support. Thus, the three are dependent in varying degrees upon one another. Moreover, while each is an outcast none is wholly evil; each has a weakness but none is entirely without worth. A fragile structure of dependence, respect, friendship and tolerance is built up; only to be destroyed when the trio becomes a quartette.

The second half, 'The Quartette', opens with an idyllic description of a remote Pacific Island:

> The isle – the undiscovered, the scarce-believed in – now lay before them and close aboard; and Herrick thought that never in his dreams had he beheld anything more strange and delicate. The beach was excellently white, the continuous barrier of trees inimitably green; the land perhaps ten feet high, the trees thirty more. . . . The isle was . . . so slender it seemed amidst the outrageous breakers, so frail and pretty, he would scarce have wondered to see it sink and disappear without a sound, and the waves close smoothly over its descent.

It is a measure of Stevenson's increasing pessimism that the discovery of this island paradise does not bring happiness but profound disillusionment. The island is not uninhabited, as first appears, but is the residence of Attwater, an Englishman who has made the place his home and has accumulated a fortune through pearl fishing.

Attwater, one of Stevenson's most profound characterisations, gives an outward impression of urbanity and confidence: he appears to be the embodiment of an English gentleman. It becomes apparent, however, that the façade of civilisation conceals a ruthless and authoritarian nature. He is a man who will brook no interference in his domain, who dispenses a puritanical order of justice over the native population and who will go to any lengths to conceal the secret of his island treasure. He magnetises the three men with the overpowering force of his personality and, whilst all three are soon consumed with hatred, it is a hatred inseparably overshadowed by fear.

Once Davis and Huish grasp that the island is a source of wealth and that Attwater has accumulated a vast treasure in pearls, they resolve to murder him and scheme how to outwit him and his native guards. From this point onwards the story becomes a complex labyrinth of relationships and uncertainties as each of the outcasts wrestles with the competing claims of greed, loyalty, remorse and cowardice. Attwater proves to be a formidable opponent and far more difficult to outmanoeuvre than the trio had assumed. When their first attempt fails Herrick wanders off alone, torn between suicide and surrender, but Huish volunteers to approach close to Attwater and maim him with vitriol. In all other respects a weak, unscrupulous, unreliable man he alone of the renegades has sufficient courage to approach the armed, merciless pearl fisher and entice him in conversation whilst scheming his death.

In this situation both Davis and Herrick, each in their different ways, cling to vestiges of morality. Herrick is confronted with the agonising choice of whether to warn Attwater of the plot against him, to join forces with Davis and Huish, or to commit suicide (and thus opt out of his moral dilemma). In deciding to throw in his lot with Attwater he is not making a simple choice between good and evil. Herrick is well aware that Attwater, for all his pose as a man of principle, is cold, ruthless and tyrannical; Davis, though weak and unprincipled, is not without virtue and there are bonds of friendship between the two men. The choice is an extremely difficult one and involves Herrick in long hours of indecision in which the urge to end his life is balanced against disgust at his inherent cowardice:

To any man there may come at times a consciousness that

there blows, through all the articulations of his body, the wind of a spirit not wholly his; that his mind rebels; that another girds him and carries him whither he would not. It came now to Herrick, with the authority of a revelation. There was no escape possible. The open door was closed in his recreant face. He must go back into the world and amongst men without illusion. He must stagger on to the end with the pack of his responsibility and his disgrace, until a cold, a blow, a merciful chance ball, or the more merciful hangman, should dismiss him from his infamy. There were men who could commit suicide; there were men who could not; and he was one who could not. . . . With the fairy tale of suicide, of a refuge always open to him, he had hitherto beguiled and supported himself in the trials of life; and behold! that also was only a fairy tale, that also was folk-lore. With the consequences of his acts he saw himself implacably confronted for the duration of life: stretched upon a cross, and nailed there with the iron bolts of his own cowardice. He had no tears, he told himself no stories. His disgust with himself was so complete, that even the process of apologetic mythology had ceased. He was like a man cast down from a pillar, and every bone broken. He lay there, and admitted the facts, and did not attempt to rise.

The moment of choice for Herrick is clearly the 'ebb-tide' of the title. 'He had complied with the ebb-tide in man's affairs,' adds Stevenson, 'and the tide had carried him away; he heard already the roaring of the maelstrom that must hurry him under.' In a wider sense the 'ebb-tide' refers to the moment of decision confronting each of the protagonists: Attwater has to decide whether or not to accept Herrick (a man whom he mistrusts) into his company; Huish has to decide whether to throw in his lot with Davis, whom he resents; Davis has to come to terms with Huish's repugnant proposal. Each of these choices involves a careful balancing of moral and personal considerations. But whereas Attwater is guided in his actions by a rigid code of religious belief, the other three have no such moral framework. The agony of being compelled to make a choice within a moral vacuum is vividly portrayed.

Davis, for all his blustering and pose as a man of decision, is at first horrified by the idea of throwing vitriol at the pearl fisher and resists it:

'I don't know what it is', cried Davis, pacing the floor, 'it's there! I draw the line at it. I can't put a finger to no such piggishness. It's too damned hateful!'

'And I suppose it's all your fancy pynted it', said Huish, 'w'en you take a pistol and a bit o' lead, and copse a man's brains all over him? No accountin' for tystes.'

'I'm not denying it', said Davis, 'it's something here, inside of me. It's foolishness; I daresay it's dam foolishness. I don't argue; I just draw the line. Isn't there no other way?'

In clinging to a semblance of a moral code, in insisting that 'it's something here, inside of me. . . . I don't argue; I just draw the line' he is instinctively recoiling from the throwing of acid though he cannot express his repugnance in coherent terms. The idea violates his fundamental conception of morality; he reluctantly gives his consent when he realises that there is no feasible alternative to Huish's plan.

The climax of the story, the attempted murder of Attwater and the shooting of Huish, is one of those scenes which are etched unforgettably on the imagination. Here, as in the storming of the stockade in *Treasure Island* and the midnight duel in *The Master of Ballantrae*, one is aware of writing of such clarity that the scene has the brilliance of a tableau: each detail is described with haunting precision. At this and numerous other stages in the narrative the reader is struck afresh with the *visual* quality of Stevenson's imagination: his gift for describing scenes and locations with photographic distinctness. Writing to Colvin on 25 April 1893 apropos illustrations for the book, he specified:

Attwater's settlement is to be entirely overshadowed everywhere by tall palms; see photographs of Fakarava: the verandahs of the house are 12ft. wide. Don't let him [the illustrator] forget the Figure Head, for which I have a great use in the last chapter. It stands just clear of the palms on the crest of the beach at the head of the pier; the flag-staff not far off; the pier he will understand is perhaps three feet above high water, not more at any price.

With the failure of the murder attempt and the death of Huish the story moves to an abrupt conclusion. Attwater spares Davis's life on condition that the captain subordinates his will to his own.

The story ends with Davis's total subservience to Attwater and his eager adoption of Attwater's evangelistic Christianity. There is a last glimpse of the captain praying passionately for forgiveness. Davis survives in the sense that he does not forfeit his life, but his survival is at the expense of his individuality. He has gained assurance, a fixed moral code, a positive belief, but he has no freedom of action. The implication is that he will live out his days on the island, content to serve Attwater and to solace himself in prayer and supplication. Herrick, a more complex figure than Davis, also joins forces with the pearl fisher but it has been clear all along that he is a man of greater intellectuality than the captain. Whether he chooses to remain on the island is left unresolved; there is a hint that he, at least, may decide to return to the world of men.

The Ebb-Tide is a tale of profound moral implications, many of which have personal relevance to Stevenson and illuminate significant aspects of his life and thought. First, the story is important since it represents his most conscious and sustained attempt to free himself from 'the dialectic of his upbringing'[57] and to come to grips with fundamental questions of human conduct. In his previous works, most notably Dr. Jekyll and Mr. Hyde and The Master of Ballantrae, he had wrestled with aspects of behaviour and morality and sought to express them in terms of man's inherent dualism. Now, in The Ebb-Tide, he went beyond the notion of duality and for the first time exposed the human dilemma in stark, existentialist terms.

In presenting the character of Attwater he went further than he had ever gone before in creating a personification of the wrathful, all-powerful God he had imbibed in his childhood. Attwater, puritanical, Calvinistic and ruthless, represents all that Stevenson found most repugnant in the rigid, orthodox Christianity of his father. But his significance lies deeper than this. Perhaps the most fascinating aspect of his character is its strong hint of deification: it is his island, his code of morality, his law. Herrick is quick to perceive his invincibility: 'O, it's no use, I tell you! He knows all, he sees through all; we only make him laugh with our pretences – he looks at us and laughs like God!' This representation of Attwater as an all seeing, all wise God-like figure makes him an interesting comparison with similar figures in our literature and a most potent symbol of the Victorian idea of God. (It is fruitful, for example, to compare Attwater with Moreau in H. G. Wells's *The Island of Doctor Moreau* (1896) and Conchis in John Fowles's *The Magus* (1966), both of whom assume the characteristics of a deity.)[58]

Yet Attwater is no mere bogy-figure. For all his cynicism, self-righteousness and intolerance he symbolises qualities which Stevenson well knew many of his readers would find attractive. Though his personality contains strong elements of megalomania he also represents order as opposed to chaos, strength as opposed to weakness. His appeal is that he stands for certainty where there would otherwise be doubt; to ally oneself with him and men of his kind is to embrace a world free of ambiguities, a world in which conduct is ruled by a rigid, authoritarian code of law. The converse situation, as symbolised by Huish, is a world devoid of restraints, a society in which there is no morality whatever. Such a society, Stevenson is at pains to stress, cannot bring happiness. In place of certainty there is merely a terrifying vacuum, an emptiness where there are no rules, no imperatives, no obligations. Faced with such a void the individual has no choice but to fall back on his inner resources: if he possesses none, the consequence is destruction or degradation. On this interpretation both orthodox religion and amorality are equally dangerous alternatives, fraught with limitations for the individual. Davis chooses the first alternative, but at the expense of the human spirit; Huish chooses the second, but at the expense of his life.

The story has a particular relevance to Stevenson's circumstances and beliefs during the closing years of his life. It has been described as 'an urban daydream',[59] for one of the most revealing aspects of the book is the implicit longing of the characters for the peace and order of England. Herrick, an Oxford graduate, dreams nostalgically of the England he has left behind: 'visions of England at least would throng upon the exile's memory: the busy school-room, the green playing-fields, holidays at home, and the perennial roar of London, and the fireside, and the white head of his father'. Even the drunken captain, John Davis, is haunted by an elusive dream of respectability:

the pictures that came to him were of English manners. He saw his boys marching in the procession of a school, with gowns on, an usher marshalling them and reading as he walked in a great

book. He was installed in a villa, semi-detached; the name,
'Rosemore', on the gateposts. . . . He saw the parlour, with red
curtains, and shells on the mantelpiece.

Not only do the protagonists find solace in dreams of England
but the island itself is depicted as a symbol of civilisation in miniature. The sand on the beach 'bore the marks of having been once
weeded like a garden alley at home'; the buildings of the settlement were 'fresh painted, trim and dandy'; all is orderly, cultivated
and urbane. Stevenson clearly intended the island to be seen as a
paradigm of Victorian civilisation.

He had come to Samoa in October 1890, at the age of forty,
mainly for health reasons but also to escape the pressures and
tensions of urban civilisation. But in doing so he was very far from
opting out of life, as some critics believed. Throughout his
residence there were rumblings of warfare in and around the
island and he found himself unwittingly at the centre of a
cauldron of unrest and conflict. Far from escaping from society,
then, he had simply exchanged one set of problems for another.
The Ebb-Tide is in a sense a dramatisation of the uncertainties
endemic in his life at this time. Implicit within it is an acknowledgement that one does not avoid the dilemmas of life simply by
residing on a remote island; always one is confronted by situations
involving a moral choice. By presenting his characters in isolation,
first on Tahiti, then on board a schooner, and finally on Attwater's
island, he is able to discuss their situation in a vacuum, freed from
distractions. The device compels the reader to look inwards, to
scrutinise his figures under a lens and to reflect on the ethical and
personal dilemmas raised by their conduct.

Stevenson's increasing awareness of the moral dilemmas of his
time is symbolised in the image which dominates the second half
of the story, that of the figure-head of a ship. When first seen by
the trio, the figure-head is described in these terms:

a woman of exorbitant stature and as white as snow was to be
seen beckoning with uplifted arm. The second glance identified
her as a piece of naval sculpture, the figure-head of a ship that
had long hovered and plunged into so many running billows,
and was now brought ashore to be the ensign and presiding
genius of that empty town.

On closer examination the whiteness of the figure is described as 'leprous'; Herrick examines the enigmatic woman with 'singular feelings of curiosity and romance'; during the final confrontation between Attwater and Davis, the pearl fisher deliberately shoots at the figure-head, symbolically destroying its mystery. It is not too fanciful to recognise in the image a symbol of that youthful optimism, that naïve yearning for adventure and romance which Stevenson was consciously rejecting in the works of his maturity. In such works as *The Ebb-Tide*, 'The Beach of Falesa' and *Weir of Hermiston* he was exploring aspects of character, morality and behaviour which had come increasingly to haunt his imagination. He recognised that the presentation of these issues in a totally realistic, contemporary setting would involve the abandonment of the buoyant optimism which had characterised his early essays and stories and an acceptance of a stark, adult, pragmatic attitude of mind: an attitude without illusions. The figure-head – which is initially regarded with awe and finally maimed without compunction – represents the destruction of his innocence, the loss of the immature, dilettante Stevenson and a conscious determination to come to terms with the problem of evil. Seen in this light *The Ebb-Tide* must be ranked as one of his most seminal works of fiction, a work which can be compared with Conrad's *Victory* as a penetrating study of the human condition.

St. Ives

When Stevenson died in December 1894 he left uncompleted two novels on which he had been working during the preceding years, *St. Ives* and *Weir of Hermiston*. *St. Ives* was begun in January 1893, initially as a diversion from one of his periodic attacks of illness, and was dictated to his stepdaughter Isobel Strong at intervals until September 1894 when, characteristically, he broke it off in a mood of dissatisfaction. His wife recorded later: '*St. Ives* was written entirely to dictation; not continuously, but at intervals, in conjunction with *Hermiston*. My husband would work on one book until he was tired or his mood changed, when he would take up the other.'[60] Working in this way he completed thirty chapters of *St. Ives*, latterly with diminishing enthusiasm as his interest flagged. The book was completed by A. T. (later Sir Arthur) Quiller-Couch and published posthumously in 1898 under the title *St. Ives: Being the Adventures of a French Prisoner in England*. The story, written throughout in the first person, narrates the experiences of a French prisoner of war, Anne St. Ives. Incarcerated in Edinburgh Castle at the time of the Napoleonic wars, the prisoner succeeds in escaping from the Castle and makes his way south to his uncle in England, pursued by a variety of followers intent on his recapture. Since he is a prime suspect in a murder — an affair of honour committed inside the Castle — he is hunted by both civil and military authorities. The plot hinges on his continual attempts to elude his pursuers, to clear his name, and to win the hand of the woman he loves, Flora Gilchrist.

In form the story follows the pattern adopted by Dickens in *The Old Curiosity Shop*: the description of a central character embarking on a long journey and an account of the experiences which befall him on the way: the companions he meets, the scenes through

185

which he travels, and his reflections on the journey. The limitation
of the genre is that it is difficult to sustain the reader's interest
without introducing diversions and incidents which almost inevitably seem contrived – Stevenson himself plainly sensed this for he
wrote at the beginning of Chapter 25 'I pass over the next fifty or
sixty leagues of our journey without comment. The reader must
be growing weary of scenes of travel' – and it is difficult to bring
the adventures to a tidy conclusion without leaving an impression
of shapelessness. He had previously adopted this form in *Kidnapped* but whereas the earlier novel was sustained by a taut, fast-
moving narrative, *St. Ives* seems slow and drawn out by comparison and lacks the exciting sea adventures of David Balfour. Once
the prisoner has escaped from the formidable castle rock – a brilliant piece of writing, comparable to the most gripping scenes in
any of his previous works – the excitement of the story is
inevitably diminished and the plot tends to become a series of
picaresque incidents, each competently written yet lacking the
overall symmetry of the earlier romances.

The story contains a number of weaknesses of characterisation
and construction of which Stevenson was probably aware. Neither
of the major characters, St. Ives and Flora Gilchrist, are drawn
with that conviction which makes *The Master of Ballantrae*, for
example, such a fascinating study of behaviour. Flora is simply a
recreation of Catriona Drummond in *Catriona* and the love scenes
between her and the Frenchman – particularly that in Chapter 26,
'The Cottage at Night', strongly criticised by Lloyd Osbourne – are
embarrassingly overwritten. Moreover, in assembling the components of his story Stevenson makes frequent use of materials
previously employed elsewhere; the escape from Edinburgh
Castle strongly recalls a similar escape in *The Black Arrow*, the
pursuit through Scotland resembles the journey of David Balfour
and Alan Breck in *Kidnapped*, and the attempt of the narrator to
return to Edinburgh to present evidence in a murder trial echoes a
similar situation in *Catriona*.

Paradoxically, the strength of the book lies in its minor characters and individual episodes rather than in the principal figures. *St.
Ives*, in common with *The Wrecker*, possesses a wealth of subordinate characters drawn with a strong sense of individuality. There is
the wily Major Chevenix, the hero's rival in love, a formidable and
gentlemanly opponent; Candlish and Sim, the drovers who
accompany St. Ives through a desolate tract of Scotland; Rowley

the engaging and exasperating boy valet; the unscrupulous
Burchell Fenn, 'a man of a gross, misbegotten face and body,
dewlapped like a bull and red as a harvest moon'; Thomas
Dudgeon, the solicitor's clerk who wins the hero's respect and
affection; Alain, the Frenchman's scheming cousin. Each of these
figures possesses the solidity and life-like quality characteristic of
the work of a major novelist. Perhaps the most memorable among
the gallery of secondary personalities is Miss Gilchrist, Flora's
redoubtable aunt. Strict, dignified, dour, yet fundamentally kind-
hearted, she is one of his most impressive creations. One of the
most dramatic moments in the story is the scene in which she
makes an unexpected entrance upon St. Ives and Flora:

> The words were still upon my lips when the door opened and
> my friend of the gold eyeglass appeared, a memorable figure,
> on the threshold. In one hand she bore a bedroom candlestick;
> in the other, with the steadiness of a dragoon, a horse-pistol.
> She was wound about in shawls which did not wholly conceal
> the candid fabric of her nightdress, and surmounted by a
> nightcap of portentous architecture. Thus accoutred, she made
> her entrance; laid down the candle and pistol, as no longer
> called for; looked about the room with a silence more eloquent
> than oaths; and then, in a thrilling voice – 'To whom have I the
> pleasure?' she said, addressing me with a ghost of a bow.

It is scenes such as this, so vividly and powerfully written, which
render the novel a rewarding experience despite the limitations of
the book as a whole. The figure of Miss Gilchrist 'surmounted by a
nightcap of portentous architecture' and surveying the room 'with
a silence more eloquent than oaths' remains long in the mind and
possesses that intense, dramatic quality of the most memorable
scenes in *Kidnapped* and *Treasure Island*.
    The book also confirmed Stevenson's mastery in the handling of
sharply evoked scenes. The story is rich in self-contained episodes,
each presented with the clarity of a short story. There is the duel
in the castle between St. Ives and Goguelat; the journey south-
wards along the Great North Road; the encounter with two
French officers in hiding; the pursuit of St. Ives by the attorney's
clerk; the encounter with the young couple bound for Gretna
Green, and many others. These incidents are so vividly conceived
and narrated that the reader is borne along irresistibly through

the convoluted plot. Moreover, the story abounds in those striking phrases which linger in the memory: 'the rain fell in crystal rods'; 'we ate like mice in a cat's ear, if one of us jingled a teaspoon all would start'; 'his head was as bald as a bladder of lard'; 'time and again we found ourselves adrift among garden borders or stuck like a ram in the thicket'. The power of the individual scenes tends to obscure the structural weaknesses inherent in the story as a whole and strengthens one's impression of a series of remarkable word-pictures executed with telling effect.

A small but interesting example of his technique is the scene in Chapter 15 in which St. Ives sets eyes on Thomas Dudgeon. The man is described as

> a long, lean, characteristic-looking fellow of perhaps forty dressed in black. . . . He seemed to value himself above his company, to give himself the airs of a man of the world among that rustic herd; which was often no more than his due; being as I afterwards discovered, an attorney's clerk.

Dudgeon is described with considerable economy of words yet the author succeeds in presenting a clear portrait of him in two or three brief sentences. The phrases 'characteristic-looking', 'he seemed to value himself above his company', and 'a man of the world among that rustic herd' convey a concise picture of a man of authority: a man accustomed to sizing up a situation and arriving at the essentials of recondite problems. The clerk occupies a comparatively minor role in the story yet he is described with the detail of a secondary character in Dickens or Thackeray. When Dudgeon decides to follow St. Ives and confront him, the hero is aware at once of a formidable intelligence, a potential adversary who is an equal match for his own cunning. Equal care is devoted to the presentation of the other subordinate characters with the result that the book is a gallery of vignettes, each drawn on a small scale yet impressive in their aptness.

A recurring theme in Stevenson's work is the manner in which human behaviour changes under the impact of stress, emotion or fear. There are a number of instances in *St. Ives* which reveal his continuing preoccupation with this theme and his fascination with questions of conduct and morality. In the third chapter, for example, there is a lengthy conversation between St. Ives and Major Chevenix. The Major suspects the prisoner of having murdered a fellow-inmate; whilst he is almost certain of St. Ives's guilt, he has no proof. His questions are therefore designed to expose the flaws in the prisoner's story and oblige the latter to confess his guilt. A second example is the conversation in a Bedfordshire inn (Ch. 15) between St. Ives and the attorney's clerk who is suspicious of his true identity. Yet another example is the dialogue between the hero and the solicitor Daniel Romaine (Ch. 18) in which St. Ives seeks to defend his conduct and the solicitor reminds him of the gravity of his predicament. Each of these conversations represents an attempt to arrive at the truth of a given situation. In each there is a constant probing of character and motive, an attempt to find the weak spot in the narrator's version of events and compel him to examine his own intentions. The effect of this is to oblige St. Ives to reassess his behaviour and examine his motives at each decisive stage of his experiences. Whilst psychologically the book lacks the depth of *Ballantrae* or *The Ebb-Tide* its characters and situations are not without interest in the light of Stevenson's continuing concerns.

One of the most interesting features of the story is the evidence it affords of his increasing nostalgia for the hills and dales of his native Scotland. As the hero journeys through the scenes which the author knew and loved, the reader senses the regret of a writer aware that he would never see Scotland again and for whom such landscapes were embedded in the memory:

A continual succession of insignificant shaggy hills, divided by the course of ten thousand brooks, through which we had to wade, or by the side of which we encamped at night; infinite perspectives of heather, infinite quantities of moorfowl; here and there, by a stream side, small and pretty clumps of willows or the silver birch; here and there, the ruins of ancient and inconsiderable fortresses – made the unchanging characters of the scene. Occasionally, but only in the distance, we could perceive the smoke of a small town or of an isolated farmhouse or cottage on the moors; more often, a flock of sheep and its attendant shepherd, or a rude field of agriculture perhaps not yet harvested.

Some of the most memorable scenes in the novel are those depicting the Scottish landscapes he had traversed so many times both in fact and imagination: Edinburgh and its surrounding terrain, the drovers' road from Edinburgh to the Border counties, Cramond on the Firth of Forth. In these passages, far more markedly than in the chapters describing English towns and scenes, there is evidence of deep familiarity and of his abiding attachment to the country of his childhood.

In an early chapter there is an idyllic description of Swanston Cottage, the small house on the slopes of the Pentland Hills which he remembered with affection from his youth. The cottage is described with an almost child-like enchantment as the narrator first approaches the scene in the grey light of an Edinburgh dawn:

> The cottage was a little quaint place of many roughcast gables and grey roofs. It had something the air of a rambling infinitesi-mal cathedral, the body of it rising in the midst two storeys high, with a steep-pitched roof, and sending out upon all hands (as it were chapter-houses, chapels, and transepts) one-storeyed and dwarfish projections. To add to this appearance, it was grotesquely decorated with crockets and gargoyles, ravished from some mediaeval church. The place seemed hidden away, being not only concealed in the trees of the garden, but, on the side on which I approached it, buried as high as the eaves by the rising of the ground. About the walls of the garden there went a line of well-grown elms and beeches, the first entirely bare, the last still pretty well covered with red leaves, and the centre was occupied with a thicket of laurel and holly, in which I could see arches cut and paths winding.

This deeply felt passage, so reminiscent of the description of Peggotty's boat-house in *David Copperfield*, is written with the sense of wonder of a young man looking back with nostalgia on the scene of lost happinesses. How vividly must he have recalled the hours he spent in and around Swanston Cottage, this remote place 'hidden away' in which he had spent so much of his early man-hood.

A curious aspect of the book which has largely escaped critical attention is the fact that the narrator, as a Frenchman, has to regard Scottish scenes and institutions with detachment *from the outside*. The effect of this is to compel Stevenson to view the customs and peculiarities of his homeland with the eye of a stran-ger, marvelling at their oddity. An interesting example of the technique is the scene in which St. Ives seeks to ingratiate himself

by attending a service at a church which he mistakenly supposes
to be fashionable:

> Mrs. McRankine inquired where I had been. I told her boast-
> fully, giving her the name of the church and the divine and
> ignorantly supposing I should have gained caste. But she soon
> opened my eyes. In the roots of the Scottish character there are
> knots and contortions that not only no stranger can under-
> stand, but no stranger can follow; he walks among explosives;
> and his best course is to throw himself upon their mercy – 'Just
> as I am, without one plea', a citation from one of the lady's
> favourite hymns. The sound she made was unmistakable in
> meaning, though it was impossible to be written down; and I at
> once executed the manoeuvre I have recommended.

The detachment of the Frenchman viewing Scottish conventions and prejudices as an outsider has its parallel in the detachment of the author writing of his homeland in voluntary exile. His
deliberate severance from the country of his birth permitted him
to view dispassionately customs and traits which would formerly
have roused deep emotions. This distancing, this continual standing back from familiar scenes and characteristics, is evident at
many points in *St. Ives*. Thus, the narrator describes wild lowland
scenery as 'extraordinarily desolate . . . an unbroken desert' and
concludes that his journeyings have given him 'a singular view of
that poor, barren, and yet illustrious country through which I have
travelled'. Implicit in the book is a tone of discovery, as if Stevenson is consciously viewing his homeland with the eyes and
attitudes of an outsider experiencing the country for the first time.
Vicariously through the observant and impressionable Frenchman he is permitted to return to the land he loved and see again
the scenes and people he knew so well. In this sense one of the
most remarkable features of the story is his total recall of the
topography of Edinburgh and its adjacent countryside. The
chapters set in and around his native city provide convincing
evidence of his deep attachment to the scenes of his childhood
and youth and of his inability to eradicate the landscape from his
mind.

As he became more and more preoccupied with *Weir of Hermiston* his interest in *St. Ives* waned to the point that he set it aside,
intending to complete it later if he could regain his enthusiasm.

He recognised that the story fell far short of his expectations. To his cousin R. A. M. Stevenson he confessed:

> I have got to a crossing place, I suppose; the present book, *Saint Ives*, is nothing; it is in no style in particular, a tissue of adventures, the central character not very well done, no philosophic pith under the yarn; and, in short, if people will read it, that's all I ask; and if they won't, damn them![61]

In drawing attention to its absence of 'philosophic pith under the yarn' he was pinpointing what is arguably its central weakness. *St. Ives* is a romance and does not claim to be anything more profound. Yet side by side with this tale he was feverishly at work on a novel in the sharpest contrast, a story which fulfilled all the expectations of his earlier work.

Weir of Hermiston

Weir of Hermiston was begun in October 1892 in a mood of great enthusiasm and worked on sporadically until the day of Stevenson's death more than two years later. Again and again it was laid aside while he was distracted with other projects – *St. Ives, The Ebb-Tide*, the proofs of *Catriona* and many short stories and articles – and it was not until September 1894 that he resumed the novel in earnest. It was his practice to dictate each chapter to his secretary, Isobel Strong, revising the work very carefully until he was satisfied. Mrs. Strong noted in her diary for 24 September 1894:

> Louis and I have been writing, working away every morning like steam-engines on *Hermiston*. . . . He has always been wonderfully clear and sustained in his dictation. . . . 'Belle,' he said, 'I see it all so clearly! The story unfolds itself before me to the least detail – there is nothing left in doubt. I never felt so before in anything I ever wrote. It will be my best work; I feel myself so sure in every word.'[62]

As he became increasingly convinced of the book's merit and reassured by his confidence in his powers of composition he worked on the novel with feverish energy. Always prone to be critical of his own work, he confessed that he was almost frightened at the ease with which the story flowed from his brain and seriously questioned whether he would be able to sustain it at the same pitch of intensity. In view of his fragile health it is more than probable that the mental and emotional strain of working on the book with such concentration hastened his death. As it was he completed nine chapters (approximately half of his original design) before his sudden demise, leaving the story as a tantalisingly incomplete fragment and a hint of the powers he had at his command.

Since it was left unfinished it has inevitably invited comparisons with *The Mystery of Edwin Drood*. Attempts to find parallels with Dickens's last uncompleted work are however misleading. Few would claim that *Edwin Drood* represents Dickens at the height of his powers or that it embodies characteristics markedly different from the novels which preceded it. *Hermiston* on the other hand occupies a distinctive place in the Stevenson canon. By common consent Stevenson's finest single achievement, it is unique in that it represents a fusion of all the diverse elements of his art. In this last unfinished work each strand of his artistry – the storyteller, the humorist, the novelist of character, the novelist of Scotland, the novelist of psychology – are brought together in a novel of epic stature which can be seen as a summation of his creative endeavour. It is also the most autobiographical of all his works, not only in the sense that it echoes themes and situations from his early life but that in writing it he was working out in fictional form the tensions which had been his emotional driving force from childhood onwards.

Before turning to a discussion of the novel itself it is worth pausing to examine its language, for in its style and vocabulary it is one of the most rewarding and carefully executed of all his writings.

It is at once apparent on opening the work that it is written in a spare, tense prose of impressive energy and power. One senses that each word, each sentence, has been considered and refined to achieve an effect of fluidity and tension unusual in his fiction. It is the style of *The Ebb-Tide* wedded to a Scottish dourness to achieve a prose of exhilarating strength. Thus, for Adam Weir 'pleasure was a by-product of the singular chemistry of life, which only fools expected'; Kirstie has 'a drawn quarrel with most of her neighbours, and with the others not much more than armed neutrality'; Christina shakes from head to foot 'with the barren ecstasy of temper'. It is a style which gains readability not merely from its economy but from its peculiar aptness to the story as it unfolds. The language has a cutting edge which permits its use as a vehicle for conveying irony, suspense or foreboding; reading it it is difficult to believe that it stems from the same pen as *Prince Otto*. The adoption of this clear, controlled, economical style permits the use of light and shade where these are appropriate and at the same

time creates the illusion of *movement*, of a journey towards a
powerful climax. At each of the crucial scenes in the story – the
painful interview between Adam Weir and his son, the encounter
on the moors between Archie and Christina, the conversations
between Archie and Frank Innes, the nocturnal visit of Kirstie
Elliott, the confrontation at the Weaver's Stone between the two
lovers – one is aware of a felicitous use of language it would be
difficult to better. The whole of Chapter 6, 'A Leaf from Christina's
Psalm-Book', could be taken as a model of the novelist's craft.
Arnold Bennett wrote apropos this chapter that it contained
'about forty pages of the subtlest, surest, finest psychological analysis that I can remember. . . . The mere writing of *Weir of Hermiston*
surpasses all Stevenson's previous achievement.'[63]

The hand of the storyteller is evident throughout the taut narrative. The opening sentence at once presages a story, a yarn set
against the background of a defined location: 'In the wild end of a
moorland parish, far out of the sight of any house, there stands a
cairn among the heather, and a little by east of it, in the going
down of the braeside, a monument with some verses half defaced.'
    At intervals during the story the reader is prepared for the
unfolding of a tragedy. Thus, in Chapter 6: 'The generations were
prepared, the pangs were made ready, before the curtain rose on
the dark drama.' And again in Chapter 7: 'Poor cork upon a
torrent, he tasted that night the sweets of omnipotence, and
brooded like a deity over the strands of that intrigue which was to
shatter him before the summer waned.' An atmosphere of brooding destiny is slowly and carefully attained – reminiscent of *The
Master of Ballantrae* though of a higher order of artistry – until at
last the reader has a sense of a Greek tragedy, of an epic in which
the emotions and conflicts of an earlier age are to be played out
again. Stevenson's intention to write 'a real historical novel, to
present a whole field of time',[64] is evident in the continual references to Scottish history and culture, in the strong sense of the
past which animates the novel and the constant reminder of qualities inherited from our forbears. Technically the book marks
a distinct advance on all his previous novels. In its construction, its
characterisation, the manner in which characters are introduced
and developed, the skill with which a cross-section of Lowland life
in the early nineteenth century is portrayed, *Hermiston* is rightly

regarded as the summit of his achievement. The previous novels – perhaps more especially *Kidnapped* – had contained indications of the range of literary powers Stevenson held at his command. But now these powers, always hitherto partially realised, came to full fruition.

Consider, for example, the scene in Chapter 6 in which Christina is lying on her bed meditating on her love for Archie Weir. She has been trying to analyse her feelings towards the young lord of the manor and is at the same time haunted by certain tales of superstition and tragedy related to her by her brother: 'You might say the joints of her body thought and remembered, and were gladdened, but her essential self, in the immediate theatre of consciousness, talked feverishly of something else, like a nervous person at a fire.'

In this one sentence Stevenson succeeds in conveying a distillation of the sense of drama which pervades the entire work. The phrase 'her essential self . . . talked feverishly of something else' is a reminder of Christina's awareness that her love for Archie can only lead to unhappiness. She senses, though she cannot formulate her intuition in rational terms, that a marriage between her and young Hermiston would be a re-enactment of tensions which had divided Scottish history for generations and that its tragic end would fulfil the ancient prophecies of the neighbourhood. The narrator likens her attitude to that of 'a nervous person at a fire', aware of the potential danger of her situation yet wilfully refusing to face realities. It is in touches such as this that Stevenson reveals his mastery of the storyteller's art and his ability to convey complex emotions and attitudes through apparently simple metaphors.

The central theme of the novel – the incompatabilities and misunderstandings between father and son – is essentially a tragic one. Despite the tragic nature of this theme the novel contains a rich vein of humour which permeates the sombre whole with a leaven of wryness. At times this takes the form of an aside inserted almost in passing, as when Stevenson speculates on the motives which could have led the dour Adam Weir to marry the pious and incompetent Jean Rutherford: 'Mr. Weir must have supposed his bride to be somehow suitable; perhaps he belonged to that class of men who think a weak head the ornament of women – an opinion invariably punished in this life.' Elsewhere it is evident as wry comment on human foibles, as in the absent-minded Robert (Hob) Elliott:

> If nobody called him in to dinner, he stayed out. Mrs. Hob, a hard, unsympathetic woman, once tried the experiment. He went without food all day, but at dusk, as the light began to fail him, he came into the house of his own accord, looking puzzled. 'I've had a great gale of prayer upon my speerit', said he. 'I canna mind sae muckle's what I had for denner.'

This sense of humour which animates the whole is never obtrusive yet one is aware of its presence as a counterbalance to the novel's underlying solemnity, as when a local wit asserts that a small religious sect dispensed sacrament 'in the form of hot whisky-toddy'. There can be little doubt that Stevenson possessed an engaging sense of humour: a sense which did not regard Scottish ways and institutions as sacrosanct. One of the many reasons why the reading of *Hermiston* is such a rewarding experience is that it contains an abundance of shrewd commentary on human character; commentary borne of years of reflection on Scottish history and people.

Hermiston is perhaps the supreme example of Stevenson's artistry as a novelist of character. Here more than in any of his other works there is a profound study of thwarted love and ambition in the relationship between an austere father and a dutiful son; there are two fully credible female characters, each drawn with sympathy and insight; and there is a love affair handled with a maturity not previously found in his fiction. There are five principal characters: Adam Weir, the Lord Justice-Clerk; his son, Archie; Kirstie Elliott, housekeeper at the Weirs' country home; Christina Elliott, a young girl to whom Archie is deeply attracted; and Frank Innes, a former college friend of Archie's who ultimately seduces Christina. Each of these possesses a living, flesh and blood quality which could only have been achieved as the result of close observation of human nature.

Adam Weir, based on the life and personality of Robert Mac-Queen, Lord Braxfield (1722–99) a man who had long held a fascination for Stevenson, is a dour, fierce, fanatically hard-working judge, a man with no time for any concern outside the strict confines of the legal profession. 'He sufficed wholly and silently to himself . . . and he went on through life with a mechanical movement, as of the unconscious, that was almost august.' He is a complex man, brilliant, merciless, intolerant, cruel; a man incapable by nature of demonstrating affection; a father who cares deeply for his son and yet cannot openly express compassion. In describing his temperament and attitudes Stevenson is drawing not only on the personality of Braxfield but on that of his own father, Thomas Stevenson, a man for whom he had a lifelong respect and admiration and yet had never fully understood. Thomas Stevenson embodied a rigid Calvinistic brand of Christianity against which Louis had rebelled as a young man; he also symbolised a way of life – that of respectable, orthodox Edinburgh society – which Louis had felt unable to accept. It is not difficult to recognise in Adam Weir a portrait of his father, drawn not with the anger and intolerance of youth but the insight of years of mature reflection.

In depicting the life and personality of Archie Weir, one of his subtlest characterisations, Stevenson drew on his deeply felt memories of himself as a young man on the fringes of respectable Edinburgh society:

> Serious and eager, he came through school and college, and moved among a crowd of the indifferent, in the seclusion of his shyness. He grew up handsome, with an open, speaking countenance, with graceful, youthful ways; he was clever, he took prizes, he shone in the Speculative Society. It should seem he must become the centre of a crowd of friends; but something that was in part the delicacy of his mother, in part the austerity of his father, held him aloof from all.

Archie, a curious mixture of compassion and intransigence, openly rebels against his father by attacking his views on capital punishment. The Justice-Clerk punishes his son by insisting that he should abandon his legal studies and be banished to the family estates at Hermiston. In this pastoral retreat Archie, removed from the pressures and distractions of urban life, withdraws increasingly into his own inner self, becoming at last a recluse. 'Young, graceful, well spoken, but always cold. . . . It was in his horoscope to be parsimonious of pain to himself, or of the chance of pain, even to the avoidance of any opportunity of pleasure.' His life is transformed by his deep emotional attraction for Christina

Elliott, but even here he finds that, such is his upbringing and temperament, he cannot give himself. He remains essentially a solitary man, bound by his own strict conventions of right and wrong. Archie should not be interpreted as a literal self-portrait in the same sense as David Copperfield or Lewisham in H. G. Wells's *Love and Mr. Lewisham*, but should be seen rather as an attempt to portray a young man embodying similar characteristics. The picture is drawn not only with care but with compassion – clearly Stevenson identified with Archie and sympathised with him in his attitude towards his father and Christina – and is all the more convincing for having been drawn with understanding.

Kirstie Elliott, a strong, passionate, warm-hearted woman, is one of his most remarkable creations, and his most successful attempt at portraying a fully-rounded picture of an emotionally unfulfilled mature woman:

Long of limb, and still light of foot, deep-breasted, robust-loined, her golden hair not yet mingled with any trace of silver, the years had not caressed and embellished her. . . . The tender ambitions that she had received at birth had been, by time and disappointment, diverted into a certain barren zeal of industry and fury of interference. She carried her thwarted ardours into housework, she washed floors with her empty heart.

A spinster, yet possessed of a fundamentally warm, kindly nature, she becomes infatuated with Archie and recognises in him an object on which all her suppressed emotions can be focused. The description of the gradual intensification of her feelings towards her young master is one of the most remarkable passages in any of Stevenson's writings, and is expressed with a profound sympathy which enables the reader to identify with her in her thoughts and actions. Kirstie is one of the most solidly drawn figures in the entire range of his fiction, not least because she is depicted 'warts and all'. She is kindly, passionate and devoted; she is also envious, irritable and outspoken. In her strengths and weaknesses she is recognisably a flesh and blood character, created with an empathy borne of close insight.

Christina Elliott, Kirstie's niece, is one of Stevenson's most credible female characterisations. Strong-willed, independent, conscious of her own power, she is deeply desirable to Archie and the two are drawn to one another with an attraction which is both

emotional and intellectual. For him she symbolises all those qualities which he had sought and failed to find in Edinburgh society –
unconventionality, independence of mind, a willingness to express
her own opinion regardless of the views of others. She also
represents his first experience of the female sex and an embodiment of woman as an enigma. The relationship between Christina
and Archie Weir is portrayed with total conviction, from their first
meeting at Hermiston church through their assignations on the
moors, to their last meeting and quarrel at the Weaver's Stone.
There is some evidence that in describing the deepening relationship between the young lovers Stevenson was echoing his own
adolescent romance with the daughter of a family acquaintance at
Buckstane near Edinburgh.[65] Certainly it is clear that in writing
Hermiston his emotions were powerfully engaged and in the
unfolding drama between the serious, proud Archie and the
vivacious Christina there are indications that he was transmuting
into fiction some of the central experiences of his own early
manhood.

Frank Innes, though in the novel's uncompleted state only
partially realised (clearly Stevenson intended to develop the
character further in the succeeding chapters), is presented as a
young Apollo:

> Frank was the very picture of good looks, good-humour, and
> manly youth. He had bright eyes with a sparkle and a dance to
> them, curly hair, a charming smile, brilliant teeth, an admirable
> carriage of the head, the look of a gentleman, the address of
> one accustomed to please at first sight and to improve the
> impression.

He is in fact an embodiment of all those qualities which Archie
does not possess. Where Frank is forthright, Archie is reticent,
where Frank is easy-going, Archie is proud and austere; where
Frank is shallow, Archie is serious. Frank is in a sense Archie's
double, a mirror-image reflecting the converse aspects of his
nature. (An interesting comparison is the relationship between Pip
and Orlick in Dickens's *Great Expectations*[66] or between William
Wilson and his counterpart in Poe's short story of that name.) He
is essential to the action of the story since he provides a reference
point against which Archie's qualities can be measured, and is a
potential rival for the affections of Christina.

Each of these characters, then, has an existence independent of the author's own and possesses a depth rarely equalled in his fiction. Their lifelike quality resides both in themselves and in their interaction with one another. Some of the most memorable scenes in the novel are those in which this interaction is displayed: in the interview between Adam Weir and his son following Archie's denunciation of capital punishment, in the conversations between Archie and Christina, in the uneasy relationship with Frank Innes, in the nocturnal discussion between Archie and Kirstie Elliott. In these and in many of the minor episodes Stevenson confirms his gift for presenting human behaviour in all its diversity and for engaging the reader's compassion and understanding.

Stevenson was pre-eminently a Scottish novelist, not only in the sense that he was born there and frequently wrote of Scottish themes, but in that he had a lifelong fascination for the history, culture and psychology of Scotland. He owed this fascination partly to his childhood nurse, Alison Cunningham ('Cummie'), who had thrilled him with tales of the Covenanters and introduced him to such stirring poems as 'The Cameronian Dream'. This poem, he later confided to Edmund Gosse, 'made the most indelible impression on his fancy, and was the earliest piece of literature which awakened in him the sentiment of romantic Scottish history'.[67] His lifelong preoccupation with the religious, cultural and political history of his homeland — which had previously found expression in such works as *Picturesque Notes on Edinburgh*, *Memoir of Fleeming Jenkin* and the novels *Kidnapped* and *Catriona* — culminated in *Weir of Hermiston*, the fullest statement of his deep emotional attachment to the country of his birth.

Stevenson's awareness of his homeland, in so far as it is possible to define a complex of responses more emotional than intellectual, lay partly in a passionate sense of history which infected all his work, and partly in an intense attachment to the moorlands where he had spent so much of his childhood and youth. The entire novel is imbued with a profound sense of the legacy of the historical past:

For that is the mark of the Scot of all classes: that he stands in an attitude towards the past unthinkable to Englishmen, and remembers and cherishes the memory of his forebears, good or bad; and there burns alive in him a sense of identity with the dead even to the twentieth generation.

This continual awareness of the past, this sense that the actions of our ancestors still impinge on our lives and shape our responses to contemporary situations, runs through the story like a leitmotiv. It is this deeply felt sense of the inheritance of former centuries which pervades the novel and infuses it with a historical consciousness from which stems much of its dramatic power. In essence, the narrator is asserting that we cannot escape from the legacy of the past: that the forces which shaped the spiritual and cultural history of Scotland continue to influence our behaviour and attitudes and will continue to do so. This is made explicit at one point when the narrator observes: 'some Barbarossa, some old Adam of our ancestors, sleeps in all of us till the fit circumstance shall call it into action'. Thus, Archie Weir would not be the man he is without the complex of temperamental and hereditary factors which had moulded his mother and father. Kirstie, in reflecting on her thwarted love for her young master, is saturated in the long history of family feuds which have marked the neighbourhood. Frank Innes, in antagonising his rival and being murdered at the Weaver's Stone, is re-enacting a tragic history of violence and hatred which characterises the lonely hollow.

There is a sense in which Stevenson did not grasp the intensity of his emotional response towards Scotland until he was exiled from it. Just as he did not appreciate the depth of his love for his father until Thomas Stevenson was dead (and as Archie does not realise until after his act of defiance how much he respects the Justice-Clerk), so he could not fully express all that Scotland meant to him until he was permanently divorced from Scottish scenes. In the lyrical descriptions of Lowland scenery − landscapes he had known and loved since childhood − can be discerned the voice of the exile recalling a picture etched irremovably on his mind:

All beyond and about is the great field of the hills; the plover, the curlew, and the lark cry there; the wind blows as it blows in a ship's rigging, hard and cold and pure; and the hill-tops huddle one behind another like a herd of cattle into the sunset. (Ch. 5, 1)

The grey, Quakerish dale was still only awakened in places
and patches from the sobriety of its wintry colouring; and he
wondered at its beauty; an essential beauty of the old earth it
seemed to him, not resident in particulars but breathing to him
from the whole.   (Ch. 6)

Frequently in reading *Hermiston* one is struck by this deep
emotional response towards the landscape. The scenery described
– which is not any particular location but rather a distillation of
the haunts of his youth, including the Lammermuirs, the Pent-
lands and Upper Tweeddale – clearly had for him a profound
emotional significance. In writing of it and seeking to express its
distinctive characteristics he was reliving the scenes of his boyhood and exorcising his yearning to see again the country of his
birth.

An examination of *Weir of Hermiston* as a psychological novel
reveals thematic affinities with *The Master of Ballantrae* and *The Ebb-
Tide* and a development of fundamental themes inseparable from
his fiction. Flowing through the dense pattern of the narrative can
be identified four main themes on which Stevenson builds the
structure of the novel: the incompatibility between father and son;
the conflict between duty and nature; the transformation of love
into a destructive force; and the complexibility and fallibility of
human nature. These strands form a framework of observation
which make the novel as a whole of continuing relevance to the
twentieth century.

The relationship between father and son is handled with rare
assurance, beautifully depicted in the description of the Justice-
Clerk and his son seated at the dining table:

The lamp shone for many hundred days upon these two at table
– my lord ruddy, gloomy, and unreverent; Archie with a potential brightness that was always dimmed and veiled in that
society; and there were not, perhaps, in Christendom two men
more radically strangers.

The phrase 'two men more radically strangers' is a perfect
description of the complex relationship between these two proud,
solitary men and the web of tensions and misunderstandings

which divides them. Each is torn between respect and dislike for the other; each disagrees profoundly with the other's opinions and attitudes yet is drawn towards him by ties of affection he is reluctant to acknowledge. It should be noted that though the dour, puritanical father is seen for the most part through the eyes of his son, there are glimpses of his personality as seen from other points of view – from that of his wife, for example, and his friend Lord Glenalmond. The result is a composite portrait of rare power, a portrait enhanced by the compassion Stevenson brought to its execution. As a young man Stevenson had been well aware that in rebelling against his father's views and against the values of Victorian Edinburgh he remained bound to his father and to the past by ties of emotion and history which could not be severed. The picture of the inflexible Adam Weir and his serious, eager, wayward son is moving in its compassion. Adam, for all his intolerance and brusqueness, is at heart a man who longs to express his emotions; his son, for all his thoughtlessness, is in essence a dutiful young man who regards the Justice-Clerk with mingled feelings of affection, respect and fear. Stevenson, looking back on his own relationship with his father, found that with the passage of time he could describe his tangled emotions with insight and with a renewed understanding of a situation which had once seemed fraught with tensions. In describing the ambivalent relationship between Adam Weir and his son, Stevenson was expressing a series of profound truths concerning human nature and in doing so was creating one of the most vital correlations in our literature.

The conflict between duty and nature is present in each of the dominant tensions of the novel: that between Archie and his father, between Archie and Kirstie, between Archie and Christina, and between Archie and Frank Innes. Thus, Archie decides to abide by his father's injunction to abandon his chosen profession and instead supervise the family estates, though this involves a violation of his natural preferences. Kirstie abandons her hopeless infatuation for him, though this demands a renunciation of her deep-felt emotions. Archie decides that he and Christina must cease their clandestine meetings, though this will involve the end of an association which has given him much happiness. He first befriends then quarrels with Innes, torn between his loyalty to a friend and his inclinations as a recluse. In each situation the character is confronted with a choice between duty and the pursuit of natural inclinations; in each the choice of duty demands a difficult balancing of competing considerations.

The dichotomy is also symbolised in the transference of Archie from Edinburgh to Hermiston. In describing Hermiston Stevenson is careful to depict the sharpest possible contrast between town and country:

Here and there, but at great distances, a byway branches off, and a gaunt farmhouse may be descried above in a fold of the hill; but the more part of the time, the road would be quite empty of passage and the hills of habitation. Hermiston parish is one of the least populous in Scotland. . . . The manse . . . is all the year round in a great silence broken only by the drone of the bees, the tinkle of the burn, and the bell on Sundays.

In the contrast between urban Edinburgh and rural Hermiston, between civilisation and primitiveness, is a symbol of the two aspects of Archie's nature struggling for expression: the one orderly, restrained, conventional; the other passionate, emotional, untamed. This again provides the novel with a tension which animates the narrative and acts as a counterbalance to the dominating personality of the Justice-Clerk.

The manner in which affection can be transformed by frustration or stiflement into a negative and ultimately dangerous emotion is amply demonstrated. Adam Weir loves his sensitive, ardent son yet cannot bring himself to express his feelings openly. Instead he presents an outward crust of aridity: 'To be wholly devoted to some intellectual exercise is to have succeeded in life; and perhaps only in law and the higher mathematics may this devotion be maintained, suffice to itself without reaction, and find continual rewards without excitement.' Adam pays the price of this repression in depriving himself of a potentially rewarding relationship with Archie. His stifled affection finds release in a fanatical devotion to his work, in a fascination with the minutiae of his profession bordering on monomania. Similarly, Kirstie's passion for Archie cannot be openly expressed; it has to be transmuted into slavish dependence, into an absorption with the mechanical routine of domesticity.

Archie's love for Christina is changed first by reticence, then by jealousy; it leads ultimately to the release of violent hatred and the murder of his rival, Frank Innes. In each instance a potentially benevolent force is thwarted and turned back on itself, finding expression on bigotry, waste or violence. One is reminded of the complex relationship between Long John Silver and Jim Hawkins in *Treasure Island*, between Uncle Ebenezer and David Balfour in *Kidnapped*, or between the two brothers in *The Master of Ballantrae*. These situations represent a series of variations on an unchanging theme: that of the limitless potentialities of human emotions and the thin dividing line which separates affection as a life-enhancing force and its expression as jealousy, devotion or anger.

A dominant theme throughout *Hermiston* is the complexity of human character. There is no single personality in the story who succeeds in wholly engaging the reader's sympathy: Adam Weir, forceful and clever though he is, forfeits much of the reader's understanding through his inflexibility and harshness; his son possesses many attractive traits but is fundamentally lacking in moral strength; Kirstie is fundamentally warm-hearted but is also hasty and ill-tempered; Christina, though beautiful and capable of experiencing deep emotion is also proud and self-willed. Each of these characters, then, has strengths and failings. Each follows his or her own impulses and has to live with their consequences. Adam has to live with the knowledge that he has forfeited his son's love and understanding; Archie with the knowledge that he can never express his true feelings towards his father or Christina; Kirstie with the awareness that her life has been wasted, that she can never display her love for Archie; Christina with the reproach that she has betrayed Archie by spurning his love. Again and again in Stevenson's work one senses that one is being presented with varieties of human temperament and behaviour and implicitly challenged to form judgements upon them. In an early chapter when Lord Glenalmond is in conversation with Archie, the learned man asks: 'Is it any less difficult to judge of a good man or a half-good man, than of the worst criminal at the bar? And may not each have relevant excuses?' Continually one is invited to acknowledge the difficulty, if not the impossibility, of forming definitive assessments of human worth, taking into account the infinite complexity of character and the acknowledgement that no one individual is wholly good nor wholly evil. At each stage of the novel one is invited to pass judgement on his characters: Where do the reader's sympathies lie? Is *X* or *Y* right or wrong to behave as he does? What can be said on his behalf? It is this constant probing of motivation and conduct which makes all his fiction, from *Treasure Island* to *Weir of Hermiston*, such a rewarding field of study and a body of work of continuing relevance to the twentieth century. Though *Weir of Hermiston* received on the whole unfavourable reviews – H. G. Wells, then a young critic for the *Saturday Review*, entitled his review 'The Lost Stevenson'[68] and lamented its departure from the pattern of his previous successes – its stature in modern times is increasingly gaining recognition. In its depth of characterisation, its psychological insight and the power of its language and narration, it is widely accepted as his most outstanding achievement, amply fulfilling the promise of the works leading up to it. Had he lived he would undoubtedly have gone on to write other novels and romances, but it may be questioned whether he could have attained the impressive literary and imaginative power of *Hermiston*. He sensed while writing it that it would be his masterpiece. One can only regret that he died before completing the book, at the early age of forty-four and whilst in the full possession of his powers. Yet this regret is tempered by the recognition that in the writing of his last book he was giving expression to his deeply felt convictions regarding the nature of the human condition and the combination of forces which had made him what he was, and that in its creation he gave of his best.

Part V
KEY TO THE CHARACTERS
AND LOCATIONS

Key to the Characters and Locations

This section consists of an alphabetically arranged dictionary of the characters and places having a significant role in the novels and stories. These are, in many cases, described in Stevenson's own words.

The following abbreviations are used throughout:

Arrow	*The Black Arrow*
Ballantrae	*The Master of Ballantrae*
Door	'The Sire de Maletroit's Door'
Ebb-Tide	*The Ebb-Tide*
'Falesa'	'The Beach of Falesa'
'Janet'	'Thrawn Janet'
Jekyll	*The Strange Case of Dr. Jekyll and Mr. Hyde*
'Lodging'	'A Lodging for the Night'
Memories	*Memories and Portraits*
'Misadventures'	'The Misadventures of John Nicholson'
Otto	*Prince Otto*
'Pavilion'	'The Pavilion on the Links'
'Suicide'	'The Suicide Club'
Treasure	*Treasure Island*
Weir	*Weir of Hermiston*
'Will'	'Will o' the Mill'
Wrecker	*The Wrecker*
Wrong Box	*The Wrong Box*

ADMIRAL BENBOW INN   Jim Hawkins's mother and father keep the Admiral Benbow inn, situated on the Devonshire cliffs on the

coast road for Bristol. After the death of his father and the discovery of the treasure map Hawkins is enlisted as cabin-boy
aboard the *Hispaniola* and leaves the inn. His mother stays on to
look after it, with a new boy as an apprentice. *Treasure*

ARBLASTER   Captain and owner of the ship *Good Hope*. He is 'a
long-faced, elderly, weather-beaten man, with a knife hanging
about his neck by a plaited cord, and for all the world like any
modern seaman in his gait and bearing'. Richard Shelton steals
his ship, intending to use it to outmanoeuvre Sir Daniel Brackley, but the scheme fails when the *Good Hope* is wrecked.
Arblaster is ruined by this loss and, when he encounters
Shelton later, seizes the opportunity to hold him prisoner.
Shelton outwits him and escapes. Following the Battle of
Shoreby, in which Arblaster fights on the Lancastrian side, he is
arrested by the victorious Yorkists and threatened with execution. Shelton, pitying him, pleads for his life, expecting grati-
tude for his reprieve. Arblaster refuses to forgive him, adding
'You have played the devil with me, and let that content you.'
Arrow

ATTWATER, WILLIAM JOHN   An Englishman who makes his home
on a remote Pacific island, fishing pearls. 'He was a huge fellow,
six feet four in height, and of a build proportionately strong.'
He had an eye 'of unimpaired health and virility; an eye that bid
you beware of the man's devastating anger'. Outwardly cultivated and urbane, he possesses a domineering and ruthless
personality and will not accept any interference with his
authority. When three strangers arrive uninvited on his island
he greets them warily; unknown to him they plan to murder
him and seize his hoard of pearls. Their attempts to outwit him
fail, however, and in the process one of the three is killed by
Attwater. Herrick, one of the visitors who befriends Attwater,
sums up his character as 'Iron cruelty, an iron insensibility to
the suffering of others, the uncompromising pursuit of his own
interests, cold culture, manners without humanity.' He is motivated in all his actions by a strict moral code which he applies
with undeviating rigour. *Ebb-Tide*

BALFOUR, DAVID   A boy of sixteen, 'the son of a poor country
dominie [schoolmaster] in the Forest of Ettrick', David journeys
to his uncle Ebenezer, of the House of Shaws, in quest of his
inheritance. He is deceived by Ebenezer who arranges for
David to be kidnapped and imprisoned aboard a brig bound for

the Carolinas. When the brig is wrecked off the coast of Mull he succeeds in escaping from his captors and, in company with Alan Breck, he makes his way on foot across Scotland. After many adventures he returns to the House of Shaws and claims his rightful inheritance from his uncle.

Whilst travelling across Scotland with Alan Breck, however, David had witnessed a political assassination and realises that he possesses vital evidence concerning the murder. When an innocent man is arrested for the crime David resolves to make a full confession, though he is aware that this may endanger Alan's safety. David is again kidnapped, this time to prevent his giving evidence at the murder trial, and is held prisoner until the trial is concluded. On his release he journeys to Holland. There he renews his friendship with Catriona Drummond, whom he eventually marries. *Kidnapped* and *Catriona*

BALFOUR, EBENEZER   The uncle of David Balfour. He is 'a mean, stooping, narrow-shouldered, clay-faced creature; and his age might have been anything between fifty and seventy'. David is both repelled and fascinated by his miserly, enigmatic character. When David attempts to claim his rightful inheritance the unscrupulous Ebenezer resolves to deceive his nephew. First he attempts to murder him then, when this fails, he arranges for him to be kidnapped. David succeeds in escaping from his captors and eventually returns to his uncle. Ebenezer realises that his scheming has come to nought and that he has no alternative but to pay to David the monies which are his due. *Kidnapped*

BASS ROCK   An uninhabited rock in the Firth of Forth, two miles off the northern tip of East Lothian. Here David Balfour is held prisoner to prevent him giving evidence at the trial of James Stewart. While on the rock, one of his captors tells him a ghost story, 'The Tale of Tod Lapraik'. David is treated kindly by his guards and has no difficulty in escaping from his confinement. (In August 1877 Stevenson considered the idea of writing an essay entitled 'Three Sea Fortalices' which would include historical and descriptive notes on the Bass Rock.) *Catriona*

BEAULIEU, DENIS DE   A young cavalier in medieval France, he enters by mistake the house of the Sire de Maletroit where he is held prisoner. Maletroit, mistaking his prisoner's identity, confronts Beaulieu with the choice of either agreeing to marry his niece or being hanged. Beaulieu and the girl, Blanche, are then

left to discuss the situation in private. During a lengthy conversation the two are increasingly drawn to one another and at last
declare their love. Maletroit then welcomes him as his new
nephew. 'Door'

BONES, BILLY   The first mate on Captain Flint's pirate ship, *Walrus*.
He was 'a tall, strong, heavy, nut-brown man; his tarry pigtail
falling over the shoulders of his soiled blue coat; his hands
ragged and scarred, with black, broken nails; and the sabre cut
across one cheek, a dirty, livid white'.

After Flint's death at Savannah, Bones is entrusted with a
map showing the location of buried treasure. Pursued by his
former associates, he takes up lodgings at the Admiral Benbow
inn but is tracked down by two of the pirates who demand the
map. Terrified by their ultimatum he dies of apoplexy, leaving
behind him a sea-chest containing his papers. *Treasure*

BRACKLEY, SIR DANIEL   The guardian of Richard Shelton. An
unscrupulous, devious man, he schemes to rob his ward of his
inherited lands. He lures Shelton into Tunstall Moat House
intending to deprive him of his life but the prisoner escapes
through a secret passage. Shelton learns of Sir Daniel's duplicity
in the civil war and determines to expose his treachery. His
determination is increased when he learns that Joanna Sedley,
whom he loves, is held captive by the knight who intends to
offer her in marriage for financial gain. Sir Daniel's schemes fail
when his house is sacked in the Battle of Shoreby and in the
confusion Joanna makes good her escape. Sir Daniel is assassinated by a member of 'The Black Arrow', a band of outlaws who
have vowed to avenge former crimes. *Arrow*

CAREW, SIR DANVERS   A Member of Parliament and respected
public figure who is savagely clubbed to death by Edward Hyde.
The murder is witnessed by a maidservant who gives a description of Hyde to the police. It is this wanton murder and the
ensuing hue and cry which compel the criminal to go into
hiding and is ultimately responsible for his downfall. *Jekyll*

CASE   An unscrupulous white trader in the Pacific islands. 'He
was yellow and smallish, had a hawk's nose to his face, pale
eyes, and his beard trimmed with scissors.' He maintains a
reign of terror over the native population by playing on their
superstitious fear of devils and witchcraft. Wiltshire, who had
initially befriended him, becomes increasingly repelled by his
unscrupulosity and resolves to bring his corrupt practices to an

end. The two meet in the bush and in the ensuing struggle Case is stabbed to death. 'Falesa'

CASSILIS, FRANK   A vagabond who travels through remote regions of England and Scotland for his own pleasure, he resolves to visit his old friend Northmour in his lonely pavilion on the Scottish coast. There he meets Clara Huddlestone, the daughter of a defaulting banker, who is seeking to protect her father and assist him in hiding. Cassilis becomes involved in the web of intrigue and mystery surrounding Northmour and his guests and, as he is increasingly attracted towards Clara, decides to join forces with them. Together with Northmour and Clara he assists in defending the banker against those pursuing him but Mr. Huddlestone is cornered and shot by Italian agents. After his death Cassilis and Clara are married. 'Pavilion'

CRABTREE, SIR JOHN   An English traveller who decides to make a study of the various courts of Europe. While visiting Grunewald in connection with his researches he is arrested on suspicion of espionage. Prince Otto reads the manuscript of his account of the Grunewald court and is uncomfortably aware of the truth of many of his observations. It is Crabtree's frank but shrewd report which forces Otto to grasp his own shortcomings and the seriousness of his predicament as the potential victim of a conspiracy. Indignant yet grateful to the baronet, the Prince orders his release from imprisonment. *Otto*

DASS, SECUNDRA   An Indian who befriends James Durie. He was 'of an extraordinarily delicate appearance, with legs like walking canes and fingers like the stalk of a tobacco pipe.' He attaches himself to James with dog-like fidelity, accompanying him on his journeys to Scotland and to the United States. His knowledge of English proves to be invaluable to his master, for it is he who discovers the address where James's brother, Henry, is in hiding in New York. When James, in quest of buried treasure, realises that he is in danger of his life at the hands of his scheming accomplices, he enlists Secundra's help in faking his own death. The attempt fails, and James is buried alive. *Ballantrae*

DAVIS, JOHN   Former captain of the American barque *Sea Ranger* he adopts the pseudonym 'Captain Brown' and lives on the island of Tahiti while in search of employment. When an opportunity arises to take a cargo of champagne by schooner to Sydney he eagerly accepts the invitation, secretly scheming to sail the ship to Peru and sell it together with its cargo. The plan goes awry when the schooner sails off course and he and his two companions, Herrick and Huish, reach a rarely visited island inhabited by an autocratic English pearl fisher, Attwater. Davis grasps that the island is a potential source of wealth and that Attwater has accumulated a valuable hoard of pearls. He resolves to murder the pearl fisher and plunder his treasure but their attempts to circumvent the Englishman end in failure. Davis is attracted by Attwater's strict, evangelistic Christianity and decides to remain on the island, solacing himself with prayer and penitence for his past crimes. *Ebb-Tide*

DODD, LOUDON   Son of an American father and a Scottish mother, he is an artistic, shy young man who travels from Edinburgh to Paris to study sculpture. There he encounters a brash young American, James Pinkerton, and is immediately attracted by his energy and confidence. Dodd joins Pinkerton in San Francisco and when his friend decides to bid for the wreck of the *Flying Scud*, convinced that the ship carries a hidden cargo of opium, readily falls in with his plans. He travels to Midway Island in search of the wreck but finds that the value of the cargo is far below Pinkerton's expectations. Dodd realises he has stumbled on a mystery, since it is clear that the original crew of the *Flying Scud* have disappeared; he devotes himself to the task of solving the riddle. *Wrecker*

DRUMMOND, CATRIONA   Daughter of James More Drummond (or Macgregor) and grand-daughter of Rob Roy. A courageous, sensitive woman, she is attracted towards the young David Balfour. Despite the fact that she is a Highlander and a Jacobite, and David is a Lowlander and a Whig, they are increasingly drawn towards one another. She assists her treacherous father to escape from prison but when he deserts her David chival-rously acts as her protector; the two fall in love and eventually marry. Two children are born of the marriage, Barbara and Alan. *Catriona*

DRUMMOND, JAMES MORE   Father of Catriona and third son of Rob Roy. A brave but deceitful man, he is held prisoner in Edinburgh Castle pending his trial for political offences. He succeeds in escaping from the Castle and makes his way to France, where he pretends to be a supporter of the Jacobite Alan Breck. In reality, however, Drummond is acting as an agent for the Hanoverian Government and seeks to trap Alan and deliver him to England; this attempt fails due to Alan's skill in outwitting him. Summing up James's character, David concludes: 'To me ... he was as plain as print; I saw him to be perfectly selfish, with a perfect innocency in the same. ... I think he was so false all through that he scarce knew when he was lying'. *Catriona*

DURIE, ALISON *(formerly Graeme)* Wife of Henry Durie. An orphan, 'and the heir to a considerable fortune which her father had acquired in trade', she is brought up on the Durrisdeer estate in the expectation that she will marry the heir to the estate, James Durie. When James is reported to have been killed at the battle of Culloden, she marries his younger brother, Henry, and has two children by him, Alexander and Katharine. She never loses her affection for James, however, and when he reappears she is openly attracted to him. Alison accompanies Henry to New York when the latter takes up his abode there. *Ballantrae*

DURIE, HENRY Younger son of Lord Durrisdeer and Ballantrae. A quiet, patient, scrupulous man, he is 'a tall dark young gentleman ... of a plain and not cheerful face, very strong in body, but not so strong in health'. The lifelong antagonism between Henry and his elder brother, James, forms the substance of *Ballantrae*. (*See* DURIE, JAMES)

DURIE, JAMES Elder son of Lord Durrisdeer and Ballantrae. Styling himself 'The Master of Ballantrae', James has 'a very handsome figure and countenance, swarthy, lean, long, and a quick, alert, black look, as of one who was a fighter, and accustomed to command'. His strong personality, unscrupulosity and demonic nature are in the strongest contrast to the gentleness and passivity of his brother. During the Jacobite rebellion of 1745 James decides to support the pretender Prince Charles, whilst his younger brother Henry remains at home, loyal to King George. The antagonism between the two brothers is strengthened when Henry marries Alison Graeme (who in reality is deeply attracted towards James), James meanwhile having been presumed killed at the battle of Culloden.

After many wanderings abroad James returns to the ancestral home, goading his brother and demanding money. After an argument Henry challenges James to a duel in the course of which James is severely wounded. He recovers from the wound and succeeds in escaping from the vicinity, only to return a second time to continue his persecution of Henry. Unable to endure the constant goading, Henry leaves for a secret destination in the United States, where he hopes to start a new life in peace; James discovers his brother's whereabouts and sets off in pursuit. Henry is now consumed with anger and a desire to humiliate his brother. James leaves in quest of a treasure he had secreted some years previously in the Adirondack mountains; Henry follows him, determined on revenge. James, realising his accomplices are secretly plotting to murder him and steal the treasure, attempts to escape by faking his own death. When his Indian servant tries too late to resuscitate the body his momentary return to life so frightens Henry that the younger brother dies of shock. The two brothers are buried in the same grave. *Ballantrae*

DURRISDEER, LORD   The father of James and Henry Durie. 'He suffered prematurely from the disabilities of age; his place was at the chimney-side; there he sat reading, in a lined gown, with few words for any man, and wry words for none ... yet his mind very well nourished with study, and reputed in the country to be more cunning than he seemed.' A shrewd, kindly bookish man, he is devoted to his two sons, especially to James. His death is hastened by the deep antagonism between the brothers. On his demise Henry adopts the title. *Ballantrae*

EARRAID   A small tidal islet off the western tip of Mull, near Iona, the scene of David Balfour's adventures in Chapter 14 of *Kidnapped*. The island is also the location of the short story 'The Merry Men'. Stevenson first visited Earraid in August 1870 to observe the construction of the Dhu Heartach lighthouse. See his essay 'Memoirs of an Islet' in *Memories*

EDINBURGH   Stevenson lived at 8 Howard Place, Edinburgh, from 1850–3; at 1 Inverleith Terrace from 1853–7; and at 17 Heriot Row from 1857–75. The Edinburgh Academy, which he attended intermittently as a boy, was situated on Henderson Row and Mr. Robert Thomson's school, where he was a pupil from 1864–7, was in Frederick Street. The old buildings of Edinburgh University where he read for the Bar and was a member of the Speculative Society are in South Bridge.

Edinburgh figures prominently in a number of his stories including most notably 'Misadventures', *St. Ives*, and *Weir*.

ELLIOTT, CHRISTINA   Niece of Kirstie Elliott. An attractive though proud and self-willed girl, she is drawn towards the young lord of the manor, Archie Weir, flattered when he pays her attentions. The relationship between the two deepens in a series of secret meetings at the Weaver's Stone but she is angered when Archie insists the meetings should cease for fear of scandal. (*See* WEIR, ARCHIE)

ELLIOTT, KIRSTIE   Housekeeper to Archie Weir on the Hermiston estates. 'Long of limb, and still light of foot, deep-breasted, robust-loined, her golden hair had not yet mingled with any trace of silver, the years had but caressed and embellished her.' Though an attractive woman she has never married and devotes her energies to the meticulous pursuit of her domestic duties. When Archie arrives at Hermiston as lord of the manor she is deeply attracted to him and tries to warn him against secret meetings with Christina. *Weir*

ENFIELD, RICHARD   A close friend and cousin of Utterson, Henry Jekyll's lawyer. It is Enfield who, while on one of his Sunday rambles about London with Utterson, relates to his friend the story of his encounter with the mysterious Edward Hyde. Hyde, threatened with exposure for his wanton assault on a child, placates Enfield by handing him a cheque for £100. Enfield notices that the signature on the cheque is that of Henry Jekyll, thus establishing some strange connection between the two men. *Jekyll*

FALESA (Tahiti)   An island in the South Pacific on which the trader John Wiltshire decides to make his home. 'Falesa might have been Fidler's Green, if there is such a place, and more's the pity if there isn't! It was good to foot the grass, to look aloft at the green mountains, to see the men with their green wreaths and the women in their bright dresses, red and blue.' 'Falesa'

FELIPE   Brother of Olalla. He is 'a diminutive, loutish, well-made country lad ... but devoid of any culture'. When a wounded officer comes to convalesce in the household of Felipe's mother the soldier is both attracted and puzzled by his mind, which is at once innocent and devious. The soldier finds Felipe in the act of torturing a squirrel; he is made to apologise and thereafter adopts an attitude of 'dog-like, adoring fidelity'. 'Olalla'

FINSBURY, JOSEPH   One of the two last survivors of the Finsbury tontine. He is a boring, methodical man, much given to tedious explanations of factual matters. When he is presumed to have died in a railway accident his nephews, Morris and John, attempt to conceal the body since they fear that otherwise they will not inherit the tontine. It subsequently becomes clear that Joseph did not perish in the accident and that the body concealed by the nephews was that of a total stranger. *Wrong Box*

FINSBURY, MASTERMAN   Brother of Joseph and one of the two last survivors of the Finsbury tontine. Masterman had led 'a model British life. Industry, regularity, respectability, and a preference for the four per cents are understood to be the very foundations of a green old age.' In advanced old age his mind fails; his nephews, Morris and John, suspect that he is dead but that his son has concealed the death in order to defraud them of the tontine. *Wrong Box*

FINSBURY, MICHAEL   Son of Masterman Finsbury. A lawyer by profession, he becomes enmeshed in a series of misunderstandings caused by an attempt to conceal a body which is believed to be that of Joseph, Masterman's brother. Michael succeeds in unravelling the legal complexities involved and apportions the tontine to the satisfaction of all concerned. *Wrong Box*.

FLORIZEL (*alias Theophilus Godall*)   Prince of Bohemia, 'formerly one of the magnates of Europe, now dethroned, exiled, impoverished, and embarked in the tobacco trade'. An adventurous, eccentric man, he has a taste for adopting disguises in order to sample a wide range of experiences. He is the proprietor of the Bohemian Cigar Divan in Rupert Street, Soho. 'Suicide' and *The Dynamiter*

GILCHRIST, FLORA   A young Scotswoman, 'about eighteen or nineteen, tall, of a gallant carriage, and with a profusion of hair in which the sun found threads of gold'. While visiting Edinburgh Castle she is attracted towards a French prisoner of war and reveals her address to him. When the Frenchman succeeds in escaping from the castle he goes into hiding in her home and she and her aunt assist him in his plans to journey to England. At length the prisoner returns to Edinburgh, a free man, declares his love for Flora and marries her. *St. Ives*

GLOUCESTER, DUKE OF   Son of Richard, Duke of York. When Richard Shelton first meets him the Duke (later King Richard III) is a young man 'slightly deformed, with one shoulder higher than the other, and of a pale, painful and distorted countenance'. Shelton is deeply impressed with his courage and shrewdness and soon has a marked respect for his qualities of ruthlessness and tenacity. The Duke knights Shelton because of his bravery during the Battle of Shoreby. *Arrow*

GODALL, THEOPHILUS: *See* FLORIZEL

GONDREMARK, BARON HEINRICH   Prime Minister of Grunewald,

'Heavily and somewhat clumsily built, of a vast, disjointed, rambling frame ... his face was marked by capacity, temper and a kind of bold, piratical dishonesty which it would be calumnious to call deceit.' An ambitious, cunning man, he schemes with the Princess Seraphina for the overthrow of Prince Otto and the declaration of a republic. Aware of Otto's neglect of his royal duties he increasingly usurps the Prince's powers and plans to declare war on the country's neighbours to further his own designs. Gondremark's schemes are temporarily thwarted when Otto vigorously reasserts his powers, but the Baron plans successfully to have the Prince abducted. He is stabbed by the Princess during an argument and is nursed back to health by his lover, Countess Rosen. *Otto*

GRADEN EASTER   A remote part of the Scottish coast, composed largely of sandhills and quicksands. Here the recluse Northmour makes his home in a pavilion of Italian design. (The location is believed to be Dirleton in East Lothian, between Tantallon and Gullane, a district familiar to Stevenson from boyhood.) 'Pavilion'

GRANT, SIR WILLIAM (PRESTONGRANGE)   Lord Advocate for Scotland. A handsome, shrewd and strong man, he listens to David Balfour's evidence concerning the murder of Captain Colin Campbell of Glenure but realises that on political grounds the testimony must be suppressed. David in his innocence fails to grasp that at the trial of a Stewart in Campbell territory before a Campbell jury any evidence which casts doubt on the accused man's guilt could not be tolerated. Grant arranges for David to be kidnapped and held incommunicado until the trial is concluded, by which time his evidence will be too late. Despite this, David respects Grant for his human qualities and concludes that 'he was at once far more sincere, and a far more artful performer, that I supposed'. *Catriona*

GRÜNEWALD   An independent East European principality, 'an infinitesimal member of the German Empire'. The reigning Prince, Otto, is neglectful of his royal duties and permits power to fall increasingly into the hands of the Prime Minister, Gondremark, and the court. Gondremark is ultimately successful in usurping the Prince and declaring a republic. Many years later the map of Europe is redrawn and the tiny state 'vanished like a morning ghost'. *Otto*

GUNN, BEN   A member of the crew of Flint's ship *Walrus*, he is marooned for three years on Treasure Island and sees no human being during that period. He lives on goats, berries and oysters and dreams of cheese – 'toasted, mostly'. He is dis-covered by Jim Hawkins running wild on the island and dressed in rags: 'Of all the beggar-men that I had seen or fancied, he was the chief for raggedness.' He befriends Hawkins and plays a leading part in thwarting the designs of Long John Silver and his accomplices. On returning to England he becomes a lodge-keeper and is 'a notable singer in church on Sundays and saints days'. *Treasure*

HANDS, ISRAEL Coxswain aboard the *Hispaniola*, 'a careful, wily, old, experienced seaman' and a confidant of Long John Silver. While Silver and his men are on the island seeking the treasure believed to be buried there, Hands is entrusted with the care of the ship. He becomes drunk on rum and the schooner sails out of control. Jim Hawkins succeeds in reaching the *Hispaniola* in a coracle, defeats Hand's attempt to murder him, and retrieves the ship for his friends. *Treasure*

HAWAII The setting of two short stories, 'The Bottle Imp' and 'The Isle of Voices'. Stevenson knew the islands well and visited them on a number of occasions during his South Sea cruises.

HAWKINS, JIM The narrator of *Treasure Island*. His father is the landlord of the Admiral Benbow inn where Billy Bones, who had served as a pirate under Captain Flint, takes up lodgings. After Bones's death a treasure map is found among his papers and Hawkins becomes cabin-boy on the *Hispaniola*, the schooner which sets sail in quest of the island. The boy is instru-mental in uncovering an attempted mutiny and in exposing the duplicity of Long John Silver. After many adventures, in which he contrives to play a leading role – displaying both courage and initiative – he and his companions defeat the mutineers and return to England with the bulk of the treasure. He is deter-mined, however, never to return in quest of the remaining silver: 'Oxen and wain-ropes would not bring me back again to that accursed island.' *Treasure*

HERRICK, ROBERT A former Oxford graduate with a penchant for Virgil, he is stranded on Tahiti without money or employment. 'With all his talent and taste (and he had much of both) Robert was deficient in consistency and intellectual manhood.' He befriends John Davis, an American sea captain, and accepts his invitation to join forces with him and Huish in a voyage aboard a schooner carrying a cargo of champagne. Davis schemes to steal the ship together with its cargo but his plan goes awry when the schooner sails badly off course. When the ship reaches a remote island inhabited by a cultivated Englishman, Attwater, Herrick is both fascinated and repelled by his personality. His colleagues plan to murder the Englishman but Herrick, after much reflection, decides that he cannot support them in their scheme. After seriously contemplating suicide he approaches Attwater alone and begs to be allowed to stay with him. *Ebb-Tide*

HOSEASON, ELIAS   Captain of the brig *Covenant*. 'He wore a thick sea-jacket, buttoned to the neck, and a tall hairy cap drawn down over his ears; yet I never saw any man, not even a judge upon the bench, look cooler, or more studious and self-possessed, than this ship-captain.' Hoseason is persuaded by the unscrupulous Ebenezer Balfour to kidnap David Balfour aboard the brig and transport him to the Carolinas. When Alan Breck, a notorious Highland Jacobite, is also taken aboard, Hoseason devises a plot to overpower Alan and steal his money. David acquaints Alan of the captain's perfidy and together they succeed in outwitting the captain and his crew. Hoseason, realising that he is no match for Alan's skill as a swordsman, displays shrewdness and realism in bargaining for terms. The attempt to kidnap David fails when the brig is wrecked off the coast of Mull. David derives from Ransome, the cabin-boy, an impression of Hoseason's roughness and brutality but concludes that the captain is not so evil a character as he has been led to believe. 'But indeed, he was neither so good as I supposed him, nor quite so bad as Ransome did; for, in fact, he was two men, and left the better one behind as soon as he set foot on board his vessel.' *Kidnapped*

HOUSTON, ALAN   An old friend of John Nicholson. When John calls at his house at Murrayfield, pleading for shelter, he finds Houston in a state of nervous tension and reluctant to admit him. The following morning John discovers the body of a murdered man in the house and no sign of Houston. Later Houston is committed to an asylum, having been certified insane. 'Misadventures'

HUDDLESTONE, BERNARD   A private banker who adopts criminal expedients in order to extricate himself from his disordered affairs. 'He had a long and sallow countenance, surrounded by a long red beard and side whiskers. His broken nose and high cheekbones gave him somewhat the air of a Kalmuck.' Fearing an attempt on his life by those he has defrauded, Huddlestone goes into hiding in a remote house in Scotland, intending ultimately to escape to the South Pacific. He is followed by Italian agents intent on revenge; his pursuers locate his hiding place and set fire to the house. The banker realises that he cannot escape and is shot dead outside the burning building. 'Pavilion'

HUDDLESTONE, CLARA Daughter of Bernard Huddlestone, a defaulting banker. 'She had a firm yet airy motion of the body, and carried her head with unimaginable grace; every step was a thing to look at, and she seemed in my eyes to breathe sweetness and distinction.' Desperately seeking for some means of protecting her father from his pursuers, she meets Northmour, a recluse living in a remote part of the Scottish coast, and accepts his offer to keep her father in hiding. The attempt fails and the banker is murdered by Italian agents. Clara then marries Frank Cassilis, an old friend of Northmour. 'Pavilion'

HUISH, J. L. A Cockney clerk who is stranded without money on the island of Tahiti. He had 'alienated all his old employers so that they passed him in the street as if he were a dog, and all his old comrades so that they shunned him as they would a creditor'. A shiftless, unreliable character, he befriends two other outcasts, Davis and Herrick, and together they commandeer a schooner, intending to sell the ship together with its cargo of champagne. The schooner sails off course and lands on a remote Pacific island inhabited by an exiled Englishman, Attwater. The outcasts scheme to murder Attwater and steal his hoard of pearls but he proves to be a more formidable adversary than they had anticipated. When all attempts to outwit him have failed Huish volunteers to approach close to him under the pretext of a parley and then maim him by throwing vitriol. Attwater sees through the plan before Huish has a chance to throw the acid and the Cockney is shot dead. *Ebb-Tide*

HYDE, EDWARD Edward Hyde was 'pale and dwarfish, he gave an impression of deformity without any namable malformation he had a displeasing smile ... and he spoke with a·husky whispering, and somewhat broken voice'. For many years this strange man is regarded simply as the friend and benefactor of Henry Jekyll, a distinguished doctor. That there is a mysterious connection between the two is known from the fact that Jekyll has prepared a will providing that, in the event of his own death, all his possessions are to pass to Hyde. Hyde's odd behaviour and unpleasant manner inspire all who encounter him with feelings of repugnance. At last he commits a brutal murder and is hunted by the police, whereupon he inexplicably vanishes from his home. It transpires that Jekyll has been experimenting with drugs in an attempt to separate the good and evil elements compounded in human nature and that Hyde is the personification of his own evil self. Jekyll, possessed increasingly by Hyde's wickedness and weary of the crimes committed under his influence, is cornered in his laboratory by his friends and commits suicide in order to put an end to him. *Jekyll*

INNES, FRANK   The son of a Morayshire laird, he befriends Archie Weir whilst a college student. 'The two handsome lads followed the same course of study and recreation, and felt a certain mutual attraction, founded mainly on good looks.' Innes's father later falls on hard times and is arrested for debt. Frank flees from the family disgrace and travels to Hermiston to join his old friend. When he learns that Archie is in love with an attractive girl, Christina, he teases him with the fact. Archie attempts to discontinue his secret meetings with Christina for fear of provoking a scandal; Innes, learning of this, woos the girl and seduces her. (The novel is left uncompleted. Innes was to have been killed by Archie after a quarrel. Archie is then arrested and condemned to death for the murder.) *Weir*

JEKYLL, DR. HENRY   A distinguished doctor and lawyer, he is described at the outset of the story as 'a large, well-made, smooth-faced man of fifty, with something of a slyish cast, perhaps, but every mark of capacity and kindness'. Born with excellent prospects in life and industrious by nature he becomes fascinated by the duality of man and has been committed for many years to 'a profound duplicity of life'. He discovers that by administering certain drugs it is possible to separate the good and evil elements within his own nature; he tries this experiment repeatedly, becoming more and more fascinated by the evil personality thus released, whom he names Edward Hyde. The selfishness and amorality of Hyde both fascinates and repels him and increasingly possesses his own character. At last, in the guise of Hyde, he commits a brutal murder and resolves to cease his experiments forthwith. However, his supply of the drug has come to an end and he is unable to achieve the transformation from Hyde to Jekyll. He is trapped in his laboratory and commits suicide, leaving behind him a written confession of his experiments and crimes. *Jekyll*

LANYON, DR. HASTIE   An old friend of Henry Jekyll. He is 'a hearty, healthy, dapper, red-faced gentleman, with a shock of hair prematurely white, and a boisterous and decided manner.' He was at school and college with Utterson, Jekyll's lawyer; thus, the two of them have a common interest in Jekyll and meet frequently to discuss the increasingly odd behaviour of their friend. After a sudden shock Dr. Lanyon sickens and dies, leaving with Utterson a long written statement. This reveals that on one occasion, at Jekyll's earnest request, he was instrumental in procuring for Edward Hyde a supply of powders from Jekyll's laboratory. Hyde drinks the potion in Lanyon's presence and is immediately metamorphosed into Henry Jekyll. Lanyon is the only person to actually witness this transformation and his narrative forms an essential element in establishing the true relationship between Hyde and Jekyll. *Jekyll*

LEYDEN   A town in Holland, the setting of the final chapters of *Catriona*. Here David Balfour settles in order to study law; he is distracted by the close physical proximity of Catriona Drummond, with whom he has fallen in love and who is staying in the same lodgings. He protects her in the absence of her father and, despite misunderstandings borne of David's shyness and innocence, the two agree to marry.

LIVESEY, DR. DAVID   The family physician and magistrate who attends Jim Hawkins's mother and father at the Admiral Benbow inn. He is described as a neat, bright man, 'with his powder as white as snow, and his bright, black eyes and pleasant manners'. When a map is discovered showing the location of buried treasure Livesey agrees to give up his practice and become ship's doctor aboard the schooner *Hispaniola*, which sets sail from Bristol in quest of the treasure. When the ship eventually returns to England he and Squire Trelawney request Jim Hawkins to 'write down the whole particulars about Treasure Island, from the beginning to the end'; the doctor himself contributes three chapters to the resulting narrative. *Treasure*

MACKELLAR, EPHRAIM   Narrator of *Ballantrae*. For nearly forty years land steward on the estate of Lord Durrisdeer, Mackellar is a dour, unemotional Scot who is devoted to the younger of the two brothers, Henry Durie. He compiles a narrative recounting the tragic story of the enmity between the Durie brothers, consisting partly of his own reminiscences and partly of letters and memoirs written by others.

MALETROIT, ALAIN (SIRE)   A nobleman in medieval France. Denis de Beaulieu, a young cavalier, enters his house by mistake and finds he is trapped in Maletroit's apartment. The nobleman, mistaking his prisoner for a captain who has been paying court to his niece, Blanche, insists that Beaulieu should agree to marry her or forfeit his life. Beaulieu and the girl are then left alone to talk over the situation. In the course of a long conversation, in which they sound out their respective personalities and attitudes to life, the two realise a mutual attraction and agree to marry. 'Door'

MARKHEIM   Posing as a customer wishing to purchase a Christmas present for a lady, Markheim visits an antique dealer when the latter is alone in his shop, secretly scheming to murder him. When the dealer's attention is distracted Markheim stabs him and commences a search of the premises, intending to rob the old man of his wealth. While he is searching and before he has had an opportunity to conceal the body a stranger enters the house and engages Markheim in conversation. The stranger reviews the murderer's past life and attempts to persuade him to murder the maid also. Markheim rejects this counsel and confesses his crime to the maid. 'Markheim'

McCLOUR, JANET   Housekeeper to Murdoch Soulis. As a young woman she has a child by a passing dragoon; because of this indiscretion she is ridiculed and threatened as an outcast. In later life her isolation and ostracism leads to a widespread belief that she is 'thrawn' [twisted, perverse]. She is persecuted by the villagers who are convinced that she is a witch. 'Janet' (*See also* the unfinished novel *Heathercat*)

MIDWAY ISLAND   An island in the Pacific Ocean on which the British brig *Flying Scud* is wrecked. It consists of a ring of coral reef over which 'innumerable as maggots, there hovered, chattered, screamed, and clanged, millions of twinkling sea birds'. Loudon Dodd and his party spend several days on the island dismantling the wreck in search of the hidden cargo of opium which they suspect it contains. *Wrecker*

MURRAYFIELD   A suburb of Edinburgh, in Stevenson's time largely rural, the home of his schoolfriend H. B. Baildon. Stevenson described Baildon's house, 'Duncliffe' in the account of 'The Lodge' in Chapter 6 of 'Misadventures'

NARES, CAPTAIN   Captain of the *Norah Creina*, in which Loudon Dodd sails to Midway Island in quest of the wreck of the *Flying Scud*. He was 'a powerful, active man ... a quick observer, a close reasoner; when he pleased, of a really elegant address; and when he chose, the greatest brute upon the seas'. He earns the respect of Dodd and his crew because of his firmness and his skill as a seaman. When Dodd realises that the wreck is almost valueless and that as a result the expedition has been in vain, Nares displays tact and shrewdness in helping him to extricate himself from a difficult situation. *Wrecker*

NICHOLSON, JOHN VAREY   Eldest son of a puritanical Edinburgh lawyer. 'He was of a fat habit, even from boyhood, and inclined to a cheerful and cursory reading of the face of life; and possibly this attitude of mind was the original cause of his misfortunes.' A well-meaning though naïve young man, he is the victim of a series of mishaps culminating in the robbery of a sum of money with which he had been entrusted. Unable to face the opprobrium of his employers and of respectable society he flees to America and finds work as a bank clerk. Ten years later he returns to Edinburgh, now a rich man. He again becomes involved in a series of misadventures but at last makes a full confession to his father and is welcomed home as a prodigal son. 'Misadventures'

NICHOLSON, MR.   A strict Edinburgh lawyer, father of three children. A dour, unemotional man, he maintains an upright home founded on religious intolerance and propriety. His eldest son, John, affectionate and impulsive, studies law in his office. When John becomes involved in a series of unlucky accidents Mr. Nicholson views with extreme disfavour the mounting evidence of his son's foolishness. Fearing a scandal and further strictures from his father, John steals some of his money and flees from the house. Years later, having in the meantime become a wealthy man, John returns home and asks his father for forgiveness. Mr. Nicholson grudgingly concedes that he has judged hastily and extends the hand of reconciliation. 'Misadventures'

NORTHMOUR   A misanthrope who inhabits a pavilion situated in a remote part of the Scottish coast. At university he befriends Frank Cassilis and the two spend some months staying in the pavilion. 'It was scarcely a companionship, but a co-existence in unsociability.' Due to Northmour's violent temper the relationship is an uneasy one; finally there is a quarrel and Cassilis departs. Nine years later Cassilis revisits the area and becomes involved in a web of intrigue surrounding his old friend. It emerges that a hunted man and his daughter are being kept in hiding in the pavilion; Northmour has agreed to assist them since he is deeply attracted towards the daughter, Clara. The attempt to conceal her father fails and he is cornered and killed by his pursuers. Northmour and Cassilis, who have mistrusted each other throughout, continue their disagreements. Finally Northmour accepts that Clara has fallen in love with Cassilis. He enlists as a soldier and is killed years later in the Tyrol. 'Pavilion'

OLALLA   Sister of Felipe and daughter of the senora of a remote Spanish residencia. When a wounded soldier arrives at the residencia for a convalescence he is immediately attracted to Olalla because of her great beauty and enigmatic charm: 'in her eyes, that hung upon mine, I could read depth beyond depth of passion and sadness, lights of poetry and hope, blacknesses of despair, and thoughts that were above the earth'. Bewitched by her strange ways and mysterious quality, the soldier increasingly seeks her company but is aware of the deep cultural differences which separate them. Repelled by the atavism of the family — her mother has tendencies towards vampirism, while Felipe takes pleasure in torturing animals — he pleads with Olalla to marry him, but when she rejects his offer he reluctantly returns to his former life. 'Olalla'

OTTO, PRINCE JOHANN FRIEDRICH   Prince of Grünewald, a principality of the German empire. 'He is not ill-looking; he has hair of a ruddy gold, which naturally curls, and his eyes are dark . . . his features are irregular, but pleasing; the nose perhaps a little short, and the mouth a little womanish; his address is excellent, and he can express himself with point.' An ineffectual Prince, neglectful of his duties, he occupies his time in hunting and travelling, bored by the intricacies of court life. While journeying incognito he learns accidentally of the contempt with which the court is regarded by his subjects and hastens back to his palace, suspecting a plot to usurp the monarchy. Aware that he has allowed many of his powers to lapse through disuse, he vigorously reasserts himself and countermands a number of decisions taken in his absence. Gondremark, the Prime Minister, is determined to overthrow the Prince and schemes to have him abducted and forced into exile. The Princess, temporarily estranged from her husband, falls in with Gondremark's plans. When Otto is in exile, however, the Princess realises the true depth of her love for him and the two are reunited. *Otto*

PARIS   Stevenson lived in lodgings in Paris at various periods between 1874–5, living as cheaply as possible whilst writing articles for magazines. His impressions of life in the artists' quarter of the city are recorded in the early chapters of *Wrecker*.

PINKERTON, JAMES   A self-educated man, brought up in America (though of English ancestry), he is 'a man of a good stature, a very lively face, cordial, agitated manners, and a grey eye as active as a fowl's'. While in Paris in pursuit of his artistic ambitions he encounters Loudon Dodd and immediately befriends him. Dodd is deeply impressed with his courage and energy and joins Pinkerton in America. When Pinkerton learns that the wreck of the British brig *Flying Scud* is for sale he becomes convinced that the ship contains opium and purchases it for an enormous sum with the aid of loans. The wreck proves to be almost worthless and he is ruined. Later he rebuilds his life and becomes a successful businessman. *Wrecker*

POOLE   The elderly and devoted servant of Henry Jekyll. Poole has served his master for twenty years but becomes increasingly disturbed by Jekyll's unaccountable behaviour and by the trust which he confides in Edward Hyde, who has access at all times to Jekyll's house. At last he can contain his fears and suspicions no longer and implores Utterson, Jekyll's lawyer, to assist him in arriving at the truth. Together they break into the laboratory at the instant that Jekyll/Hyde commits suicide. *Jekyll*

PRESTONGRANGE: *See* GRANT, SIR WILLIAM

QUEENSFERRY   A town in West Lothian, on the south bank of the Firth of Forth. At the Hawes Inn at Queensferry (which still exists) David Balfour meets Hoseason, Captain of the brig *Covenant*. From here David is lured aboard the ship and kidnapped. After many adventures he succeeds in making his way across Scotland and eventually returns to Queensferry, where he calls on the solicitor Mr. Rankeillor and claims his inheritance. *Kidnapped*

RANKEILLOR, MR.   Lawyer to Ebenezer Balfour. He is 'a shrewd, ruddy, kindly, consequential man in a well-powdered wig and spectacles'. When David Balfour returns to Queensferry after the abortive attempt to kidnap him, he meets Rankeillor and tells him the full story of his adventures and of his uncle's deceit in seeking to deprive him of his inheritance. The lawyer, having satisfied himself of the genuineness of David's legal claims, accompanies David to the House of Shaws where Ebenezer is confronted and tricked into making a confession. *Kidnapped*

ROSEN, COUNTESS ANNA   A member of the court of Grünewald and mistress of Gondremark, the Prime Minister. She is 'tall, slim as a nymph, and of a very airy carriage; and her face, which was already beautiful in repose, lightened and changed, flashed into smiles, and glowed with lovely colour at the touch of animation'. She is secretly in love with Prince Otto and, while pretending to fall in with Gondremark's schemes to overthrow the Prince, acquaints Otto with the plot to abduct him. After the declaration of the republic she realises that her true loyalties lie with Gondremark and is reunited with him. *Otto*

ST. IVES, VISCOUNT ANNE (*alias* CHAMPDIVERS)   A French prisoner of war who is held captive in Edinburgh Castle. After killing a fellow prisoner in a duel he succeeds in escaping from the Castle and goes into hiding, assisted by the woman he loves, Flora Gilchrist. He determines to make his way to his uncle in Bedfordshire, masquerading as an Englishman, but is pursued by followers intent on his recapture. After many adventures he is successful in outwitting his pursuers and in clearing his name of the charge of murder. He returns to Edinburgh to marry Flora and settles in England with her. *St. Ives*

SAN FRANCISCO   Stevenson lived in lodgings in San Francisco from December 1879–May 1880, living as frugally as possible whilst earning a precarious living from journalism. His impressions of the city and its picturesque waterfront are recorded in the early chapters of *Wrecker*.

SEDLEY, JOANNA   Ward of Lord Foxham. A courageous, attractive and strong-willed young woman, she is caught in the turmoil of the Wars of the Roses and aware that she could become a pawn in civil war rivalries. Accordingly she disguises herself as a boy and assumes the name John Matcham. She is held prisoner by the unscrupulous Sir Daniel Brackley who schemes to marry her to Lord Shoreby in return for financial gain. Joanna has fallen in love with Richard Shelton who assists her in escaping from Sir Daniel and making her way across country. She flees from Shoreby, which is sacked in the civil war, and is reunited with Shelton, who has meanwhile been knighted by the Duke of Gloucester. She is married in Holywood Church with the bless-ing of her guardian. *Arrow*

SERAPHINA, PRINCESS   Wife of Otto, Prince of Grünewald. 'Her forehead was perhaps too high, but it became her; her figure somewhat stooped, but every detail was formed and finished like a gem; her hand, her foot, her ear, the set of her comely head, were all dainty and accordant.' She and Otto are estranged and, while she remains faithful to him, she permits it to be rumoured that she and Gondremark, the Prime Minister, are lovers. Discontented with her life, she schemes with Gondremark for the overthrow of the Prince and the declara-tion of a republic. When Otto is abducted by his usurpers she realises the depth of her love for him and joins him in exile. They live peaceably in retirement, writing poetry. *Otto*

SHAWS   An estate in the parish of Cramond (a town on the Firth of Forth, close to Edinburgh) the home of Ebenezer Balfour. The surrounding countryside is pleasant but the house itself 'appeared to be a kind of ruin; no road led up to it; no smoke arose from any of the chimneys; nor was there any semblance of a garden.' David Balfour is the rightful heir to the estate and, after first attempting to deprive him of his inheritance, Ebene-zer eventually agrees to pay to his nephew two thirds of the yearly income of Shaws. *Kidnapped*

SHELTON, RICHARD (DICK)   Ward of Sir Daniel Brackley and son of Sir Harry Shelton. He is 'a young fellow not yet eighteen, sun-browned and grey-eyed, in a jacket of deer's leather, with a black velvet collar, a green hood upon his head, and a steel crossbow at his back'. Shelton mistrusts Sir Daniel since he suspects him of having been implicated in the death of his father. Learning of Sir Daniel's plans to rob him of his birth-right he attempts to flee from his guardian but is imprisoned in Tunstall Moat House. With the assistance of his lover, Joanna Sedley, he succeeds in escaping through a secret passage and makes his way across country, intending to expose Sir Daniel's treachery. Richard becomes closely involved in the civil war, fighting bravely for the House of York and taking an active part in the Battle of Shoreby. After the battle he is knighted by the Duke of Gloucester and reunited to Joanna, whom he marries in Holywood church. *Arrow*

SILVER, JOHN   The landlord of the Spy-Glass inn, Bristol, and formerly quartermaster aboard Captain Flint's pirate ship *Walrus*. He is 'very tall and strong, with a face as big as a ham – plain and pale, but intelligent and smiling'. His tallness earns him the nickname 'Long John'. Learning of Squire Trelawney's plan to fit out a schooner in search of Flint's treasure he applies for the post of ship's cook, scheming secretly to organise a mutiny and seize the treasure for himself. The plot is, however, discovered in time and the mutiny is temporarily thwarted. On reaching the island Silver and the men loyal to him do their utmost to defeat the Squire and his men but are unsuccessful in locating the treasure. Realising at length that he cannot possibly succeed in his designs, he joins forces with the Squire in return for a promise that he will not be prosecuted. When the schooner reaches the mainland of South America en route for England Silver succeeds in escaping and is heard of no more. *Treasure*

SMOLLETT, ALEXANDER   Captain of the *Hispaniola*. Engaged by Doctor Livesey to take command of an expedition in search of buried treasure, he soon expresses his unease regarding the enterprise. He is disturbed by the fact that the treasure hunt is common knowledge among the crew and suggests certain precautions in the event of mutiny. When it becomes apparent that a mutiny is indeed being planned Smollett displays great resourcefulness and courage in thwarting the designs of the mutineers. He proves to be a formidable adversary for Long John Silver and together with Squire Trelawney, Doctor Livesey and Jim Hawkins succeeds in defeating the pirates and returning to England with the treasure. *Treasure*

STEWART, ALAN BRECK   A Highland Jacobite outlaw who befriends David Balfour and accompanies him in his journey across Scotland. 'He was smallish in stature, but well set and as nimble as a goat; his face was of a good open expression, but sunburnt very dark, and heavily freckled and pitted with the smallpox; his eyes were unusually light and had a kind of dancing madness in them, that was both engaging and alarming. . . . Altogether I thought of him, at the first sight, that here was a man I would rather call my friend than my enemy.' When Alan is taken aboard the brig *Covenant* the captain and crew scheme to overpower him and steal his belt of gold; David warns him of the Captain's perfidy and together they succeed in foiling the attempt. After the loss of the brig off the coast of Mull David and Alan travel across Scotland together: David in quest of his inheritance, and Alan en route for the Firth of Forth, from where he aims to escape to France.

When Captain Colin Campbell of Glenure (the 'Red Fox') is assassinated at Appin, Alan immediately becomes the prime suspect since he is known to have been in the vicinity at the time of the murder. With David's assistance he succeeds in making his escape to France, where he is reunited with a Scots battalion of Louis XIV. *Kidnapped* and *Catriona*. (The character is based on an actual person. For information on the real Alan Breck see G. E. Brown, *A Book of R. L. S.* (Methuen, 1919) pp. 40–2.)

TRELAWNEY, JOHN   A local squire and close friend of Dr. David Livesey. He was 'a tall man, over six feet high, and broad in proportion, and he had a bluff, rough-and-ready face, all roughened and reddened and lined in his long travels'. When the squire learns of the existence of a map showing the location of buried treasure he decides at once to organise an expedition to retrieve it. He purchases and equips a schooner for this purpose and personally selects the crew. He engages as ship's cook an old seafaring man, Long John Silver, unaware that Silver had been quartermaster aboard Captain Flint's pirate ship, *Walrus*, and is plotting to seize the treasure for himself. The squire is reluctant to admit that his judgement of human nature has in this instance been misplaced, but on receiving irrefutable proof of Silver's duplicity he concedes his error and is at length successful in thwarting the pirate's designs. *Treasure*

UMA   A young Kanaka girl, a native of the island of Falesa. 'She was young and very slender for an island maid, with a long face, a high forehead, and a shy, strange, blindish look, between a cat's and a baby's.' John Wiltshire, a white trader, is physically attracted to her and goes through a form of wedding ceremony with her, secretly intending to desert her at the first opportunity. He quickly becomes aware of her total devotion and affection for him and these qualities, combined with her simplicity and innocence, bind the two closer together. Wiltshire eventually decides to settle permanently with

Uma on the island. 'Falesa'

UTTERSON, GABRIEL JOHN   Henry Jekyll's lawyer and a friend of many years standing. He is 'a man of a rugged countenance, that was never lighted by a smile; cold, scanty and embarrassed in discourse; backward in sentiment; lean, long, dusty, dreary and yet somehow lovable'. As Jekyll's legal adviser he is greatly disturbed when his old friend prepares a will which provides that, in the event of his decease, all his possessions are to pass into the hands of Edward Hyde. Utterson becomes increasingly alarmed by Jekyll's inexplicable behaviour and, at the climax of the story, it is he who is instrumental in cornering Hyde in the laboratory. *Jekyll*

VILLON, FRANCIS   An unscrupulous poet living in medieval Paris. A thief and a rascal, Villon flees from the scene of a murder in which he fears he is implicated. The night is bitterly cold and he is unable to find shelter. Without money and fearful of pursuit, he knocks on the door of a stranger and begs for hospitality. The stranger is suspicious of his intentions but offers him supper; the two embark on a lengthy conversation on their respective attitudes to life. 'Lodging' (*See also* the essay 'François Villon: Student, Poet and Housebreaker')

WEIR, ADAM   Lord Justice-Clerk of Scotland. A dour, serious man obsessed with the study of the law to the exclusion of all other considerations, 'he did not try to be loved, he did not care to be; it is probable the very thought of it was a stranger to his mind'. Between Adam and his son, Archie, there is little understanding. Where the son is questioning the father is dogmatic; where the son is interested in culture the father is contemptuous of the humanities. When Adam Weir sentences a criminal to death, Archie, who is deeply opposed to capital punishment, speaks out against the sentence. The Justice-Clerk hears of his son's rebellion and banishes him to the family estates at Hermiston. *Weir*

WEIR, ARCHIE   Son of Adam Weir, the Lord Justice-Clerk. A serious, eager young man who inherits his father's sternness and his mother's tenderness, he is brought up in a rigid, conventional household, fearing and respecting his dogmatic father. When Archie dares to challenge his father's views in public he is banished to the family estates at Hermiston to learn the duties of a laird. Here he meets and falls in love with Christina Elliott, the daughter of his housekeeper's brother. Though

she is deeply attracted to him the lovers quarrel, Archie pleading for their secret meetings to cease for fear of scandal. (The
novel is left uncompleted. Stevenson intended Christina to be
seduced by Archie's rival, Frank Innes. Archie, learning of this,
confronts Innes with the accusation and murders him. Archie is
arrested and tried before his own father, found guilty and
condemned to death. He is rescued from prison by Christina's
brothers and the two succeed in escaping to America.) *Weir*

WILL   The adopted son of a miller. He is brought up in a remote
valley, content to remain in the valley but continually seeking
information concerning the world of the cities outside. At the
age of thirty he begins courting the parson's daughter, Marjory,
but due to his slowness their relationship does not progress
beyond a polite friendship. When Marjory marries another
man Will reconciles himself to the life of an innkeeper and
spends the remainder of his life in the valley. He dies never
having ventured outside his own surroundings, content in his
philosophy of quiet resignation. 'Will'

WILTSHIRE, JOHN   A trader in the South Pacific islands. He arrives
on the island of Falesa where he befriends an unscrupulous
Englishman, Case. He is impressed by Case's courage and
shrewdness but does not at first realise the extent of his duplicity. Wiltshire marries a native girl, Uma, intending to desert
her at the earliest opportunity; as time passes he is increasingly
impressed with her loyalty and devotion. He is affronted by
Case's corruption and determines to bring to an end the
Englishman's reign of terror over the natives. Uma risks her life
in order to warn him of Case's whereabouts. At night in the
bush he and Case meet, there is a fight and Case is stabbed to
death. Wiltshire, now convinced of Uma's total love and faith-
fulness, settles down with her on the island. 'Falesa'

Appendix

1. FILM VERSIONS

Numerous film adaptations have been made of Stevenson's novels. By common consent the most successful have been the 1932 version of *Dr. Jekyll and Mr. Hyde*, memorable because of the outstanding performance of Fredric March as the tormented Henry Jekyll; the 1945 version of *The Body Snatcher*, worthy of a niche in cinematic history for its remarkable evocation of Victorian Edinburgh; and Walt Disney's 1950 production of *Treasure Island*, indelibly associated with Robert Newton's fine performance as Long John Silver. It is perhaps inevitable that of all his stories *Dr. Jekyll and Mr. Hyde* has attracted most attention from film producers, but it is arguable that no version has yet succeeded in conveying the atmosphere of brooding suspense which pervades the novel, or in presenting the complexity of the Jekyll–Hyde relationship.

The following is a list of the principal film adaptations based on Stevenson's stories.

1920   *Treasure Island*
       Starring Charles Ogle as Long John Silver and Shirley Mason as Jim Hawkins
       Directed by Maurice Tourneur.
1920   *Dr. Jekyll and Mr. Hyde*
       Starring Conrad Veidt.
       Directed by F. W. Murnau
1921   *Dr. Jekyll and Mr. Hyde*
       Starring John Barrymore
1932   *Dr. Jekyll and Mr. Hyde* (Paramount)

Starring Fredric March, Miriam Hopkins and Rose Hobart. (Fredric March won an Academy Award for his performance). Cast also included Holmes Herbert, Halliwell Hobbes, Edgar Norton
Directed by Rouben Mamoulian
The screenplay with 1400 frame blow-ups was published in 1976 in the *Film Classics Library* (editor Richard J. Anobile).

1934   *Treasure Island* (Metro-Goldwyn-Mayer)
Starring Wallace Beery as Long John Silver and Jackie Cooper as Jim Hawkins
Cast also included Lewis Stone, Lionel Barrymore, Otto Kruger, Douglass Dumbrille, Nigel Bruce, Chic Sale
Directed by Victor Fleming.

1938   *Kidnapped* (TCF)
Starring Warner Baxter and Freddie Bartholomew
Cast also included Arleen Whelan, John Carradine, C. Aubrey Smith, Nigel Bruce, Reginald Owen
Directed by Alfred Werker.

1941   *Dr. Jekyll and Mr. Hyde* (MGM)
Starring Spencer Tracy, Ingrid Bergman and Lana Turner. Cast also included Ian Hunter, C. Aubrey Smith, Donald Crisp and Sara Allgood
Directed by Victor Fleming.

1945   *The Body Snatcher* (RKO)
Starring Henry Daniell
Directed by Robert Wise
Produced by Val Lewton.

1948   *The Black Arrow* (Columbia)
Starring Louis Hayward and Janet Blair. Cast also included George Macready, Edgar Buchanan, Paul Cavanaugh
Directed by Gordon Douglas.

1950   *Treasure Island* (Disney Studios)
Technicolor
Starring Robert Newton as Long John Silver and Bobby Driscoll as Jim Hawkins. Cast also included Walter Fitzgerald, Basil Sydney, Denis O'Dea, Geoffrey Wilkinson, Ralph Truman
Directed by Byron Haskin
(N.B. In 1954 Robert Newton played the same role in a feature film made for television, *Long John Silver*, and in 26 half-hour television programmes filmed in Australia.)

1953   *The Master of Ballantrae* (Warner Brothers)
       Technicolor
       Starring Errol Flynn and Anthony Steel. Cast also included
       Roger Livesey, Beatrice Campbell, Felix Aylmer, Mervyn
       Johns, Jacques Berthier, Yvonne Furneaux, Ralph Truman
       Directed by William Keighley.
1959   *Kidnapped* (Disney Studios)
       Technicolor
       Starring Peter Finch and James MacArthur. Cast also
       included Bernard Lee, John Laurie, Finlay Currie, Niall
       MacGinnis, Peter O'Toole, Miles Malleson, Oliver Johnston,
       Duncan Macrae, Andrew Cruickshank
       Directed by Robert Stevenson.
1960   *The Two Faces of Dr. Jekyll* (Hammer)
       Starring Paul Massie
1966   *The Wrong Box* (Columbia Pictures Corporation)
       Technicolor
       Starring John Mills as Masterman Finsbury, Michael Caine
       as Michael Finsbury and Tony Hancock as the detective.
       Cast also included Ralph Richardson, Wilfrid Lawson,
       Nanette Newman, Peter Cook, Dudley Moor, Peter Sellers,
       Thorley Walters, Cicely Courtneidge, Irene Handl, John Le
       Mesurier, Gerald Sim, Norman Bird, Tutte Lemkow
       Directed by Bryan Forbes.
1971   *Kidnapped* (Movielab)
       Panavision
       Starring Michael Caine and Lawrence Douglas. Cast also
       included Trevor Howard, Jack Hawkins, Donald Pleaseance,
       Gordon Jackson, Freddie Jones, Jack Watson
       Directed by Delbert Mann
       (Based on *Kidnapped* and *Catriona*.)
1971   *Treasure Island* (Massfilms)
       Starring Orson Welles as Long John Silver. Cast also
       included Kim Burfield, Lionel Stander, Walter Slezak, Rik
       Battaglia
       Directed by John Hough.

2.   POSTHUMOUSLY PUBLISHED WORKS

In recent years a number of Stevenson's writings, some unpublished during his lifetime, have been issued in scholarly editions. Details are as follows:

Our Samoan Adventure. Edited, with an introduction and notes, by Charles Neider (Weidenfeld & Nicolson, London, 1956). This is a transcription of a diary kept by Stevenson and his wife and covering the period September 1890–December 1894. The diary throws much interesting light on the Stevensons' pattern of life in Samoa and is accompanied by numerous rare photographs from family albums.

The Cevennes Journal: Notes on a Journey through the French Highlands. Edited, with an introduction and notes, by Gordon Golding (Mainstream Publishing, Edinburgh, 1978). This reproduces the text of the manuscript journal of the walking tour, 22 September–2 October 1878, which formed the basis for *Travels with a Donkey in the Cevennes.*

An Old Song. Edited, with an introduction and notes, by Roger G. Swearingen (Archon/Wilfion, USA, 1982). The discovery of Stevenson's first novel, published anonymously in *London* magazine in 1877, was an important literary event. The story, set in Scotland, concerns the rivalry of two cousins brought up by a dour uncle and anticipates the theme of *The Master of Ballantrae.* The volume also includes an early fictional fragment, 'Edifying Letters of the Rutherford Family', apparently based on Stevenson's youthful experiences in Edinburgh.

References

The following abbreviations are used throughout:

Balfour   Graham Balfour, *The Life of Robert Louis Stevenson* (one volume edition, Methuen, 1910).

Furnas   J. C. Furnas, *Voyage to Windward* (Faber & Faber, 1952).

PART I

1. 'Rosa Quo Locorum: Random Memories'.
2. For a detailed discussion of the two Edinburghs see Moray McLaren, *Stevenson and Edinburgh* (London: Chapman and Hall, 1950).
3. See, for example, Jenni Calder, *RLS: A Life Study* (London: Hamish Hamilton, 1980) pp. 53–7, and Paul Binding, Introduction to *Weir of Hermiston and Other Stories* (Harmondsworth: Penguin Books, 1979) pp. 15–16.
4. RLS to Charles Baxter, 2 February 1873.
5. Janet Adam Smith, *R. L. Stevenson* (London: Duckworth, 1937) p. 79.
6. RLS to Mrs. Sitwell, June 1875.
7. RLS to Henry James, August 1890.
8. RLS to R. A. M. Stevenson, June 1894.
9. Quoted in Smith, op.cit., p. 126.
10. RLS to Charles Baxter, 1 December 1892.
11. RLS to Colvin, August 1879; RLS to Miss Monroe, June 1886.
12. RLS to R. A. M. Stevenson, June 1894.
13. 'A College Magazine'.
14. RLS to Baxter, 5 December 1881.
15. Cf. Wells, *The Island of Doctor Moreau* and *The Croquet Player*; Golding, *The Lord of the Flies*.
16. See, for example, *Heathercat*, *The Young Chevalier* and *The Great North Road*.
17. Henry James, 'Robert Louis Stevenson', *Century Magazine*, April 1888, xxxv, pp. 869–79.
18. RLS to Marcel Schwob, 19 August 1890; RLS to Colvin, 29 April 1891.
19. Cf. RLS to Colvin, 1 May 1892.
20. Henry James, op.cit.
21. On his death Stevenson left eight unfinished novels, in addition to *Weir of*

Hermiston and *St. Ives*. These fragments are reprinted in Volume 16 of the Tusitala Edition.

22. Conan Doyle, *Through the Magic Door,* p. 245.
23. G. B. Stern, Introduction to *The Tales and Essays of Robert Louis Stevenson*.

PART II

1. The final chapter of *An Inland Voyage*.
2. RLS to his mother, September 1878.
3. Quoted in Maixner, *Robert Louis Stevenson: The Critical Heritage* (London: Routledge & Kegan Paul, 1981) p. 8.
4. RLS to R. A. M. Stevenson, April 1879.
5. RLS to J. A. Symonds, Spring 1886 (apropos *Dr. Jekyll and Mr. Hyde*).
6. *Academy*, 9 July 1881, xx, pp. 21–2.
7. Preface, *Familiar Studies*.
8. Cf. Edgar Allan Poe, 'Twice-Told Tales', *Graham's Magazine*, May 1842.
9. *Academy*, 1 April 1882, xxi, p. 224.
10. Quoted in G. E. Brown, *A Book of RLS* (London: Methuen, 1919) p. 161.
11. See John Fowles, 'Afterword' to Alain-Fournier, *Le Grand Meaulnes* (New York: New American Library, 1971).
12. RLS to James, 29 December 1890.
13. RLS to Colvin, 2 December 1889.
14. Janet Adam Smith, *R. L. Stevenson*, p. 109.
15. Colvin records that Conrad preferred *In the South Seas* to *Treasure Island* (introductory note to RLS's letter to Colvin, 29 April 1891).
16. RLS to Colvin, 1 May 1892.

PART III

1. RLS to William Archer, February 1888.
2. RLS to W. E. Henley, October 1879.
3. See also Doyle to RLS, 30 May 1893 and Barrie to RLS, 8 May 1891.
4. Balfour, p. 160.
5. Roger G. Swearingen, *The Prose Writings of Robert Louis Stevenson: A Guide* (London: Macmillan, 1980) p. 28.
6. RLS to J. A. Symonds, spring 1886.
7. Quoted in George E. Brown, *A Book of RLS*, p. 157. For a fuller discussion of this matter see Irving S. Saposnik, *Robert Louis Stevenson* (New York: Twayne Publishers, 1974) pp. 75–9.
8. Cf. H. G. Wells's short story 'The Country of the Blind' in which a similar moral dilemma is posed.
9. RLS to Lady Taylor, January 1887.
10. RLS to Colvin, 2 November 1890.
11. RLS to Colvin, 28 September 1891.
12. The first unexpurgated edition was that published by Penguin Books in 1979, edited by Jenni Calder.
13. Cf. David Punter, *The Literature of Terror* (London: Longman, 1980) pp. 239–67.

14. Cf. H. G. Wells, *The History of Mr. Polly*, Ch. 7: 'it never palled upon him that in the dusky stabbing of the "Island of Voices" [sic] something poured over the stabber's hands "like warm tea".'
15. RLS to Colvin, 14 December 1886.
16. 'The Works of Edgar Allan Poe', reprinted in *Essays Literary and Critical* (Tusitala Edition, vol. 28).

PART IV

1. 'My First Book', *Idler*, August 1894. Reprinted in *Essays in the Art of Writing*.
2. Ibid.
3. See, for example, Robert Kiely, 'Adventure as Boy's Daydream', in *Robert Louis Stevenson and the Fiction of Adventure* (Cambridge, Mass.: Harvard University Press, 1964) and W. W. Robson, 'The Sea Cook: a Study in the Art of Robert Louis Stevenson' in *On the Novel* (London: J. M. Dent, 1971).
4. RLS to Henley, October 1884.
5. *Great Expectations*, Ch. 2: 'I was in mortal terror of the young man who wanted my heart and liver; I was in mortal terror of my interlocutor with the iron leg.'
6. 'My First Book', op.cit.
7. RLS to Henley, May 1883.
8. 'My First Book', op.cit.
9. 'The Sea Cook: a Study in the Art of Robert Louis Stevenson', op.cit.
10. RLS to Sidney Colvin, 9 March 1884.
11. RLS to W. H. Low, December 1883.
12. Cf. Letters and reviews quoted in Maixner, *Robert Louis Stevenson: The Critical Heritage*, pp. 176–87.
13. Furnas, p. 217.
14. Ibid., p. 218.
15. RLS to J. A. Symonds, spring 1886.
16. *The French Lieutenant's Woman*, Ch. 49.
17. See Robert M. Philmus, 'The Satiric Ambivalence of *The Island of Doctor Moreau*' in *Science Fiction Studies*, 23, vol. 8, March 1981.
18. RLS to his father, 25 January 1886.
19. Cf. 'Memoirs of an Islet' in *Memories and Portraits*.
20. Cf. David Lodge, '*Tono-Bungay* and the Condition of England', in *Language of Fiction* (London: Routledge & Kegan Paul, 1966).
21. Henry James, 'Robert Louis Stevenson', *Century Magazine*, April 1888.
22. H. B. Baildon, *Robert Louis Stevenson: A Life Study in Criticism* (London: Chatto & Windus, 1901) p. 230.
23. Quoted in Balfour, p. 233.
24. September 1886. Cf. Stevenson's essay 'Some Gentlemen in Fiction', *Scribner's Magazine*, June 1888: 'In one of my books, and in one only, the characters took the bit in their teeth; all at once, they became detached from the flat paper, they turned their backs on me and walked off bodily; and from that time my task was stenographic – it was they who spoke, it was they who wrote the remainder of the story.' See also John Fowles, *The French Lieutenant's Woman*, Ch. 13.
25. RLS to S. R. Crockett, 17 May 1893: 'I shall never see Auld Reekie [Edinburgh]. I shall never set my foot again upon the heather. Here I am

until I die, and here will I be buried.'

26. G. E. Brown, *A Book of RLS*, p. 49.

27. James to RLS, 21 October 1893; Vernon Lee, *Contemporary Review*, September 1895, pp. 404–7.

28. James to RLS, 21 October 1893.

29. *Catriona*, Ch. 20: 'And till the end of time your folk (who are not yet used with the duplicity of life and men) will struggle as I did, and make heroical resolves, and take long risks.'

30. RLS to Colvin, October 1883.

31. Quoted in F. Masson (ed.), *I Can Remember Robert Louis Stevenson* (London: Chambers, 1922) pp. 206–8.

32. RLS to William Archer, March 1894.

33. See, for example, V. B. Lamb, *The Betrayal of Richard III* (London: Coram Publishers, 1959); Josephine Tey, *The Daughter of Time* (London: Peter Davies, 1951); Paul Murray Kendall, *Richard III* (London: Allen & Unwin, 1955).

34. *The Times*, 25 May 1919.

35. 'The Genesis of *The Master of Ballantrae*'; reprinted in *Essays in the Art of Writing*.

36. RLS to Colvin, 24 December 1887.

37. *Letters of Henry James*, ed. Percy Lubbock (1920) vol. I, p. 157; W. E. Henley: 'A Masterpiece in Grime', *Scots Observer*, 12 October 1889.

38. RLS to Colvin, 24 December 1887.

39. Quoted in Kiely, op.cit., p. 204.

40. RLS to Adelaide Boodle, December 1887.

41. Cf. H. G. Wells, *The Time Machine*, Ch. VII: 'The Time Machine was gone! At once, like a lash across the face, came the possibility of losing my own age, of being left helpless in this strange new world. The bare thought of it was an actual physical sensation. I could feel it grip me at the throat and stop my breathing.'

42. The influence of Poe on *The Master of Ballantrae* is remarkable throughout. There is, for example, the antagonism between the two brothers ('William Wilson'); the voyage of the *Nonesuch* in Ch. 9 (cf. *The Narrative of Arthur Gordon Pym*); and the melodramatic ending which hinges on the idea of burial alive ('The Fall of the House of Usher' and 'The Premature Burial').

43. RLS to James, March 1888.

44. RLS to Colvin, 14 January 1889.

45. David Daiches, *Robert Louis Stevenson and his World*, p. 74.

46. Swearingen, op.cit., p. 126.

47. Preface to Tusitala Edition.

48. Epilogue to *The Wrecker*.

49. RLS to Colvin, 24 October 1891.

50. G. E. Brown, *A Book of RLS*, p. 285.

51. *The Wrecker*, Ch. 10.

52. RLS to Colvin, 24 October 1891.

53. G. B. Stern, Preface to *RLS: An Omnibus*.

54. RLS to Colvin, 25 April 1893.

55. RLS to Colvin, 29 May 1893.

56. 'In Defence of Ebb-Tide', New York *Critic*, November 1894.

57. Jenni Calder, Introduction to *Dr. Jekyll and Mr. Hyde and Other Stories* (Harmondsworth: Penguin Books, 1979).

58. Cf. H. G. Wells, *The Island of Doctor Moreau*, Ch. 14: 'They build themselves their dens, gather fruit, and pull herbs – marry even. But I can see through it all, see into their very souls, and see there nothing but the souls of beasts, beasts that perish – anger, and the lusts to live and gratify themselves.' (Wells may have derived some of the details of Moreau's island from New Island in *The Ebb-Tide*.)

59. Kiely, op.cit., p. 181.

60. Preface to Tusitala Edition.

61. RLS to R. A. M. Stevenson, 17 June 1894.

62. Isobel Strong and Lloyd Osbourne, *Vailima Memories of R. L. Stevenson* (London: Constable, 1903) pp. 69–71.

63. Arnold Bennett, *Journals* (1932) vol. I, p. 206.

64. RLS to R. A. M. Stevenson, June 1894. The phrase refers to *Heathercat*, another uncompleted novel, but could equally well be applied to *Weir of Hermiston*.

65. See Compton Mackenzie, *Robert Louis Stevenson* (London: Morgan-Grampian Books, 1968) appendix.

66. For a discussion on the relationship between Pip and Orlick see H. M. Daleski, *Dickens and the Art of Analogy* (London: Faber & Faber, 1970) pp. 242–4.

67. Balfour, op.cit., Ch. 3.

68. *Saturday Review*, 13 June 1896. Included in Parrinder and Philmus (eds), *H. G. Wells's Literary Criticism* (Brighton: Harvester Press, 1980) pp. 99–103.

Select Bibliography

THE WORKS OF ROBERT LOUIS STEVENSON

The following editions are recommended:

The Tusitala Edition (London: Heinemann, 1923–4) 35 vols.

The Skerryvore Edition (London: Heinemann, 1924–6) 30 vols.

The Vailima Edition, edited by Lloyd Osbourne (London: Heinemann, 1922–3) 26 vols.

The Collected Poems, edited, with an introduction and notes, by Janet Adam Smith (London: Rupert Hart-Davis, 1971).

The Stories of Robert Louis Stevenson (contains the complete short stories) (London: Gollancz, 1928).

RLS: An Omnibus, selected and edited by G. B. Stern (contains a representative selection of essays, short stories, sketches and fables) (London: Cassell, 1950).

Weir of Hermiston and Other Stories, selected and edited with an introduction by Paul Binding (Harmondsworth: Penguin Books, 1979). (This also contains 'Will o' the Mill, 'Thrawn Janet, 'The Misadventures of John Nicholson' and 'The House of Eld'.)

The Strange Case of Dr. Jekyll and Mr. Hyde and Other Stories, edited with an introduction by Jenni Calder (Harmondsworth: Penguin Books, 1979). (This also contains 'The Beach of Falesa' and *The Ebb-Tide*.)

THE LETTERS

The Letters of Robert Louis Stevenson to his Family and Friends, selected and edited with notes and introductions by Sidney Colvin (London: Methuen, 1899) 2 vols. New edition, rearranged in four volumes and containing 150 new letters (1911).

Vailima Letters, being correspondence addressed by Robert Louis Stevenson to Sidney Colvin, November 1890–October 1894 (London: Methuen, 1895).

Henry James and Robert Louis Stevenson: A Record of Friendship and Criticism, edited by Janet Adam Smith (London: Rupert Hart-Davis, 1948).

246

BIBLIOGRAPHY

W.F. Prideaux, *Bibliography of the Works of Robert Louis Stevenson* (London: Hollings, 1903; revd edn, 1917).

Roger G. Swearingen, *The Prose Writings of Robert Louis Stevenson: A Guide* (London: Macmillan, 1980).

BIOGRAPHY

Graham Balfour, *The Life of Robert Louis Stevenson* (London: Methuen, 1901). This is the authorised biography in the sense that it was written with the co-operation of Stevenson's widow and stepson and was intended to complement the volumes of letters edited by Sidney Colvin. It is an extremely readable, competent and well-researched account of Stevenson's life and times, written by one who knew him well and possessed a deep insight into his character. It suffers, however, from having been prepared so soon after Stevenson's death and parts of it border on hagiography. Since the author was an intimate friend of Stevenson and his family – particularly during the Vailima period (he lived in the same household for some years) – the biography remains an indispensable account of Stevenson and his circle, though inevitably some of Balfour's judgements have been superseded by later scholarship. There is an excellent bibliography of Stevenson's writings and a comparison of four drafts of the opening paragraphs of *Weir of Hermiston*.

Janet Adam Smith, *R. L. Stevenson*, Great Lives series (London: Duckworth, 1937). The author, well known for her scholarly edition of the *Collected Poems* and her fascinating study of the friendship between Stevenson and Henry James, here contributes an excellent introductory account of his life and times. Written at a time when uncritical adulation of Stevenson was no longer fashionable, and after a number of derogatory studies had been published, this is a refreshingly balanced appraisal which separates the man from the legend.

Lettice Cooper, *Robert Louis Stevenson*, European Novelists series (London: Arthur Barker, 1947). Studies of novelists written by other novelists are usually extremely interesting and this one is no exception. Within the compass of 100 pages Lettice Cooper succeeds in presenting a balanced appraisal of Stevenson's achievement as essayist, romancer and novelist, steering a middle course between enthusiasm and judicious criticism. Her discussion of the psychological aspects of the novels and romances is particularly stimulating and her overall assessment is a useful contribution to Stevenson studies.

J. C. Furnas, *Voyage to Windward: The Life of Robert Louis Stevenson* (London: Faber & Faber, 1952). This is a very full, detailed and reliable account of Stevenson's life and background, based on many years of travel and research. Though not as readable as Graham Balfour's biography, it clearly stems from an intimate knowledge of Stevenson and his milieu, particularly of his years in the South Seas. This was widely accepted as the 'definitive' biography until the publication of James Pope Hennessy's in 1974. There is a full scholarly apparatus including detailed references, bibliography and appendices, including an assessment of Stevenson's literary achievement and a discussion of the main points of controversy.

Compton Mackenzie, *Robert Louis Stevenson*, International Profiles series (London: Morgan-Grampian Books, 1968). As a Scot, a novelist and a friend of some of Stevenson's closest associates Compton Mackenzie was well placed to write this short critical biography. It vividly conveys the flavour of his life and milieu and is excellently illustrated with contemporary photographs and prints. There are stills from film and television adaptations and a summary of the principal events in the life.

Margaret Mackay, *The Violent Friend: The Story of Mrs. Robert Louis Stevenson 1840–1914* (London: J. M. Dent, 1970). This is a fascinating account of the background, life and times of Stevenson's wife, Fanny Vandegrift Osbourne. The book contains *inter alia* an excellent description of Stevenson's life and achievement. It is particularly valuable for the insight it affords into Fanny's character and the unique blending of personalities which resulted in such an unusual marriage.

James Pope Hennessy, *Robert Louis Stevenson* (London: Jonathan Cape, 1974). Written by the author of a distinguished study of Anthony Trollope, this fine biography is based largely on the collections of letters in the National Library of Scotland in Edinburgh, the Beinecke Library at Yale University and the Houghton Library at Harvard. Mr. Hennessy's outstanding achievement is to bring fresh and original insights to each stage of the work and to present Stevenson as an important writer who demands serious reassessment. Since the book is intended for the general reader rather than the scholar, the author has omitted references for the numerous extracts from letters and diaries; some readers may find this a serious limitation. The lucidity, depth and thoroughness of this work make it an essential text for students of Stevenson.

Jenni Calder, *RLS: A Life Study* (London: Hamish Hamilton, 1980). Written by the daughter of David Daiches and a noted Stevenson scholar, this study aims 'to explore and explain a man and writer rather than produce a final round-up of evidence'. The book complements James Pope Hennessy's study since the former concentrates on Stevenson as a literary figure whereas Jenni Calder primarily explores the factors which shaped his personality and outlook. It is an impeccably researched account which brings vividly to life his engaging personality and the impact of his family and friends on his complex temperament.

CRITICISM

G. B. Stern, *Robert Louis Stevenson*, Writers and their Work series (London: Longmans Green, 1952). This is a useful introductory essay, which aims to summarise Stevenson's life and art and place him in his literary context. The discussion of the novels and stories is competently handled and Miss Stern displays an acute understanding of his strengths and weaknesses as man and writer. There is an excellent bibliography of Stevensoniana and a useful index to the Tusitala Edition.

Robert Kiely, *Robert Louis Stevenson and the Fiction of Adventure* (Cambridge, Mass.: Harvard University Press, 1964). One of the finest critical works on Stevenson to appear in recent times, this is a comprehensive study of the fiction including both the novels and the short stories. The author places Stevenson in his literary context as a writer of 'fiction of adventure' but also demonstrates his significance as a precursor of Conrad. The study is particularly valuable for its discussion of Stevenson's preoccupation with moral ambiguity and the recurrence of this theme throughout his fiction. There is an excellent critical apparatus.

Dennis Butts, *R. L. Stevenson*, The Bodley Head Monographs series (London: The Bodley Head, 1966). This is a short introduction to Stevenson's life and works, written by a scholar with a deep understanding of the nature of his artistic achievement. The discussion of the principal novels and stories is thorough and stimulating, and at each stage of the analysis his work is placed in context against the background of his circumstances and intentions. There is a short but useful bibliography of works by and about Stevenson.

David Daiches, *Robert Louis Stevenson and his World* (London: Thames & Hudson, 1973). This is a carefully written and well-researched study of Stevenson and his circle, written by a scholar possessing a deep insight into the man and his works. The book affords a useful introduction to Stevenson's life and times illuminated by sympathetic understanding and critical balance.

Jenni Calder (ed.), *The Robert Louis Stevenson Companion* (Edinburgh: Paul Harris Publishing, 1980). This is an anthology comprising appreciations from a number of leading contemporary figures including Sidney Colvin, J. M. Barrie, W. E. Henley and Henry James. Jenni Calder contributes an introductory essay which provides an overview of Stevenson's life and achievement.

Paul Maixner (ed.), *Robert Louis Stevenson: The Critical Heritage* (London: Routledge & Kegan Paul, 1981). This volume brings together in a convenient format a mass of contemporary criticism, letters and book reviews ranging from *An Inland Voyage* (1878) to *St. Ives* (1897). The collection is excellently edited by Paul Maixner who contributes a fascinating scholarly introduction.

ADDITIONAL RECOMMENDATIONS

Boodle, Adelaide A., *RLS and his Sine Qua Non* (London: John Murray, 1926)
Brown, George E., *A Book of RLS* (London: Methuen, 1919)
Eigner, Edwin, *Robert Louis Stevenson and the Romantic Tradition* (Princeton University Press, 1966)
McLaren, Moray, *Stevenson and Edinburgh: A Centenary Study* (London: Chapman & Hall, 1950)
Simpson, E. Blantyre, *Robert Louis Stevenson's Edinburgh Days* (London: Hodder & Stoughton, 1898)
Simpson, E. Blantyre, *The Stevenson Originals* (London: T. N. Foulis, 1912)
Stevenson, Fanny and Robert Louis, *Our Samoan Adventure*, edited by Charles Neider (London: Weidenfeld & Nicolson, 1956)

Index